Dissonan

Voices

RACE, JAZZ, AND

INNOVATIVE POETICS IN

MIDCENTURY AMERICA

JOSEPH PIZZA

University of Iowa Press, Iowa City

University of Iowa Press, Iowa City 52242
Copyright © 2023 by the University of Iowa Press
uipress.uiowa.edu
Printed in the United States of America

ISBN 978-1-60938-911-6 (pbk)
ISBN 978-1-60938-912-3 (ebk)

Design and typesetting by Ashley Muehlbauer

Printed on acid-free paper

Cataloging-in-Publication data is on file
with the Library of Congress.

Portions of the preface, chapter one, and chapter
five provided courtesy of the Western Regional
Archives, State Archives of North Carolina.

For Ali

Contents

Acknowledgments ix

Preface: Integrating Black Mountain xi

INTRODUCTION Dissonant Voices: Race, Jazz, and the New American Poetics of Breath 1

CHAPTER ONE Form Is Never More Than an Extension of Bird: Projective Verse as Jazz Poetic 23

CHAPTER TWO Outside Boston: Stephen Jonas in the Poetry of John Wieners and Jack Spicer 57

CHAPTER THREE Howling Parker: Jazz, Race, and Beat Performance 94

CHAPTER FOUR Broadening the Voice: Amiri Baraka among the Hipsters 129

CHAPTER FIVE Spitting Fire: The Black Arts Movement and the New American Poetry 155

Conclusion: Out and Gone 189

Notes 209

Works Cited 215

Index 233

Acknowledgments

This book arrived after a long and winding journey. Consequently, many individuals have contributed to it, both directly and indirectly. My thinking here likely has its origins in my earliest experiences growing up in mixed neighborhoods and schools and in the example of teachers like John Hulsman and Gary Barricklow, undergraduate mentors at Rider University, who labored to enrich our community discourse through a distinguished speaker series that brought influential African American and Afro-Caribbean writers like Derek Walcott, Amiri Baraka, John Edgar Wideman, and Edwidge Danticat, among others, to campus. In each of these instances, the promise and possibility of alternative, integrated communities spurred my imagination and inspired my research.

Fortunately, such enthusiasms were nurtured throughout my graduate and early teaching careers as well. While a graduate student at Oxford, I had the benefit of learning from Nick Shrimpton, Matthew Reynolds, Christopher Ricks, and the late Eric Griffiths, among others, about the joys and rigors of scholarly discourse. Though their interests and specialties lie far afield from my work here, my approach to scholarship and my understanding of poetic voice was largely forged in response to their excellent examples. Without the support of colleagues and administrators, however, that approach would have never found its way into print. As a result, I would like to thank Laura McLean, Matthew DeForrest, and Melita Mitchell for the opportunity to teach courses in African American Studies at Johnson C. Smith University. Meanwhile, Farrell O'Gorman, my department chair at Belmont Abbey College, provided the institutional support needed to complete a long writing project. In more ways than one, colleagues old and new have sustained me as well. In particular, I'd like to extend my gratitude to Nathalie Cote, Rajive Tiwari, Bill Van Lear, Angela Mitchell, Al Benthall, Erin Jenson, Troy Feay, Daniel Hutchinson, Patrick

Wadden, and Simon Donoghue for their conversations, professionalism, and, occasionally, much-needed drinks! Of course, my students have also played an integral role in my research. Though there are too many to name, my American Identity, African American Literature, and Contemporary Poetry students have contributed directly to my understanding of the material that follows. So, too, have the creative writers and editors whom I've had the good fortune to work with in the 4:30 a.m. group and at Agora.

A good number of scholars, librarians, and society friends have contributed to this study as well. Chief among them, Piers Pennington deserves special recognition for the many hours of conversation we've spent discussing the manuscript and related topics; my thinking has been aided at several turns by his insight and suggestions. Heather South at North Carolina's Western Regional Archives has also been an invaluable resource in navigating the Black Mountain College Collection. Alice Sebrell, Brian Butler, Jeff Arnal, and everyone at the Black Mountain College Museum and Arts Center deserve a special thanks for organizing the annual ReVIEWING conferences where a good portion of this study was debuted. In presenting and publishing parts of this material there and elsewhere, I have been aided by Thomas Frank, Carissa Pfeiffer, John Roche, Michael Kindellan, Joshua Hoeynck, Jeff Davis, Jeff Gardiner, and many others. I would also like to thank Aldon Lynn Nielsen and the manuscript's anonymous second reader for enhancing this study through their detailed feedback and support. Most of all, however, I am grateful for the patient reading and steady encouragement of the Contemporary North American Poetry Series editors, Dee Morris, Alan Golding, and Lynn Keller, and for Meredith Stabel's hard work and guidance throughout the publication process.

Finally, I would be remiss if I did not mention that this study was completed during the years of the COVID-19 pandemic. As such, it owes its contours and shape, in ways that I still haven't fully grasped, to various periods of isolation and lockdown. Naturally, a longing for community loomed large at that time. Thankfully, I had the comfort of virtual chats with a large and extended family, including my parents, Joe and Anna-Marie Pizza, grandmother, Ann Tramontana, brothers, and in-laws. Even more so, though, I was blessed with the immediate company of my children, Sera, Tommy, and Ella, and my wife, Ali, whose support, encouragement, and cheerful perseverance exceeded any reasonable expectation. It is unlikely that this project would have ever come to completion without the help of my first community, whose voices resonate with the humor, tension, and affection that I'd be lost without.

Preface

INTEGRATING BLACK MOUNTAIN

In February of 1949, Langston Hughes visited one of the first integrated higher education institutions in the Jim Crow South, Black Mountain College. Though scholars have had little to say concerning the visit, it reflects the larger, and little known, networks of community extending beyond the college's isolated campus. As Hughes reported in a subsequent postcard to the photographer Carl Van Vechten, Black Mountain was "just about the most amazing campus I have seen in my natural life—and interracial too" (Hughes, postcard to Van Vechten). Hughes's enthusiasm here cannot be overstated. In retrospect, the commingling of modernism's preeminent African American poet with the community that served, in many ways, as incubator to the postwar avant-garde, looked ahead to the integrated communities of writers who would flourish elsewhere in the following decade. As biographer Arthur Rampersad frames it, the visit was part of a Negro History Week speaking tour that had brought Hughes to Washington, D.C., as well (*Life of Langston Hughes*, 163). Although Black Mountain had welcomed lecturers for Negro History Week since at least 1943, integrated in 1944, and become known as a haven for Black travelers, hosting an interracial group of

Freedom Riders from the Congress of Racial Equality (CORE) during their 1947 "Journey of Reconciliation" through the South, its role in the process of desegregation was and remains largely unknown (Wilkins, "Social Justice at BMC before the Civil Rights Age"). In this context, Hughes's visit marks a pivotal moment in that struggle, one that would reverberate well beyond the Black Mountain campus.

Behind the scenes, the circumstances that made Hughes's appearance possible were the product of an almost decade-long conflict between various factions of Black Mountain faculty and students. At its best, the college, like other experimental communities, offered students and faculty the rare adventure of living out their ideals. As Jon Horne Carter writes, Black Mountain "was assembling an entirely new community, built of political refugees and cultural exiles—creating a world rather than preserving one" ("Community Far Afield," 60). During the school's early years, it became increasingly clear that integration was essential to the creation of this new world; however, the path to achieving integration remained uncertain. As Martin Duberman records the situation, by the early 1940s the entire community wanted to pursue some form of integration on campus, but the college split over the question of how to do so (Duberman, *Black Mountain*, 213). For their part, the students broadly supported the idea of immediate and full admission of Black students and instructors; meanwhile, the faculty were divided over the timing of such a plan (Duberman, 213–18). Though many sided with the students, some faculty took to heart Zora Neale Hurston's advice when she wrote to one of the school's founders, theater instructor Bob Wunsch, that "even at this distance I can see the dynamite in the proposal to take Negro students *now*" (Hurston, Letter to Robert Wunsch, February 21, 1944). Hurston believed that the timing of such a plan appeared more like a publicity stunt for ambitious "Left-wing" faculty than a genuine attempt to assist African American students (Hurston, Letter to Robert Wunsch). Such concerns were echoed in faculty debates. As Mary Emma Harris has written, despite sharing a common commitment to desegregation, faculty discussions concerning the best process by which to achieve it "were often bitter, and charges of racism, political intrigue, and opportunism were exchanged" (*Arts at Black Mountain College*, 70).

Despite the rancor of such debates, they revealed one common denominator among faculty and students alike: the shared belief that integration was essential to the school's progressive pedagogy and avant-garde aesthetics. For the vast majority of faculty and students, their urgency to begin this project in earnest stemmed from their own experiences as strangers in the South. As castaways on an island of progressivism, the community perceived itself from the very beginning as threatened and harassed by the same cultural forces that instituted and maintained racial segregation. Consequently, many northerners recounted their shock and dismay at witnessing first-hand—and for the first time—the farcical inequities of southern racial attitudes by aligning their own plight with that of African Americans. Fielding Dawson and Michael Rumaker, for instance, whose extensive biographical accounts provide essential context for Black Mountain's theoretical experimentation, dwell on their early encounters with and opposition to segregation at ball parks and on trains (Dawson, *Black Mountain Book*, 30–31; Rumaker, *Black Mountain Days*, 40–43). As Rumaker frames it, he felt that his homosexuality should have placed him in the segregated cars at the back of the train as well, musing, in the bracing language that the community often encountered when leaving campus, that as "a criminalized faggot" and "a writer, an artist" he "belonged in the back cars too" (42). The braiding together here of race, sexuality, and artistic vocation was common among both students and faculty at the college during this time. Politically progressive and aesthetically experimental, Black Mountain prided itself on attracting figures from the margins of American society, many of whom aligned their own aspirations with the quest for racial integration.

In addition to white Americans such as these, the European refugees who sought shelter in Black Mountain's community frequently aligned themselves with African Americans as well. In fact, for a good portion of the college's history, a significant number of its instructors were German, including refugees from the famed Bauhaus fleeing political and religious persecution. For many of them, and the European students who followed, southern segregation seemed frighteningly similar to their experiences with totalitarian regimes in Europe, uniting them with Northerners who shared an impatience with the school's deliberations over integration. Zoya Sandomirsky Slive, a student at the 1941 summer institute, recalls her first encounter with segregated drinking fountains in nearby Asheville:

I roamed around, stopped at a five-and-ten store, and in the back of the store had a drink from a water fountain. Suddenly I felt dozens of eyes piercing my back. I turned around and saw people staring at me. What

did I do wrong? A sign above the water fountain read: "For Colored."
(Slive, "Another Kind of Hoe Down," 97)

Working on campus shortly afterward, Slive couldn't escape the irony of the situation: "I had come seeking freedom [from a country that] at the same time denied freedom to a large portion of its own citizens" (97). This recognition, like those of Rumaker and Dawson a decade later, proved an essential part of Slive's Black Mountain experience, informing her subsequent work as a civil rights activist (97).

Despite these commitments, integration was a fraught process. For instance, by the time the college did finally agree on a plan to integrate, several faculty members who had advocated for it earlier in the decade had either resigned or been forced out (M. E. Harris, *Arts at Black Mountain College*, 70–71). Such disagreements aside, the school did welcome its first African American student and faculty members in the summer of 1944, accepting Alma Stone Williams, a Spellman alumna and valedictorian, and hiring artist Carol Brice and singer and composer Roland Hayes (C. Clark, "Black Mountain College"). As Williams recalled, the debate leading up to her matriculation was painfully ironic:

> [Black Mountain] could expect fellow Americans to have no special
> problems in transporting fleeing European scholars to work or study in
> a Southern place of refuge. Problems of nationality, religion, language,
> political allegiance, and money—these the college could handle on its
> resilience and its progressive, democratic design. But the college leaders
> were not sure in the spring of 1944 that they could bring, or desired to
> bring, an American Black person to join their ranks and study beside
> them. (Williams, "Opening Black Doors at Black Mountain College," 41)

Fully aware of the situation on campus, Williams nonetheless took up the pioneering work of integrating Black Mountain and found the experience rewarding: "[t]he timing was perfect. I had an exhilarating, unforgettable eleven-weeks experience that helped shape my life" (41). She found that a shared passion for experiment in art created a space where the participants' cultural differences could intersect and create new forms of community:

> I was at home among these people: students and teachers, Northern
> and Southern, regulars and institute members, Americans and foreign-

ers, Thomas Mann's daughter and Sigmund Freud's daughter-in-law. The arts brought us together, and differences were not so much threatening as they were attracting. (41)

Williams's reflection here marks perhaps the high point in Black Mountain's struggle to integrate, a testament to the school's ability to live out its ethos. Clearly, the experiment was a success, with African American students continuing to attend Black Mountain throughout the remaining decade and into the 1950s.

For his part, Langston Hughes was certainly inspired by this, as his subsequent account of the visit in the *Chicago Defender* attests. Expanding upon his postcard to Van Vechten, Hughes praised Black Mountain's ambition to realize a living democracy, insisting that its interracial composition emanated from its democratic way of life: "There are no discriminations of any sort on its campus. Democracy in action is its way of life. . . . It does not talk about decent race relations. It lives them" ("Democracy Is Not a Theory at Black Mountain College," 6). Though the school had struggled to maintain a significant number of African American students—Hughes's article may even have been conceived, at least in part, as a recruitment letter—it is nonetheless true that the Black Mountain community braved segregationist ire and political intrigue in its attempts to live out these convictions. As Hughes writes, the college's pedagogical practice was shaped by a thoroughly integrationist ethic: "Teaching in the usual academic sense is transcended at Black Mountain where the accent is rather on student and teacher living and exploring and working together inside the classroom and out . . . one race or social background with another" ("Democracy Is Not a Theory," 6). The choice of "accent" here is fitting, revealing the focus of the community's rhythm of life as a kind syncopation of Jim Crow norms. In fact, the ambition to integrate avant-garde aesthetics and progressive politics at Black Mountain instanced a larger struggle at the heart of modernism's experimental practice: namely, the extension of such experiments into the political sphere. From Ezra Pound's espousal of Italian Fascism to the Bauhaus's various relations to democratic socialism, Soviet Communism, and German Nazism, the exchanges between innovative arts and reactionary or radical politics in this period has been well-documented.[1] In contrast to this, Black Mountain's political legacy, like Hughes's involvement with the avant-garde, has been largely overlooked. As Aldon Lynn Nielsen and Lauri Ramey have shown, contrary to the assumptions of many scholars, Hughes took great interest in avant-garde developments and defended African American writers who shared this perspective ("Introduction: Fear of a Black Experiment" xiii–xv). Additionally, as Nielsen has demonstrated, Hughes's concern for the work of innovative poets was related directly to his larger attempt to claim a space for his writing, and that of his successors, at the cutting edge (*Black Chant*, 38–39). Such delayed recognition of Hughes's avant-garde interests has hindered not only our understanding of his work, but also our understanding of experimental communities like Black Mountain, where aesthetics and politics were interwoven in ways still not fully understood. As a result, Hughes's interest in the college, and its alignment with his own concern for the potential future of innovative African American art, has gone unnoticed. One of the central aims of this study is to bring such convergences to light by exploring the aesthetic and ideological interchanges that shaped the college's legacy as a major influence on America's first truly integrated avant-garde in the late 1950s and early 1960s. Read in the context of this larger history, then, Hughes's presence at Black Mountain serves as a locus of these gathering concerns, a harbinger of the work and debate to come.

Dissonant Voices

Introduction

DISSONANT VOICES

RACE, JAZZ, AND THE NEW AMERICAN POETICS OF BREATH

Toward the end of his life, Amiri Baraka found himself reflecting on the attempts to forge an integrated avant-garde in midcentury New York. Diagnosing the ills of that scene, Baraka insisted that "[i]f you cannot make the connection that is between Olson and Sun Ra, you cannot understand the pathology of that time" ("Charles Olson and Sun Ra," 00:00:52–7). Though they were contemporaries, Sun Ra's experimental jazz has rarely been considered in relation to Charles Olson's innovative poetics. In fact, while some of Ra's poetry bears a relation to Olson's experiments in typography, the two are rarely conjoined. Instead, discussions of postwar jazz poetics typically focus on Olson's close collaborator Robert Creeley, on better known Beat poets like Allen Ginsberg, on African Americans like Bob Kaufman, or even on Baraka himself. Despite their overlapping interests, these writers are typically read in isolation, cut off from the integrated communities that fostered their work by the subsequent scholarly habit of segregating poets in a fashion strikingly similar to the era's predominant culture. To remember such circumstances as pathological accurately names the unfettered racism plaguing the period, while also suggesting its chronic endurance today.

In fact, Baraka's metaphor draws on another key element in both New American and Black Arts poets' enthusiasm for jazz: its foregrounding of the body, of the tactile and the haptic, over and against the more abstract and cerebral approach of the period's academic poetry. This embodied approach based its understanding of performativity on the conjunctive notion of space, of the space of the page in Olson's typographic score, and of the space created by the galactic rhythms of Ra's avant-garde jazz. Breath, in this case, attunes the individual to what Ra described as a "Cosmic Equation," an equalization or perception of equality syncopated via a nascent Afrofuturism predicated upon the beautiful dissonance of cross-cultural, alien encounters with the sounds of others (*Sun Ra: The Immeasurable Equation*, 110). In this way, Baraka frames the creation of a thoroughly integrated poetics as an honest attempt to respond to the era's pathology. As he noted, for a poet at this time—whether Black or white—"Sun Ra and Olson were perfect mentors" ("Charles Olson and Sun Ra," 00:22:45–47).

Taking its cue from Baraka, *Dissonant Voices* seeks to trace the effects of such tutelage through an integrated reading of the work of New American and Black Arts Movement poets at midcentury. For the writers involved in the burgeoning artistic scenes developing across the country at this time, the marriage of innovative poetics and avant-garde jazz provided a basis for both physical solidarity and imagined communities of common interest. Whether in North Carolina, Boston, San Francisco, the Village, or Harlem, an emerging avant-garde, sharing an embodied poetics of breath rooted in jazz, spread through a mix of personal contacts, café readings, and small press publications. Poets at Black Mountain like Olson, Creeley, and Robert Duncan simultaneously participated in and presided over growing scenes on the West Coast and in the Northeast, while little magazines like *Origin* and the *Black Mountain Review* provided forums for sympathetic writers in each locale to share their work. In fact, *Black Mountain Review* 7, the final issue of the magazine, would prove particularly important in this regard. Often referred to as the "Beat" issue, it presented a mix of Beat and Black Mountain writers and was guest edited by Allen Ginsberg. Though integration debates did not find their way into these publications, the crucial role of African American culture, and particularly jazz, appears repeatedly as a common ground of inspiration and a unifying force drawing together avant-garde artists and writers from across the map. These cultural alignments, coupled with an increasingly progressive politics actively involved in desegregation efforts in the South, led many younger African American writers in the 1950s and the 1960s to discover the emerging poetics of breath and voice as a natural extension of earlier attempts to marry literary modernism with the musical modernism of jazz.

Scholars, too, have noted these connections. The poet Lorenzo Thomas, for instance, in his study *Extraordinary Measures: Afrocentric Modernism and Twentieth-Century Poetry*, recalls that "Black Arts poets maintained and developed the prosody that they had acquired from Black Mountain and the Beats" (201). While Thomas combines Black Arts poets with Black Mountain and the Beats here, his focus elsewhere in his study is with the performative approach to typography that Black Arts writers developed from Olson's well-known essay "Projective Verse" (Thomas, 211). He goes on to describe the typographic practices of Sonia Sanchez, Johari Amini, and Askia Muhammad Touré as creating specifically Olsonian scores for performance (211–12). In a related way, Daniel Kane has shown that the focus on breath of "Projective Verse" provided an impetus for the many community readings that brought poets together in a physical space and so helped to define the interracial New York scene in this period (*All Poets Welcome*, 29–30). In addition, Kane has also argued that Olsonian approaches to typography were essential for Umbra poets, many of whom would play important roles in the Black Arts Movement later in the decade (84). Similarly, Tyler Hoffman has noted the influence of Olson's projectivist poetics in exploring the performance styles of Black Arts Movement poets (*American Poetry in Performance*, 171–72). As Hoffman admits, "[i]ronically, it is in many ways the white poet Charles Olson's essay 'Projective Verse' . . . that opened up these avenues of expression" (171). Meanwhile, Raphael Allison's *Bodies on the Line* examines two dominant strains of the 1960s-era poetry reading that he terms the "humanist" and the "skeptical" approaches to performing a text (xiii, xv). Though not primarily concerned with either the New American Poetry or the Black Arts Movement, many figures involved in, and indebted to, both groups appear throughout Allison's study. Though the focus is different, his critique of the era's naïve faith in presence, particularly in the "humanist" approaches of Ginsberg and Olson, aligns with many of the background assumptions supporting this study. Olson's valorization of the body, his haptic poetics, as I understand them, thus form a hinge between his interests and the jazz inspiration that augments mine.

Like Thomas, Kane, Hoffman, and Allison, Aldon Lynn Nielsen includes Olson's poetics on his list of key influences on the work of African American poets in early 1960s New York (*Black Chant,* 53). In addition, Nielsen, whose pioneering scholarship has done more to recover the work of overlooked African American poets in this period than that of any other scholar, is also quick to assert that such poetry was in no way derivative and that, in fact, Black poets lent invaluable support to their better-known white peers:

> They were not a newer, postmodern mockingbird school, merely adopting the fashionable trimmings of newly notorious white writers, such as the Beats. Instead, these new black writers were often providing leadership and places to publish to white writers, such as Olson and Ed Dorn and Diane di Prima. (*Black Chant,* 54)

Once again, Black Mountain and Beat examples are cited, though, crucially, in this case, the work of white poets appears dependent on their interracial friendships. Nielsen's defense of African American writers and their contributions to the New American Poetry hints at the larger fault lines troubling the communities studied here. As Michael Davidson has written, "[d]espite the rhetoric of tribalism or mutual aid adopted by many of the writers during this period, the actual development of community was not always so egalitarian" (*San Francisco Renaissance,* xi). Despite the democratic ethos taken up by many African American writers seeking to help their white peers at this time, this sense of mutual aid did not always carry over when the same white writers gained fame in later years. Such "dissonant companionship," as Andrew Epstein, following Robin Blaser, has termed it, thus describes well the abiding interest and defensive posturing that frequently characterized friendships within these communities (Epstein, *Beautiful Enemies,* 28).

Taken together, then, the critical discussion begs a host of questions. For instance, to what degree should the work of these poets be read as constituting an integrated or allied poetics? What positionalities did Black and white poets alike adopt in response to the racial politics of the period? How should the lasting effects of their collaborations be understood? Such questions—and there are surely others—loom especially large at present, as institutions across the United States attempt to reckon with the enduring legacy of segregation and with the long march that some have begun to call a Second Civil Rights era. Up to this point, however, such concerns remain largely unexplored. Yet while no detailed study of these relationships has yet been undertaken, the work of Thomas, Kane, Hoffman, Nielsen, and Epstein, among others, attests to a considerable, and growing, consensus concerning the interracial context necessary for understanding avant-garde poetic communities at midcentury.

As Thomas's example shows, however, scholars are not the only ones who have recognized the significance of this subject. Perhaps no major contemporary poet has addressed this topic as fully as has Nathaniel Mackey. Beginning with the early essays collected in *Discrepant Engagement* and continuing in his recently published Robert Creeley Lecture titled "Breath and Precarity," Mackey has returned frequently to the imaginative spaces where innovative poetics meet jazz aesthetics, with regular attention to Black Mountain and the Beats. For example, in the introduction to *Discrepant Engagement*, he notes that while the "Jazz Age and the Beats offer the best-known examples" of the convergence between poetics and jazz, "the Projectivists can be seen as having been touched as well" (8). He goes on to quote, at length, Olson's and Creeley's enthusiasms for Charlie Parker, asserting that the latter's prose demonstrates a "syncopated, 'offbeat' quality" akin to bebop (8–9). More recently, Mackey has explored the combined influence of "Projective Verse" and Ginsberg's "Notes for *Howl*" as forging a poetics of breath and voice allied with then new developments in jazz ("Breath and Precarity," 2–3). As he recalls in the same lecture, the confluence of Black music and innovative poetics is instructive:

A poetics of breath is all the more palpably evident in black music, particularly the music of wind instruments, a radical pneumaticism in which the involuntary is rendered deliberate, labored, in which breath is belabored, made strange. . . . I especially heard this in Sonny Rollins' version of "On Green Dolphin Street". . . . I could never get over and still can't get over the hectored, put-upon way he opens the piece, running the gamut between stop-and-go, halting attack, a tossed, asthmatic shortness of breath, a catching of breath, and a relaxed assurance of breath so nonchalant as to barely evince effort. . . . I used to play this track for poetry classes when I began teaching in the mid-seventies. I would say, "This is projective verse." ("Breath and Precarity," 9)

While Mackey's point here is anecdotal, it is nonetheless crucial to the readings pursued in this study. Though the range of reference is somewhat larger, Olson, Creeley, Ginsberg, and many of the younger poets whom they inspired at midcentury would learn the same lesson regarding Rollins, Parker, Chano Pozo, Billie Holiday, John Coltrane, and others. As I intend to show in subsequent chapters, the New American Poetry's poetics of breath and voice would not have been possible without such an analogical understanding of the Black music that inspired it.

Recognizing this influence requires, at least in part, grappling with the long history of the terrain shared by poetry and music. While space precludes an exhaustive discussion of the subject here, it is helpful to recall that it was central to the Modernist poets whose work inspired the midcentury avant-garde. Since at least Walter Pater's *The Renaissance*, with its famous declaration that *"All art constantly aspires towards the condition of music"* in its attempt to "obliterate" the distinction between form and content, the musical horizon has marked one end of the spectrum for poetic expression (106). Inspired, in part, by Pater, but taking a more pragmatic approach, Ezra Pound famously described "melopoeia" as one of the three kinds of poetry, defining it as a type of writing where "the words are charged, over and above their plain meaning, with some musical property, which directs the bearing or trend of that meaning" ("How to Read," 25). Pound's sense of melopoeia's capacity to exceed the "plain meaning" pairs well with Pater's understanding of music as defying the need to categorize. Both, no doubt, contributed to Louis Zukofsky's formulation in *A-12*:

I'll tell you.
About my *poetics*—

$$\int_{\text{speech}}^{\text{music}}$$

An integral
Lower limit speech
Upper limit music (*A-12*, 138)

Working the speech-music axis thus suggests the latter be taken as the poetical apotheosis of spoken language. As Bob Perelman has written, however, such "utopian" thinking ignores practicalities: "The simultaneity of sound and significance that constitutes music and allows for single lines to build up into immediately perceptible chords does not occur with words" (*Trouble with Genius,* 185). While Perelman is certainly correct, Zukofsky's ambition need not be read in the extreme. As Zukofsky wrote elsewhere, a poem can be defined as "a context associated with a 'musical' shape, musical with quotation marks since it is not of notes as music, but of words more variable than variables, and used outside as well as within the context with communicative reference" ("An Objective," 16). Here, Zukofsky is careful to distinguish "musical" from music, suggesting a figurative treatment that perceives verbal art as abiding "with communicative reference," while also possessing the capacity to exceed the merely referential. The New American poets' interest in jazz can be read similarly, with the musical impulse pushing the referential stasis of language into action, moving it to exceed or explode linguistic and cultural codes through an alignment of poetry with Black music. As Jacques Attali has written, Black music—and jazz, in particular—engaged in this period in a longstanding struggle "to win creative autonomy" and so "build a new culture" (*Noise,* 138). This alternative culture would be based upon what Michel Serres called "the multiple," on the chaos that predates the one-dimensional representations of an orderly cosmos (*Genesis,* 101). In fact, by reimaging the alternative value of such noisy discord, the jazz-inflected poetics of midcentury innovators would emerge as a rallying point for integrated communities across the country.

In seeking to explore the New American Poetry and, by extension, the poets of the Black Arts Movement, in this way, I have borrowed throughout from the insights of scholars specializing in the fields of jazz studies, sound studies, and critical race theory. In particular, Paul Berliner's influential *Thinking in Jazz* has shaped my approach to Black Mountain and Beat understandings of improvisation. As Berliner shows, improvisatory thought begins with considerations of rhythm: "[p]erhaps the most fundamental approach to improvisation emphasizes rhythm, commonly known in the jazz community as time or time-feel" (Berliner, *Thinking in Jazz,* 147). This sense of rhythm as "time-feel" is seconded by many of the poets considered in this study. In addition, many poets in the period also assumed an analogous relationship between the articulation of musical phrases in time and the rhythmic shape punctuation lends to writing:

Miles Davis once advised Tommy Turrentine that players could "play simple and sound good," if they understood how to "phrase." Turrentine elaborates, explaining that improvising "linear or melodic" ideas is like "writing a sentence. The commas, the periods, and the exclamation points have to be very pronounced." (Berliner, 157)

In other words, the rhythm of a sentence bears some comparison with the improvised articulation of a melodic phrase in music. In both cases, timing is a crucial source of inventiveness and originality. Such "language metaphors," as Berliner terms them, recur throughout his discussions of musical improvisation, suggesting a fruitful correspondence between the different arts: "[a]s individual figures encounter one another in thought, they can produce various types of imaginative unions whose precise features may have unexpected implications for artists, suggesting a wealth of derivative ideas for consideration and pursuit" (185). Ultimately, these derivative ideas share, across media, a grounding in physicality reminiscent of both Olson's and Ginsberg's preoccupations with the possibilities and limitations presented by a poetics centered in breath and the body:

> When leading, the body pursues physical courses shaped not only by the musical language of jazz, but by idiomatic patterns of movement associated with the playing techniques of an instrument. These, in turn, reflect the instrument's particular acoustical properties, physical layout, and performance demands. Ultimately, all of these factors define the body's world of imagination, inviting it to explore their relationships. (Berliner, 190)

Similarly, projectivist and Beat poets alike cultivated a performative approach to composing that drew on their own physical capabilities and limitations. Whether understood as a form of improvisation or in the more traditional sense of composition and revision, the demands of such performances shape their poetics at each stage of the writing process.

Additionally, the jazz poetics pursued by the poets considered in this study address the audience in a physical way as well. As Erik Redling has argued, such texts approach the reader through an art that goes beyond metaphor in its demand on audience participation:

Jazz poems, however, not only document the poets' resourcefulness of transforming jazz into a written shape, but they also call on the readers to participate in the creation of music. The typographical "anomalies" ask readers to imagine a certain portion of the text or even the whole poem as a musical performance. . . . The readers cannot simply read over such typographical signals but need to imagine themselves as partaking in the poem's musical performance. Perhaps more than other types of poetry, jazz poetry allows readers to become active and "compose" their own aesthetic experience. (*Translating Jazz into Poetry*, 7)

These metaphorical performances practiced by writer and reader effectively create meaning through a collaboration unique to jazz poetry. Interestingly, Redling's primary example is a projectivist poem, Paul Blackburn's "Listening to Sonny Rollins at the Five Spot," which merges Olson's typographic practices with Ginsberg's jazz-inflected approach to performance. Like the poems featured throughout this study, Blackburn's work employs Black Mountain and Beat poetics to render a reading experience that crosses multiple media as part of its attempt to parallel jazz performance conventions. Following the pioneering work of cognitive linguists George Lakoff and Mark Johnson, Redling shows that such collaborative performances create an "intermedial" text, one where poetic innovation "creates" an experience of "the saxophonist's music," rather than simply imitating or describing it for the reader (*Translating Jazz*, 9). In approaching both Black Mountain and Beat-inspired poetry as instances of a jazz poetic, I have understood them accordingly, as intermedial texts constructed along the basis of rhythmic improvisation engaging the reader as participant. In this way, I believe, the rhetoric of "breath" identified by Mackey, and the physical implications it carries for writers of differing genders and racial groups, can be best understood.

In drawing on this performative aspect of New American and Black Arts Movement poetics, I have also been informed by sound studies, and particularly by investigations of the way breath manifests itself through more recent understandings of textual voice. Though literary-critical discussions of voice have too often appealed to the very New Critical habits of reading that Olson's, Ginsberg's, and Baraka's poetics opposed, or blindly celebrated the poets' often uncritical adoption of performance practices meant to reveal a hidden or unitary self, recent critical investigations have witnessed a broad expansion and complication of the subject. In his introduction to the influential collection *Close Listening*, Charles Bernstein builds upon Garrett Stewart's exploration of the phonotext of poetry, arguing for critical attention to the poetry reading as, crucially, "its own medium" (Bernstein, 12).[1] In this way, he pursues an "audiotext," an understanding of aurality that is, as he notes, "proprioceptive in Charles Olson's terms," and thus congruent with the exploration of voice proposed here (13). So, too, is Brent Hayes Edwards's recent discussion of the materiality of voice: "What one hears in singing, then, is . . . the unique ways that a particular human body . . . gives resonant form to a particular language" (*Epistrophies*, 18). Such embodied performance marks for Edwards "the space where music and language coincide," an overlapping that signals "the paradigm of innovation in black art" (19). This paradigm has been explored thoroughly in Henry Louis Gates, Jr.'s foundational account of the "Talking Book" and "Speakerly Text" traditions of African American Literature, which hover in the background of subsequent discussions of voice in this study (Gates, *Signifying Monkey*, xxv–xxviii). These perspectives anticipate and complement more recent philosophical revaluations of voice by writers like Stanley Cavell, as well as by prominent theorists like Shoshana Felman and Judith Butler, among others.[2] Of particular relevance here, Adriana Cavarero, drawing on the work of Olson's near contemporary, Hannah Arendt, has explored voice's obstinate physicality through the sexual and racial dissonances that such physicality sounds. For Cavarero, even contemporary discussions of voice that attempt to register its embodied uniqueness, like Roland Barthes's "grain" or Hélène Cixous's *"languelait,"* abstract this quality, converting it into "the voice," a singular and disembodied subject of discourse (Barthes, *Pleasure of the Text,* 184; Cixous, *Entre l'écriture des femmes,* 32; Cavarero, *For More Than One Voice,* 143). According to Cavarero's analysis, it is only in polyvocal song and in certain strands of innovative poetry that such qualities become apparent. Following these qualities, she approaches the voice as a "vocalic matrix" where "relationality," the act of saying, rather than the message of what's said, holds sway: "The voice not only announces this relation, but it announces it as corporeal, material, and rooted in the always embodied singularity of an existent that convokes the other with the rhythmic and sonorous breath of his or her mouth" (200). Her use of "breath" here parallels in many ways Olson's and Ginsberg's, as does her concern for the politics that emanate from such a position:

"Wherever you go, you will be a polis," says Arendt, citing a famous sentence that bears witness, according to her, to the way in which for the Greeks the political consists in a space created by acting and speaking together "which can find its proper location almost any time and anywhere." The *polis*, according to Arendt, is not physically situated in a territory. It is the space of interaction that is opened by the reciprocal communication of those present through words and deeds. (Cavarero, *For More Than One Voice*, 204, citing Arendt, *Human Condition*, 198)

Similarly, as will be shown with Olson, Arendt's attitude toward racial integration could at times be inconsistent, condemning the horrors of the Holocaust on one hand, while, as Fred Moten reminds us, opposing school desegregation in the United States on the other (Moten, *The Universal Machine*, 65–139). Countering the racism apparent in this aspect of Arendt's thought, Cavarero instead focuses on the capacity of her work to foreground, perhaps despite herself, the mutual exchange of breath, the reciprocal recognition of the physical diversity that abstraction elides. For Cavarero, this relationality forms the basis of her larger argument:

the speakers above all make heard a mutual dependence on a voice that is invocation . . . an acoustic dialogue that takes its cadences from the very rhythm of breath. Their logos is oriented toward resonance, rather than toward understanding. Like a kind of song "for more than one voice" [*come una specie di canto a più voci*] whose melodic principle is the reciprocal distinction of the unmistakable timbre of each—or, better, as if a song of this kind were the ideal dimension, the transcendental principle, of politics. (Cavarero, 200–201)

This shift toward "resonance" and away from "understanding" alters typical approaches to dialogue. Rather than express or convey a message, voices resonate in a call-and-response fashion. It is a distinction that holds equally true in the world of post-World War II poetry, where the obsessive focus on traditional lyricality, on first-person monologue, characteristic of neo-formalists and confessional writers alike, might be contrasted with the dissonant poetics of breath espoused by New American and Black Arts poets in much the same way. In this regard, the musical metaphor she invokes is telling. Music was essential to innovative poets at midcentury in their attempts to elaborate a poetics of breath and voice. For now, it is perhaps enough to note that such an approach to voice as physical embodiment is aligned in important ways with Olson's larger conception of context as haptic, as the "touch on all sides" that constitutes the interacting relations of a polis (Olson, *Special View of History*, 25).

Interestingly, one of Cavarero's prime examples is the work of Edward Kamau Brathwaite. Brathwaite's poetry, it should be noted, is also in dialogue with innovative American writing that shares much with the poetics of the Beats, Black Mountain, and the Black Arts Movement. According to Cavarero, Brathwaite's reading style "restores the voice to the text" through its use of typeface as scoring and its dissonant, polyvocal performance (*For More Than One Voice*, 150). Consequently, she insists that a dialogic resonance persists in his work, one whereby "meaning resides precisely in this vocalic continuum of the community" (150). In making her case, she appeals frequently to the example of Black music, arguing that for various African-derived musical traditions in former British colonies (including the U.S.), such music stands "in direct and explicit contrast to the sonorous universe that is transported by the English language" (149). In a similar way, Brathwaite's recovery of the voice's embodied dissonance opposes the English literary tradition's bodiless interest in received forms. Brathwaite himself notes that "the hurricane does not roar in pentameter" (*History of the Voice*, 10). As I will be arguing throughout, there is something similar at work in the jazz-inflected poetics of voice offered by Black Mountain and the Beats and adapted by a younger generation of African American poets in the 1960s. It is a poetics where the attention to breath and voice introduces a vernacular difference that declares a body, and so requires our recognition, as readers, of this specific person, and of their ability to perform a politicized marginality otherwise rendered silent by the standards of conventional, printed discourse. In this way, these poets share with Olson and Ginsberg a clear opposition to the Eurocentric tendency to privilege a generic voice as such, a disembodied voice that is nonetheless indexed as that of the white, affluent, cisgender male, unless otherwise interrupted by vernacular.

Such interruptions are explored in Fred Moten's *In the Break: The Aesthetics of the Black Radical Tradition*. There, African American vernacular expression indexes a body at once at odds with, while also folded into, hegemonic cultural codes. For instance, in rereading Aunt Hester's primal scream as described in the opening chapter of Frederick Douglass's *Narrative*, Moten reveals what

Marx thought of as an "impossible example," the speaking commodity (*In the Break*, 11). As such, Aunt Hester's scream represents "[t]he commodity whose speech sounds embody the critique of value, of private property, of the sign" (12). This critique aligns well with Cavarero's understanding of voice as the body's stubborn resistance to metaphysics, its insistence on marking her specific materiality, over and against the disembodied voice of the western philosophical tradition. As Moten observes, "the revolutionary force of the sensuality that emerges from the sonic event Marx subjunctively produces"—produces subjunctively, in other words, by assuming the would-be impossibility of the speaking commodity—is precisely the performative aesthetic that his study so astutely details (*In the Break*, 12). Accordingly, he describes such resistance in terms of Black music: "the universalization or socialization of the surplus, the generative force of a venerable phonic propulsion, the ontological and historical priority of resistance to power and objection to subjection, the old-new thing, the freedom drive that animates black performances" (12). Moten's phrasing here evokes well both the "New Thing" of 1960s avant-garde jazz and, in its hyphenation, the "Changing Same" detailed by a writer central to this study and his own: Amiri Baraka.[3] Just as Aunt Hester's scream resists objectification, Baraka's work functions as a resistance to the alienation of commodification, dwelling literally "in the break," echoing the study's title (*In the Break*, 85). As such, Moten reads Baraka's early career as a site where "[s]yncopation, performance, and the anarchic organization of phonic substance delineate an ontological field wherein Black radicalism is set to work" (85). In subsequent chapters, I will attempt to bring this reading to bear on Baraka's syncopation of Black Mountain and Beat poetics, corroborating and extending the perspectives of Moten and Cavarero by bringing them into contact with the poetics that both led to and followed from Baraka's representative break.

More recently, Moten has revisited these topics in *Black and Blur*, the first part of his trilogy, *consent not to be a single being*. As he attests, the essays collected in the volume search out the problematics of *In the Break*'s omitted opening sentence: "Performance is the resistance of the object" (*Black and Blur*, vii). In doing so, Moten returns to Aunt Hester's scream, rereading it as "not simply unrepresentable," but as "an alternative to representation" (*Black and Blur*, ix). The trauma of her scream cannot be healed. Instead, Moten urges us to read it as "a perpetual cutting, a constancy of expansive and enfolding rupture and wound" (ix). This unavoidable physicality persists as "serration," as a "disruption of meaning, of the modality of subjectivity or subjective embodiment . . . [of the] proprioceptive coordination that constitutes what Amiri Baraka might call the 'place / meant' of possessed and / or possessive individuation" (ix). This charting or inscripting leads to a larger perception of Blackness as collective "estrangement," as "the displacement of being and singularity" (xiii).

Consequently, when Moten returns to the subject of voice, it is through an exploration of the problems of phonography, of its would-be elision and displacement of the body in Theodor Adorno's approach to "structural listening" (*Black and Blur*, 119). Focusing on a 1993 recording of the opera singer Jessye Norman's performance of Arthur Schoenberg's *Erwartung*, Moten hears "the mellifluous off inside the drama; the montagic, dissonant, syncopated abstract . . . the Black performance of narrative; the irreducible trace of (slave) narrative" (120). Such dissonances attend upon the physical interruption of voices that require a body. In Adorno's ideal form, phonographs exhibit a kind of writing whereby the listener reads imaginatively, without the mediation of a performer's physical presence. As Adorno argues, this is more the case with male than female voices: "Male voices can be reproduced better than female voices . . . in order to become unfettered, the female voice requires the physical appearance of the body that carries it" ("Curves of the Needle," 54). Moten rightly reads this passage as an instance of "pathologized racial and sexual difference," and subsequently demonstrates that, as an African American woman, Norman's performance disrupts the abstraction of disembodied structural listening through its very sonic difference:

> Her phonographic re*mate*rialization of *Ewartung* disrupts discontinuity with the radical force of an objective and objectional continuance, thereby requiring a reconfiguration of the concept of writing as that which occurs where performance and recording converge at the site of a *bodily* inscription. (*Black and Blur*, 129)

Such convergences insistently broach the "fugitive thingliness of a black performing body," and so, as Moten shows, disrupt not only Adorno's understanding of the record's capabilities for graphic reproduction but also, as with his earlier critique of Marx, reveal a gap or break in the theorist's failure to recognize the significance of racial and sexual difference (*Black and Blur*, 132). Referencing Adorno's well-known antipathy to jazz, Moten concludes by asserting that such misperceptions blind him to the body's stubborn import:

[J]azz moves within the history of a resistant, however commodified, objecthood, the history of an aggressive audiovisual objection that constitutes nothing other than the black and animating presence of *Erwartung*, the black thing that Adorno wouldn't understand, that Norman's objectional audiovisuality animates or reproduces with each encounter. (133)

A similarly "objectional audiovisuality" recurs throughout this study, irrupting and so interrupting the dominant narrative of a predominantly white avant-garde in midcentury American poetics. Drawing upon Moten's and Cavarero's estimations of the body's thingliness, its resistant materiality, the succeeding chapters of this project investigate the ways in which the necessarily racialized discourse of jazz inspired an integrated poetics resonant with these concerns.

In reading race, therefore, as a discourse that both unites and divides these writers, I have drawn on Moten's formulation of syncopated performance, threading his understanding of Blackness as a "consent" "to the displacement of being and singularity" with the well-known work of Kimberly Benston, Stuart Hall, and, more recently, that of Meta DuEwa Jones. As Benston has argued, for African American poets in the postwar era, the "performative ethos" of Black modernism informed the practice of racial identity in strategic ways (Benston, *Performing Blackness*, 1–2). This theme echoes Hall's well-known reading of race. In his famous formulation, the "Blackness" of various forms of popular culture, including Black music, "is this mark of difference *inside* [such] forms . . . which are by definition contradictory and which therefore appear as impure, threatened by incorporation or exclusion" (Hall, "What Is This 'Black' in Black Popular Culture?," 110). Such contradiction runs in at least two directions. First, in its very terms, "black popular culture" denotes the "engagement across cultural boundaries" and consequent "confluence of more than one cultural tradition" that complicate any essential reading of race in such forms ("What Is This 'Black,'" 110). Second, vulnerable to both appropriation and neglect, such difference also risks contradiction by pivoting on a "strategic essentialism," on, in other words, an assertion of Blackness as a unified discourse in order to resist the monolithic designs of the dominant culture, despite the fact that, ultimately, the "essentializing moment is weak because it naturalizes and dehistoricizes difference, mistaking what is historical and cultural for what is natural, biological, and genetic" ("What Is This 'Black,'" 110, 111). Instead, Hall shows that "[w]e are always in negotiation, not with a single set of oppositions that place us always in the same relation to others, but with a series of different positionalities," ones which, in Moten's terms, displace "singularity" and so "are often dislocating in relation to one another" (Hall, "What Is This 'Black,'" 112). In this way, Hall encourages us to understand such strategies henceforward as instances of resistance performed at various points by multiple positionalities. In reading African American poetry here, I explore the various negotiations authors made as part of the process of articulating such strategic forms of resistance. As Meta DuEwa Jones has shown, in her own exploration of jazz poetics, African American poetry is an "ultra-discursive field of signification," one where the "multivocal" and "improvisatory performance of identities can be heard" (Jones, *The Muse Is the Music*, 6). Listening to the dissonance inherent in these performances, therefore, will be a central aim of this study.

So, too, however, will be the parallel and often appropriative performances of whites. In a study that seeks to integrate scholarly understandings of innovative poetics at midcentury, it is necessary to problematize this work as a poetry that involves, in Hall's terms, an "engagement across cultural boundaries" ("What Is This 'Black,'" 110). As Matthew Frye Jacobson has written, one side of that boundary is inhabited by white writers who similarly sought to swim against the "complex crosscurrents at the confluence of capitalism, republicanism, and the diasporic sensibilities of various racially defined groups themselves" (*Whiteness of a Different Color*, 19). Many of the writers considered here were positioned at the margins of whiteness, negotiating working-class positionalities alongside homosexual or bisexual identities, and hailing from Irish or Jewish ancestries, ones, in other words, that only recently were admitted to the fullness of white privilege. As historians like David R. Roediger have forcefully argued, of course, class alone does not negate such privilege.[4] Still, these considerations add nuance to discussions of their writings as racial performances, particularly where those very performances struggle to overcome appropriative tendencies and stereotypical posturing. This is another way of saying that I read these writers in part as attempting to locate strategies for rethinking and resisting the array of privileges that whiteness confers. While the success of these attempts remains debatable, they present fruitful complications of the origins and development of postwar American poetics.

Weaving these strands together, then, this study seeks to address the interracial dialogue at the heart of New American and Black Arts Movement poetics, with particular attention to the formation, dissemination, and refashioning of the Black Mountain and Beat poetics of breath and voice. Part of that task involves extending the work of previous scholars by recovering the writing of overlooked African American poets. At the same time, however, the other part involves examining the poetry of their white peers as parallel racial performances, ones that depend upon the acknowledged precedent of Black cultural expressivity for their force and reference. To date, no study presents this dialogic dimension in its fullness. Instead, white practitioners, with Baraka typically listed as the sole exception, continue to be presented in various subgroupings—Beat, New York School, Black Mountain, and so on—while the works of Umbra and Black Arts Movement poets tend to be viewed as offering alternatives or supplements to these. As a result, this study proposes to break down that partition by rereading three moments in its construction. First, I attempt to unearth the appropriative roots at the ground of Black Mountain and Beat poetics; second, I detail the interracial collaborations that, however briefly, grew out of them; and third, I explore the essentialism of Black Arts Movement poets as a strategic response that effectively refashions the earlier work of their white peers.

In each case, jazz provides the meeting ground for these writers. Whether styled as Bop, Cool Jazz, or the New Thing, works by musicians in these genres and subgenres supplied analogous examples for artistic creation that captivated and inspired virtually all of the writers considered in this study. In fact, for each of the white writers discussed, their encounters with Black poets were often shaped by their enthusiasm for Black music. From Olson, Creeley, and Ginsberg, to Baraka, Sanchez, and Cortez, jazz concepts thus play an essential role in constructing their poetics and thereby govern their contacts and associations. As a result, the chapters that follow explore the pairing of jazz and interracial friendship at the heart of Black Mountain and Beat poetics, tracing these as a means for asserting the centrality of race in the construction and reception not only of Black Arts Movement writing but of major currents within the New American Poetry as well.

Though Beat poetics may appear directly relevant to such an investigation, Black Mountain's central presence, and the absence of other important poets, may be questioned. Certainly, arguments can be made in favor of a wider inclusion of writers in such a study. Frank O'Hara, for instance, played an important role in the New York scene where so many poets, Black and white, encountered each other. His enthusiasm for jazz and his friendship with Amiri Baraka have been well-documented. For this very reason, however, it is unnecessary to repeat the excellent work of scholars like Michael Magee and Andrew Epstein.[5] Similarly, the lack of female poets in the book's opening chapters may also concern some. While women were certainly present and actively involved in the scenes surveyed here, their engagement with interracial collaboration appears, in retrospect, less pronounced than that of many of the male poets examined in the chapters that follow. Of course, as equally marginal figures seeking admittance to the predominantly white male avant-garde of the time, the work of female poets in these communities poses its own set of complex questions and difficulties. While many of these questions are addressed in chapter five, in a study that seeks to foreground race, space precluded a larger discussion of these issues in earlier chapters. Still, it is worth noting one representative example here. Diane di Prima frequented the Beat, Black Mountain, New York School, and San Francisco scenes throughout her career, both as a writer and as a publisher of the important newsletter *The Floating Bear* and of the independently run Poet's Press. She was also involved in a long-running affair with Baraka, conceiving a child, Dominique, with him in the early 1960s. Reflecting on the era, her subsequent attitude toward its men appears mixed. On the one hand, she recalled that the "male cabal" now known as the New American Poetry was simply annoying:

> I realize that there truly was this determinedly male community of writers around me in the 50s. . . . I saw these guys, myself and the others, as artists simply. All the striving was for and of the Work, and I loved them for it. I loved them at their best and beyond their best as fellow companions of the Road. My choice: to overlook their one-upmanship, their eternal need to be *right*. Or I took it in stride as not important. A minor part of their Act. (*Recollections of My Life as a Woman*, 107)

In this spirit, di Prima denies any form of passive victimization, asserting instead her "choice" to accept her peers' chauvinism as merely a minor flaw. As she frames it, such attitudes were simply an "Act," not the heart of their relationship, which instead was centered on the "Work." And yet, on the other hand, such attitudes clearly affected the development of her own work:

> I had taken it as a matter of course when Donald Allen stopped in a doorway at a party at Roi's [Baraka's] house, to tell me that he wouldn't be including my work in the *New American Poetry* anthology.... Because of my ongoing affair with LeRoi ... there was implicit my ever-present acceptance that I would carry the guilt for the affair: LeRoi's poems could be included, but not mine. He was married, which made me, by implication, the home-breaker, the scarlet woman. It was all very matter-of-course. (*Recollections of My Life as a Woman*, 238)

Though presented sarcastically as "matter-of-course," di Prima's memoir reveals a much deeper wound. Her struggle to come to terms with the situation in her prose could be contrasted with her approach to it in her poetry. As can be shown, many of her poems from the period—works such as "Minor Arcana" or "The Practice of Magical Evocation"—engage directly in a feminist revision of New American poetics. In such poetry, the double standard present in scenes such as the one noted is confronted and resisted. There, her peers' chauvinism is framed as a "matter-of-course" that is, nonetheless, complicit in the injustices of the status quo. As Rachel Blau DuPlessis has termed it, the persistence of such chauvinism represents a "lost opportunity" in confronting a hegemonic patriarchy that the work of many otherwise innovative male poets and editors of the period inadvertently recreates (*Purple Passages*, 116). These questions remain timely and important, but they do not necessarily cross over into the terrain of race and thus remain on the periphery of this study until chapter five, in which female African American poets link di Prima's concerns over gender to questions of race and advance both through their own work.

As for Black Mountain, little to date has been written concerning the roles of integration and jazz in the formation of Olson's and Creeley's poetics. A central ambition of this study, therefore, is to recover this essential context. Additionally, through Black Mountain, writers from the San Francisco and Boston scenes also enter the study. Still, important poets like Larry Eigner, John Ashbery, Barbara Guest, Robert Duncan, and Denise Levertov are not included. While these poets certainly occupied significant spaces in Donald Allen's anthology and exercised influential roles in the subsequent development of postwar American poetry, their work proves only tangential to that studied here. Surely, a closer reading of race in the poetics of each would repay the effort; however, given the book's focus, space did not allow for such explorations in this study. Plus, as scholars and poets like Thomas, Nielsen, and Mackey have shown, the poetics of breath that inspired Black and white writers alike was drawn predominantly from Black Mountain and the Beats. For this reason, in the succeeding chapters I have focused on those poets whose work actively engaged with and responded to these groups.

Building upon the background sketched here, then, the first chapter details an unacknowledged source for the poetics that would become synonymous with Black Mountain: Charlie Parker. Over the course of the ten published volumes of their correspondence, Olson and Creeley repeatedly refer to Bird's music as the primary influence on their shared conception of rhythm, on its advance upon Ezra Pound's approach to measure, and on the sense of possibility it offered for further elaboration and exploration. In doing so, questions of race come to the fore, revealing the ways in which Olson's and Creeley's attitudes demonstrate both a clear commitment to formulating an inclusive poetics, one opposed to Pound's antisemitism and responsive to Black Mountain's larger drive to integrate, while also struggling to overcome commonly held prejudices and stereotypes. Applying this perspective to "Projective Verse" augments our understanding of their work in this period, showing the degree to which Olson and Creeley shared parallel concerns with Beat writers and with the work of unacknowledged predecessors like Langston Hughes, as well as with a younger generation of emerging poets elsewhere.

In a related way, the second chapter of this study explores the poetic friendship between Stephen Jonas, John Wieners, and Jack Spicer. As homosexual poets and interracial friends in mid-1950s Boston, Jonas and Wieners established a connection based on shared interests and common contacts, attending Olson's famed 1954 reading at the Charles Street Meeting House. Afterward, Jonas's understanding of Federico García Lorca's theory of *duende* would become the hinge linking Olson's projectivist poetics to their own nascent, jazz-inflected postmodernism. Though more often associated with the San Francisco Renaissance, Jack Spicer's brief time in Boston would prove formative as well. His friendship with Jonas would lead him to adopt a version of projectivist *duende* that, in his poetry from the period and, most notably, in his subsequent work, *After Lorca*, would chart a course for the remainder of his career. Through a consideration of their collaboration, then, the chapter demonstrates Jonas's unrecognized influence on both Spicer's and Wieners's burgeoning careers, while also demonstrating the Boston group's unique development of principles derived from Black Mountain and the Beats.

Following this, projectivist poetics are joined with Beat prosody through an examination of the conjunction of race and performance in the work of Allen Ginsberg and Bob Kaufman. While Black Mountain writers may have been the first to fully theorize a poetic analogy for jazz composition, Ginsberg's parallel approach to the poetics of breath proved equally important, and perhaps even more influential, for African American poets in the period. Though often associated with the Beats, Kaufman shared with Ginsberg—as well as with Olson and Creeley—a deep affection for and aesthetic reliance on the music of Charlie Parker. Consequently, their writing demonstrates a deeper affinity than their casual friendship suggests. By examining the shouts, screams, and howls of Kaufman's work, the chapter unearths one aspect of this affinity, exploring, on one hand, the influence of Black music on Ginsberg's poetics, while revealing, on the other, the degree to which Kaufman's work adapts and responds to Ginsberg's complicated example.

Building upon this, the fourth chapter focuses on the integrated group of avant-garde writers gathered around Amiri Baraka in late 1950s and early 1960s New York. Reading Baraka's early poetry in light of his exchanges with Olson and Ed Dorn, this chapter aims to capture a fuller picture of Black Mountain's role in his early poetic development, one that also reveals important, and overlooked, aspects of the interracial community brought together by his work as writer, editor, and publisher. Through these encounters, he gradually reworked projective verse, drawing out the racial implications, and contradictions, inherent in the poetics of breath devised at Black Mountain and adopted by his fellow poets in New York. In doing so, Baraka's negotiation of projective poetics not only advanced key elements of the New American Poetry, but also founded important principles that would guide poets engaged in the Black Arts Movement later in the decade.

The final chapter in this study then explores the ways in which poets associated with the Black Arts Movement reimagined important principles of projective verse, creating, in its place, a poetry whose attention to line, enfranchisement of blank space, and valorization of breath formed the ideal score for a Beat-derived performance art. This reimagining of projectivist poetics and Beat performance is widespread among writers who participated in the Umbra Workshop, the Black Arts Repertory Theatre, and related groups further afield. By focusing on poetry by Lorenzo Thomas, Sonia Sanchez, and Jayne Cortez, the performative element of their writing reveals a hitherto unexplored extension of the New American Poetry, while, at the same time, rewriting our understanding of the dissonant Americanness of postwar avant-garde poetics, bringing it into contact with the racial politics of the late 1960s and early 1970s. While poetry and theory by Baraka and Thomas set the stage, Sanchez's writing can be seen as an exemplary re-imagining of the performative ambitions at the heart of a poetics of breath. Ultimately, though, Cortez's collaboration with her band the Firespitters marks perhaps the furthest extension of this element of the New American Poetry. In this way, the chapter brings the book's concerns to a conclusion, having paused at a moment when avant-garde poetics began to shift away from Olson and Ginsberg through a critique of the poetics of breath that characterized their influence.

Later developments aside, the poetry considered in *Dissonant Voices* evinces the first substantial attempt at pursuing a thoroughly integrated poetics of breath and voice, one based upon a shared enthusiasm for Black music. While subsequent reflection shows that the challenges involved in this attempt overcame the ambitions of many involved, their body of work continues, nonetheless, to inspire today. As Mackey has written, "[b]lack music says, as does an allied, radically pneumatic poetics, that breath, especially imperiled breath, matters" ("Breath and Precarity," 18). In the chapters that follow, I explore the precarious situation of writers who attempted to create spaces for realizing just such a radically pneumatic, allied poetics.

Chapter One

FORM IS NEVER MORE THAN AN EXTENSION OF BIRD

PROJECTIVE VERSE AS JAZZ POETIC

Charles Olson's Black Mountain years encompass his most determined push to enact a definitively "post-modern" poetics of breath and voice ("The Present Is Prologue," 207). In concert with a young Robert Creeley, Olson's published and unpublished work from this period demonstrate his various attempts to realize the implications of his influential essay, "Projective Verse." Often taken as the definitive statement of the New American poetics of breath and voice, the essay was written with assistance from Frances Boldereff and Creeley, with the latter contributing the crucial insight that "[f]orm is never more than an *extension* of content," which Olson immediately credited as "beautiful, and most USABLE" (Creeley, *O & C Cor*, 1:79; Olson, *O & C Cor*, 1: 85).[1] Creeley's insight quickly took on the status of dictum in their correspondence, appearing in the published version of "Projective Verse" in the spring of 1950 and referenced subsequently as a guiding principle of the poetics that would shape the New American Poetry.[2] That the principle arose in the context of Creeley's larger engagement with jazz aesthetics, with the bop rhythms of Charlie Parker, Max Roach, Thelonious Monk, Miles Davis, and others, however, has remained largely unexplored. In fact, jazz listening sessions became woven into both the curricular and the extracurricular experience at Black Mountain during Olson's tenure. In this way, jazz can be seen as part of the larger attempt to engage the writing and literature students there with the distinctiveness of American culture, with its various "departures from the Western norm" (Olson, Literature Program Catalogue Description, 7). For his part, Olson certainly understood the import of jazz on the poetics of "Projective Verse" and on the so-called "Black Mountain School" of poetry it inspired. In fact, his initial response to Creeley's poetry borrowed a phrase from Fats Waller's swing-era hit "The Joint Is Jumpin" to emphasize this: "[T]he verse of, my poultry man: two strings, and the joint was jumpin" (*O & C Cor,* 1:86). As he reflected in a 1968 interview, projective verse was indebted chiefly to jazz: "Poetics? Boy, there was no poetic. It was Charlie Parker. Literally, it was Charlie Parker" (Olson, *Muthologos,* 71).

Scholars of Olson and Creeley have not entirely ignored this context. In his introduction to the ten-volume Olson-Creeley correspondence, George Butterick suggests that the letters show "both men," in Creeley's terms, "'looking for a language,'" and addresses the two poets' shared interest in jazz as a basis for it:

> Creeley keenly participated in the rhythms of the new speech that issued parallel to jazz, and while Olson had relatively little experience of jazz (limited, perhaps, to Fats Waller and the stride and boogie-woogie pianos of Greenwich Village Café Society days of the late thirties), he trusted his American speech in whatever forms he heard it. (Introduction, *O & C Cor,* 1:xiv)

Though cautious, Butterick's note concerning Olson encourages further research. The letters themselves are filled with references by both Creeley and Olson that reveal the latter's engagement with jazz even more fully than noted here. In a short, but more revealing comment, Sherman Paul has considered the analogous relationship between dance, action painting, jazz, and Olson's poetics, claiming that these arts "offered the instruction they [Creeley and Olson] wanted," and adding that, "Charlie Parker reminds us that Olson more than any of his predecessors stresses breath" (Paul, *Olson's*

Push, 39). Though Paul doesn't expand upon or follow up on these notes, there is ample evidence that both Olson's and Creeley's approach to "breath" and "rhythm" owe a significant debt to Parker and bebop. In a similar way, Tom Clark has provided additional context on the subject. With Olson, he records the poet's involvement in the jazz scene presided over by Amiri Baraka in Greenwich Village (T. Clark, *Charles Olson*, 298–99). In regard to Creeley, Clark introduces the poet's commentary on "The Whip" by claiming that "[t]he imagination of a cool, angular, driving jazz, punctuated with anxious, staccato accents and playing at moderated volume somewhere off in the backdrop, is an important element in the existential *ambience* of much of Creeley's earliest serious writing" (T. Clark, *Robert Creeley*, 46–48). As I have argued elsewhere, Creeley's jazz poetic developed through his Black Mountain contacts, first via his correspondence with Olson and, later, through his friendship and collaboration with trumpeter and painter Dan Rice.[3] This chapter will thus attempt to fill in the picture by exploring Olson's and Creeley's letters and critical prose in the light of jazz histories and critical studies of jazz poetics.[4] As these letters reveal, jazz music marks a rich and undervalued context for the poetry and prose that the two poets would pursue together at Black Mountain College and later, in the aftermath of its closure, throughout the late 1950s and 1960s.

Such analogies, however, are always situated within and mediated by the poets' understanding of jazz as an African American art form, as, in Baraka's terms, "Black Music."[5] Consequently, I will be examining the conjunction of jazz aesthetics and integrationist pedagogy, as well. Ultimately, I hope to show here that projective verse ought to be read alongside Beat aesthetics as another kind of midcentury jazz poetic, as, in other words, one more extension of Charlie Parker's trailblazing music. At the same time, however, projective verse's participation in African American cultural traditions occurred via a very different context, namely the debates concerning integration at Black Mountain College. In creating, therefore, the kind of integrated aesthetic that could account for America's "departures from the Western norm," Olson and Creeley pioneered a poetics of breath and voice that was clearly aligned with the interests of a younger generation of jazz-inspired poets, both white and Black. By rereading the origins and inspirations of this poetic, this chapter seeks to revise our understanding of projective verse, augmenting the claims of previous scholars and poets while recovering its place in the creation of an interracial, postwar avant-garde.

Though often misread as avoiding politics altogether in this period, Olson was actively involved in the struggle for racial integration. Having found his way to Black Mountain in 1948, Olson worked to advance such efforts while pushing writing to the center of the college's curriculum through his marathon workshops and larger-than-life personality. After spending the early 1940s working for the American Civil Liberties Union, the Office of War Information, and Roosevelt's reelection campaign, as Director of the Foreign Nationalities Division for the Democratic National Committee, he knew well the challenges involved in bridging racial divides and building coalitions (T. Clark, *Charles Olson*, 76–89). However, after Roosevelt's sudden death in April 1944, Olson came to view Washington under Truman and especially later into the Eisenhower era, in terms of Pound's "pejorocracy," and so chose to weave his political concerns into an ambitious and burgeoning poetics (Olson, *Maximus* I.3). As scholars like Ben Hickman and Lisa Siraganian have recently argued, rather than turn his back on politics entirely, these experiences led Olson to think more deeply about poetry as a different kind of political arena, as an alternative path to enact change (Siraganian 148); Hickman, *Crisis and the U.S. Avant-Garde*, 66). In this way, too, the question of integration became for him intertwined with the development of projectivist poetics. Not surprisingly, then, in addition to recruitment trips to African American schools and plans to attract Black veterans via the G.I. Bill, Olson can be found during his Black Mountain tenure exploring ways in which to further integrate the college and its curriculum.

Consequently, the subject of Southern segregation was never far from Olson's mind. According to students, his remarks turned often to the subject of the campus's surrounding environment, with special attention to questions of race. As Michael Rumaker recalled, students and faculty alike were regularly regarded as "Nigger lovers" by the surrounding community (Rumaker, *Black Mountain Days*, 267). Olson's responses to this were various, though always measured, tempered by the college's marginal status as an island of progressivism. On one occasion, he reportedly opined to students that "[t]he tragedy of blacks is that they can't play it across the board," meaning, in other words, that they were the victims of structural inequalities (quoted in Rumaker, 268). Consequently, he encouraged his white class to see that "[b]etween whites and blacks there needs to be a coalescence" (Rumaker,

268). Of course, it is fair to ask why the school itself did not become more of a space for such a coalescence under Olson's tenure. In part, the answer may lie in Langston Hughes's estimation that Black Mountain's progressive pedagogy and lack of a traditional degree program would appeal only to a very few, regardless of race ("Democracy Is Not a Theory," 6). Olson himself offered a similar perspective in a 1951 faculty meeting, where he argued that since the college purposely catered to the "marginal area" of society with its experimental philosophy and only occasional conferment of degrees, it was unethical not to make this situation clear to prospective African American students, regardless of the college's financial situation and consequent need of tuition dollars (Black Mountain College, Faculty Minutes).

Despite such challenges, Olson and his colleagues demonstrated a dogged persistence in arguing for the virtues of integration during the meeting's four and a half hours of discussion. Biology professor Victor Sprague, for instance, began with a report on his trip to Shaw University, a historically Black university in Raleigh. In particular, Sprague praised the school's new president for his inauguration speech's actual "interest in education" and for leaving out "the usual crap" that often fills such artificial addresses (Black Mountain College, Faculty Minutes). For his part, Olson shared details of his trips to Asheville's Allen School, a prestigious high school for African American girls—where a young Nina Simone would have been in attendance at this time—and Stevens Lee High School, the city's only black public high school (Black Mountain College, Faculty Minutes). As reported, he criticized the United States government at home and abroad, taking special aim at the Truman administration's "Johnny Appleseed policy in the Orient" and to what he saw as America's hegemonic battle against communist forces in Korea. Despite this, and despite the reign of Jim Crow at home, Olson assured those in attendance that Black Mountain "welcomes a student without any question of race, religion, or politics" (Black Mountain College, Faculty Minutes). When asked by colleagues why recruitment efforts focused on "all Negro schools," Olson angrily retorted "because they invite us," adding that it was essential to Black Mountain's pedagogy: "[T]hey are alert and know they'll get straight statements from us, they know about us; it is important that we do this extension of the educational act" (Black Mountain College, Faculty Minutes). Such exchanges attest to the continuing debate at Black Mountain over integration, even into the school's final years. For Olson, these concerns were clearly a natural extension of not only his work in the

Roosevelt administration but of the larger poetics and pedagogy he hoped to instill at Black Mountain College. In fact, he encouraged students to see that Jim Crow was analogous to Nazi antisemitism, and as such posed the dire question that they all must confront about the fate of their situation in the segregated South: "'How do we defend ourselves, any of us, from what's just over the hill'" (quoted in Rumaker, 138–39).

Though efforts toward furthering campus integration would continue, another mode of defense for Olson and his students would be to integrate the intellectual life of the college through a direct encounter with the diversity of American culture in art and writing. As his catalogue description for the four-year "Writing and Literature" course has it, the emergence of a distinctively American culture, rather than classic European texts, would be the primary object of students' attention:

> Rather than the "history" of English and American literature by periods, centuries, and forms, the 4-year discipline is organized on the premise that the American language and culture are departures from the Western norm, and that both the use of language and the position of man [*sic*][6] as individual and in society is undergoing change. (Olson, Literature Program Catalogue Description, 7)

Such change was apparent in Olson's teaching in many ways, from his freewheeling digressions on primary interests like anthropology, linguistics, and contemporary politics to his occasional interest in the music of Charlie Parker, all of which served to connect the relatively isolated campus experience with the diversity and vitality of the world beyond its borders. As Fielding Dawson writes, the Americanness of Olson's pedagogy lay in its diversity, its ability to weave together "Europe . . . the Orient, and in a direct line Kline, Pollock . . . Charlie Parker, Miles Davis . . . Raymond Chandler's mythic women, *The Lady from Shanghai*," and so get past the merely personal to an "intuitive mystery beyond" (78). More than any other, Charlie Parker's music became the primary example of "departures from the Western norm" at Black Mountain during Olson's tenure, offering the community a window into the eclectic, integrated postmodernism that Dawson's description conjures.

In this regard, Rumaker's recollections of jazz's importance for the college community in this period are especially vivid. In keeping with the intensity of campus life, parties featured regular listening sessions to what students perceived as exciting new experiments in jazz:

> Practically everybody living on campus showed up at our Saturday night parties. The music—Miles Davis and Charlie Parker and Bud Powell and Stan Getz (whom Ed Dorn didn't like)—blared away on the Magnavox phonograph in its walnut cabinet, or on one of the new LP record players borrowed for the occasions, and everybody danced to it or listened, really *listened*, to the music in a very serious, if stoned, way—so typically Black Mountain, so typically the attentions of most of the people there, at the cutting edge, ahead of what was being broadcast in the rest of the land. (*Black Mountain Days*, 161)

Such close listening, while remaining ahead of popular culture in many ways, also offered new methodologies to apply to their own art and writing. Nor were such interests confined to students. Creeley's classes, for instance, often returned to jazz musicians as allegorical models, placing them on the same plane as major modernist poets:

> In Creeley's class we read and discussed at length William Carlos Williams' earlier poems as points of departure towards our own possibilities in American speech, as well as the poetry of Hart Crane . . . and the jazz of Charlie Parker, Bud Powell and Miles Davis, whose records could be heard playing late into the night from Creeley's apartment in the rear of the Studies. (Rumaker, 345)

Rumaker, of course, was not alone in sharing such memories. Dawson similarly recalled the ubiquity of jazz beyond the classroom, where "Stan Kenton, Woody Herman . . . [and] Miles Davis" records were commonly played by students and faculty alike (*Black Mountain Book*, 191). In this way, both inside the classroom and out, Creeley's enthusiasm for jazz became a much admired and imitated model for the apprentice writers at Black Mountain. As Rumaker observed, "Creeley preferred to work, like Olson, late at night, jazz blaring on his phonograph (the same as his beloved Hart Crane did in his time), and then only in erratic fits and starts, finding a consistency of rhythmic work difficult" (*Black Mountain Days*, 347). In all of these ways, then, the politics of integration and the rhythms of jazz were effectively woven into the life of Olson's Black Mountain.

The ten-volume Olson-Creeley correspondence, running from April 1950 to July 1952, focuses throughout on the possibility of a postmodern poetics that could build upon the work of William Carlos Williams and Ezra Pound, while omitting, as Creeley called it, the latter's "bigotry & pettiness" (Creeley, *O & C Cor*, 1:119). This tension between Olson's and Creeley's admiration for Pound's poetics and their disgust at his racism also recurs throughout the correspondence. Consequently, Creeley's insistence on the lessons to be learned from bebop, or modern jazz, appear all the more significant. As an African American art form, jazz and, in particular, bebop represented not simply popular music, but music made by, and largely for, the marginalized. Developed through late-night jam sessions and by small combos in cramped nightclubs, far from the shining dance halls and national broadcasts of Depression-era and wartime swing, bebop forged an aggressive new sound.[7] Insurgent, revolutionary, and socially aware, bebop musicians sought not only to reinvent jazz, but to do so as part of a larger cultural resistance to Jim Crow–era segregation in America. As John Lowney has written, bebop emerged as a radical alternative to swing, one possessed of an "oppositional consciousness" and a political "militancy" that were instrumental to the burgeoning movements for civil rights at home and abroad (*Jazz Internationalism*, 17). In this way, bebop musicians provided a crucial inspiration for Olson, Creeley, and their poetic disciples. As the drummer Kenny Clarke put it, "[t]here was a message to our music. . . . The idea was to wake up, look around you, there's something to do" (quoted in Gillespie and Fraser, *To Be, or Not . . . to Bop*, 142). As a result, in mixing Pound and jazz, Olson and Creeley could hardly avoid questions of race in constructing their poetics.

Or so it would seem. Despite Olson's and Creeley's shared concerns for the injustices of racism—indeed, in addition to attempts to integrate Black Mountain, such concerns became central to their disagreement with Pound—they often seem unaware of their own racist tendencies. In fact, in a manner akin to Pound's and Eliot's minstrel performances of Br'er Rabbit and Ol' Possum in their correspondence, Creeley often shifts into African American Vernacular English to praise Olson's poetry: "That poem today: too much . . . like a pile driver, or what they say: Man, you are breaking it up, you are in yr crib. Real groovy. Anyhow, very good" (*O & C Cor*, 1:48). The praise here is racialized in two ways: first, its racism is brought into focus by "they," by the unidentified other—presumably, African Americans—whose language becomes the vehicle for an inside joke; second, it can be read as praising what Creeley finds to be the distinctively jazzy aspects of Olson's writing, its "grooviness," in a hipster slang derived from African-American Vernacular English (AAVE). For his part, Creeley certainly identified with the latter meaning, remarking in a 1965 interview on his introduction to the "whole cult of the hipster" while a student at Harvard, and of the good fortune of experiencing it "when a lot of the idiom got located" (*Tales Out of School*, 3). Either way, the usage is appropriative and marks a tension at the heart of the hipster culture of the period, one which connects it in many ways to the minstrel enthusiasms of Pound and Eliot. As Eric Lott has observed in his study *Love and Theft*, the history of minstrelsy reveals, among many other things, the white admiration that often lies at the heart of cultural appropriation.[8] Similarly, Creeley's hipster slang in this period appears to be deployed most often in admiration, as though he were unaware of its appropriative reach.

For Olson's part, the language was initially confusing. In a reply to the letter cited, he asks in the postscript, "[w]hat does the tag 'too much' that you use, mean?" (Olson, *O & C Cor*, 1:52). Creeley responded by offering a gloss, along with a larger rationale:

> Well: "too much." A coincidence that made its mark: that abt all the close friends thru the college yrs, and later: were musicians or were making sounds, etc. It was a shortcut to speech, understanding, to make use of the words running with same / or: the worst, crazy, too much, gone, the thing, goofed, in his crib, dig, etc., etc. I.e., had lived for about a yr, right there, and was talking most the time / with that lang. (*O & C Cor*, 1:62)

Interestingly, Creeley links the phrasing to his friend's music. In his brief "Autobiography," Creeley recalls his Harvard days as being populated with jazz musicians who were "very close friends—Buddy Berlin, Race Newton, and Joe Leach," adding that "[i]t was Buddy and Race who first played me Charlie Parker, and Joe . . . actually knew Milt Jackson, Howie McGhee, and many more" ("Autobiography," 131). In this context, the "lang" appears to be an attempt to reproduce the angular, staccato playing of bebop musicians. As Geneva Smitherman has argued, however, such hipster terms as "*cool, dig,* jazz," etc., are rooted in African American communities: "Initially these latter terms moved out of the black community via white musicians and others of the artsy Hip Set (whom Mailer referred to as 'white Negroes')" (*Talkin' and Testifyin,'* 69). I will have occasion to comment on Mailer's controversial essay. For now, I simply want to show that Creeley's explanation largely omits the racial and ethnic source of such expressions. Instead, this omission, taken together with the fact that such appropriations offered poetical soundings, linguistic shorthand for arcane knowledge, frames the dualism at the heart of Creeley's adoption of jazz idioms and aesthetics in his early poetry, and so offers an important context for understanding his approach in this period. From here, he goes on to note his Harvard sojourns among the impoverished of Boston, around "Columbus Avenue," the "railroad Station," and the "parts where the colored live," a map that Olson would have recognized, if not fully understood, from his own experiences there a generation earlier (Creeley, *O & C Cor,* 1:62).

In these ways, Olson's and Creeley's engagement with hipster culture shares important aspects with what Norman Mailer would later define in his controversial essay, "The White Negro." Published in 1957, the same year, notably, as the obscenity trial for Allen Ginsberg's "Howl,"[9] the piece attempts to shed light on what Creeley termed the "cult of the hipster." As W. T. Lhamon, Jr., has shown, the hipster is in many ways a direct descendant of the blackface performer:

> The post–World War II era of rock 'n' roll and the populist core of postmodernism (from bebop and funk jazz to Mailer's essay "The White Negro" to the substitutions for vaudeville found in talk shows and stand-up comedy) are all, at least in part, heirs of blackface performance. (*Raising Cain,* 215)

As Lhamon demonstrates, in partaking of this lineage the hipster occupies a complicated racial space, a mix of admiration and appropriation that looks back to the "positive cultural codes" of the "earliest blackface performers," to an era before capital and the cultural elite conspired to flatten such interracial aspirations into one-dimensional racial stereotypes (215). Paradoxically, in returning to the racial ambiguity of an earlier period, the "White Negro" appears to Mailer as a new creature in midcentury America: "[s]o there was a new breed of adventurers . . . with a black man's code to fit their facts.

The hipster had absorbed the existentialist synapses of the Negro, and for practical purposes could be considered a white Negro" (Mailer, "White Negro," 303). White face, Black code, Mailer's hipster dwells in a new form of double-consciousness, one where "energy," "movement," and the "search for the good orgasm" predominate (303). The terms hearken back to the larger preoccupations Olson and Creeley shared in their deliberations over the kinetics of "Projective Verse." The connections, however, go further.

Before explaining hipster slang in lingo strikingly similar to that shared by Creeley in his letters to Olson, Mailer situates jazz at the heart of this new cultural experience. In doing so, Mailer claims that the hipster adopts jazz as essential to a "primitive" way of life:

> Knowing in the cells of his existence that life was war, nothing but war, the Negro (all exceptions admitted) could rarely afford the sophisticated inhibitions of civilization, and so he kept for his survival the art of the primitive, he lived in the enormous present, he subsisted for his Saturday night kicks, relinquishing the pleasures of the mind for the more obligatory pleasures of the body, and in his music he gave voice to the character and quality of his existence, to his rage and the infinite variations of joy, lust, languor, growl, cramp, pinch, scream and despair of his orgasm. For jazz is orgasm, it is the music of orgasm, good orgasm and bad, and so it spoke across a nation, it had the communication of art even where it was watered, perverted, corrupted, and almost killed, it spoke in no matter what laundered popular way of instantaneous existential states to which some whites could respond, it was indeed a communication by art because it said, "I feel this, and now you do too." ("White Negro," 303)

Much of this resonates with Olson's attitudes toward race, jazz, and hipster practice. In fact, Olson demonstrated his admiration for Mailer on several occasions, quoting from memory terms coined in *Advertisements for Myself*, in which "The White Negro" was reprinted, and even going so far as to regard Mailer, without irony, as, "the All-American Male" (*Muthologos*, 263, 281).[10] Indeed, just after exclaiming that Black Mountain had no poetics save for the example of Charlie Parker, Olson held up Mailer and Robert Duncan as these "two big American poets," these "American men," on par with W. B. Yeats, and whose writing broke through the darkness of the period (*Muthologos*,

280–81). In the second volume of *The Maximus Poems*, he appears to allude directly to the passage from "The White Negro" when he asserts that "jass is gysm," echoing both Mailer and a conjectured etymological root for the word "jazz" (Olson, *Maximus*, II.23).

Alongside such signs of influence, however, it must be stressed that Mailer's reductive portrait of African American males invokes a stereotypical racism of its own in his praise of the "primitive" and in its concomitant abandonment of the "intellectual." As Ralph Ellison noted, the piece invoked "[t]he same old primitivism crap in a new package. It makes you hesitant to say more than the slightest greetings to their wives lest they think you're out to give them a hot fat injection. What a bore" (Ellison and Murray, *Trading Twelves*, 197–98). Similarly, James Baldwin, in his famous response to Mailer, complained that the essay's depiction of African American men rested on white male insecurities: "It is still true, alas, that to be an American Negro male is also to be a kind of walking phallic symbol: which means that one pays, in one's own personality, for the sexual insecurity of others" ("The Black Boy Looks at the White Boy" 269–70). As Lott has demonstrated, such fascinations with Black male sexuality are rooted in homosexual structures of feeling passed down by the legacy of minstrelsy: "Mailer and other white Negroes down the years inherited a structure of feeling that no doubt preexisted but was crystallized in the responses of the first minstrel performers to the allure of black men" (Lott, *Love and Theft*, 55). In this way, Mailer's essay frames the difficulties inherent in attempting to understand Olson's and Creeley's reliance on hipster cultural codes throughout their correspondence. Unfortunately, such codes often reveal the tension inherent in cross-cultural influence, even in this otherwise progressive subculture. As Baldwin concluded, "[t]he relationship, therefore, of a black boy to a white boy is a very complex thing" ("The Black Boy Looks at the White Boy," 270).

Such exchanges of hipster lingo, then, can be shown to lay bare the complicated racial situations shared by Olson and Creeley at this time. The ambivalence that they display can be observed more fully in an early and uncollected poem by Creeley, titled, "The Primitives / Poem from a Photograph: East African Natives," published later in the first volume of his correspondence with Olson (*O & C Cor*, 1:73–74). An instance of ekphrasis, the poem's speaker ponders the image of seven East Africans whose "fourteen eyes" scrutinize him as he gazes on their photo (*O & C Cor*, 1:73). The piece's tension heightens as the speaker scans the photo in hopes of getting to know these "primitives" in some more intimate, more human way. Thankful that they are not "an archaic white," he still struggles to empathize with their humanity:

> I expect that they
> are people but I do not
> know. It is
> yet to be seen. (*O & C Cor*, 1:73)

Despite its date, the hesitation over the humanity of these "people" is disturbing. The formal accomplishment of the writing only adds to this. Even in this early poem, Creeley's care for what Lynn Keller has termed his "intraphrasal line-breaks," and the "desperate" pauses that they enact, reveals a host of suggestions (*Re-Making It New*, 141). The emphasis put on "they," for instance, calls attention to the otherness of these characters that is so crucial to the poem. Contrasted with "I," "they" exist in a manner "yet to be seen," despite the photographic evidence. Such confusion is apparent in the second line, where the subject has been separated from its clause, leaving the "people" with a merely negative identity. The full stop after "know" works similarly, halting any attempt to understand the subject of the passage.

The poem closes with a reiteration of the East African people's essential otherness. Once again, Creeley's handling of line breaks highlights the border that separates the speaker from the subjects of the photograph:

> we know. So, too,
> with these irrefutable others,
> notwithstanding
> the very odd look. (*O & C Cor*, 1:74)

Here, the stanza itself begins with an awkward enjambment, carrying over from the previous one the clause that completes the sentence, "What we can argue / depends on what / / we know" (*O & C Cor*, 1:74). Borrowing a move from William Carlos Williams's "The Red Wheelbarrow," Creeley hangs the import of the sentence on "depends," but, unlike Williams, the conclusion fails to deliver (W. C. Williams, "Red Wheelbarrow," 224). The "we" who shape the perspective of the poem reveal the author's lack of insight; this "we," after all, appears to be white Americans whose gaze Creeley has constructed as the normative view of the poem. In this regard, the "irrefutable others," then, turn out to be a matter of viewing position, of situation. To be situated in any social context is, for Creeley's speaker, to stand apart—"notwithstanding"—from those who are not a part of one's immediate community; it is to give a "very odd look" to all of the "others" one encounters. In this way, the piece broaches the larger, and abiding, concern throughout his later poetry with lyric subjectivity; however, this concern is registered here through a striking meditation on race. Although it is a flawed poem, "The Primitives," as its title suggests, offers another instance of Creeley's attitudes toward race in the period. Caught between denunciations of Pound's overt racism and his own hipster appropriations, Creeley's poem offers a studied ambivalence: cultural difference appears here as an unbridgeable chasm. Despite the reflexivity of the concluding lines, with their suggestion that "The Primitives" could just as well be white Americans—it all depends on who is in the subject position—it nonetheless asserts a racialized "we" and "they," "[p]rimitives" and human beings, deeming such gaps "irrefutable." The racism implicit in this, as in the speaker's wincing inability to "know" that "they are / people," with all the weight that the enjambment suggests, makes for difficult reading. That Creeley never sought to publish or later collect the poem may be seen as a renunciation of the racial views it implies. Certainly, he had opportunities to print it shortly afterward, in *Origin* II's special feature of his work, or a couple of years later in one of the early poetry collections that he began publishing almost annually in the middle and late-1950s. Whatever reservations he may have had about it later, however, the poem's understanding of race demonstrates many of the same tensions inherent in his adoption of the "cult of the hipster" and concomitant enthusiasm for jazz at this time.

EXTENDING THE FORM

A few weeks before writing the letter we have been considering, Creeley had combined these concerns in his first appeal to Olson to consider bebop's analogous approach to form. In offering "[s]ome notes on the thing abt the projective vs. non-projective," his first comments on Olson's draft copy of the essay that would become "Projective Verse," Creeley focuses on the problem of the "musical phrase":

> that wd point to the "voice" or what constitutes, better, more exact:
> what is to be heard (this to be taken as "analogy"). Two things we have

yet to pick up on—with the head: a feel for TIMING, a feel for SOUND
. . . & when, at those times of practice, you hit: these were an overt
part of it. (*O & C Cor*, 1:38–39)

His first impression of projective verse, then, is an apprehension of its implications for breath and voice, for the "TIMING" and "SOUND" of speech's
syncopated rhythms. For Creeley, Olson's poetics "hit" when the attention
focused on such musicality. The insight, moreover, is valuable, since there
is "[n]ot much to go on, now: other than Williams, or EP. THO: a listening
to Gertrude Stein will demonstrate a damn clear grip on just this thing you
are writing abt" (*O & C Cor*, 1:39). By situating Olson's advance on the musical phrasing of Williams, Pound, and Stein, Creeley places him within his
own modernist pantheon. Their subsequent correspondence bears out the
sincerity of such praise. Going one step further, however, he offers Olson
the first of several jazz "analogies" for projective verse:

An analogy: viz current "hatred" of this man: Charlie Parker: even
among his own group: and to be put with him, Max Roach, Miles Davis, Bud Powell, et alia: the point: here, TOO, a hatred for that which
breaks out, or extends the FORM, the only FORM:—what IS there, in
any given instance. Granted: we cannot take over exactly: this example, of what timing, variation, & a sound-sense can COMPLETE: it is
worth the time & trouble to listen, since it in the case of Bird, etc.: is
a precise example of the consciousness necessary, in a basic form: or
character. (*O & C Cor*, 1:39)

The extension of form will be a central concern of Creeley's later contributions to "Projective Verse." Here, the phrasing strives to make plain Parker's
ability to reveal the possibilities inherent in a given form, "what IS there,
in any given instance," through his manipulation of rhythmic breathing,
"timing, variation," and etc. Take, for example, his reported 32-bar solo on
the standard "Honeysuckle Rose," which would eventually be reimagined
as his own original composition, "Scrapple from the Apple."[11] Stretching
time in this way, Parker's playing "breaks out" of the given, inherited form,
as part of the process of creating the "only FORM," that is, the only appropriate, living realization of what for the poet is typically called content. To
link Parker's bebop aesthetic with Olson's poetics in such a way expands

both the influence of bebop, which is typically limited to the Beats, and the program of projective verse. Such grand claims may have embarrassed the twenty-four-year-old Creeley, writing to Olson, his forty-year-old senior. After typing the letter, he hand-wrote in the margin, "All this: a tangent" (Creeley, *O & C Cor*, 1:38). Nevertheless, his future attempts to contribute to Olson's project return to these concerns.

Creeley's later commentary on Olson's subsequent draft of the "Projective Verse" essay continues this train of thought. In a follow-up letter, Creeley credits Olson's method with foregrounding the problem of formalist poets like W. H. Auden:

> the intelligence that had touted Auden as being a technical wonder, etc. Lacking all grip on the worn & useless character of his essence: thought. An attitude that puts weight, *first:* on form/ more than to say: what you have above: will never get to: content. (*O & C Cor*, 1:78)

In terms of the letter cited, Auden's attachment to "inherited forms" prevents his poetry from achieving the "only FORM" (*O & C Cor*, 1:39). In fact, for Creeley, such adherence to traditional or closed forms negates the possibility of any authentic "content," and so marks Auden's poetry as "worn & useless." Though harsh, his judgment here may also be directed at the formalism of contemporary Americans as well, of southern Agrarians like John Crowe Ransom and Allen Tate, while looking ahead to tensions between disciples of open form poetics and formalists like the Movement poets in Britain.[12] In concluding the passage, Creeley offers up a critical dictum that would become a central tenet of projective verse: the improvisation of form at the service of content.

> Anyhow, form has now become so useless a term/ that I blush to use it. I wd imply a little of Stevens' use (the things created *in* a poem and existing there . . .) & too, go over into: the possible areas or methods for a way into/ a "subject": to make it clear: that form is never more than an *extension* of content. An enacted or possible "stasis" for thought. Means to. (*O & C Cor*, 1:79)

As opposed to Auden's use of inherited forms, Creeley calls for a poetics that, like the music of Parker, Roach, Davis, et al., "extends the form, the only

FORM" by breaking out of the constraints imposed by traditional metrical schemes (*O & C Cor*, 1:39). His reference to Wallace Stevens's comments in a published symposium on "The State of American Writing" bears this out. There, Stevens offers a cavalier definition of poetic form: "Poetic form in its proper sense is a question of what appears within the poem itself. . . . By appearance within the poem itself one means the things created and existing there" ("State of American Writing," 885). That poetic form consists of "the poem itself" may appear tautological; however, taken in the context of Stevens's work, it is a definition at once as simple and as complex as his well-known *ars poetica*, "Of Modern Poetry," where the distinctively modern work is the "poem of the mind in the act of finding / [w]hat will suffice" (Stevens, "Of Modern Poetry," ll.1–2). Creeley's admiration for Olson's draft essay of "Projective Verse" comes from his reading of it as advancing upon the poetics of Stevens, Williams, and others, as he notes in the same letter: "What can I say: I take you to put down here movement beyond what the Dr., Stevens, etc., have made for us. Wonderful things" (*O & C Cor*, 1:21). In trying to pinpoint subsequently what, exactly, that advance consisted of, Creeley found himself expounding upon Olson's approach to rhythm, detailing the "analogy" offered by bebop (*O & C Cor*, 1:39). That analogy gave him the conceptual framework to understand projective verse as a bebop poetics, one that would enable him to take his hipster experience and translate it into a postmodern poetry that could advance upon the work of poets like Stevens, Williams, and Pound. For Creeley, the postmodern poetry he imagined at this time could be described as the poem, not "of the mind," but of the voice, in the act of improvising itself.

As his reply to Creeley's first mention of a jazz analogy shows, Olson appreciated the "equivalence" and its accompanying praise:

cree-
ley:
tanks,
tanks
           especially wish i had sd (you will, you will!)

           "Two things we have yet to pick up on—with the head:
           a feel for TIMING, for
           SOUND

        & when you hit,
        these are an overt part, they
        were in it"

      say, why don't I slug that in, in copy? any objections? introduced
thus: "Creeley's gloss, here, is helpful: . . ." ?

. . .

      also like yr equivalence of consciousness & character in:

        "is a precise example of the consciousness necessary,
        in a basic form: or character" (*O & C Cor*, 1:50)

Olson's projective response, replete with allusions and rhythmic variations, indicates the measure of his enthusiasm for Creeley's reading of the draft in the light of a possible jazz poetics. The staccato opening, followed by the shifting margins of the verse paragraph, staggers the reading experience, imitating a rhythmic technique common to Parker and other bop performers, while the allusive layering of his reference to Oscar Wilde graphs an earlier period's aesthetic revolution onto Creeley's and Olson's present experience, again in a move similar to Parker, Gillespie, and others' reworking of popular standards.[13] While "tanks, / tanks" can be read simply as an informal way of offering "thanks" in a dialectical form, the usage creates a homonym for military tanks, suggesting the larger import of their accord, that it positions them as allies in a battle against the poetic establishment. In approving of the "equivalence of consciousness & character" that Creeley drew with Parker, Olson lends his support for the larger jazz analogy with projective verse. Going forward, they would continue their pursuit of a postmodern poetics with the tacit agreement that jazz offered a rich and suggestive parallel, especially in terms of creating a rhythmic scoring for the voice, though Creeley's enthusiasm for this would typically exceed Olson's.

    In fact, Olson's later focus on "breath" appears to be modified by Creeley's suggestions. About a month later, he worked through the significance of breath in resolving the "whole damned problem" of the "line" (*O & C Cor*, 1:127). There, Olson's approach echoes Pound while also looking ahead to Creeley's understanding of Parker:

THE LINE, comes (I swear
it) from the *breath*, fr the breathing of the man who writes. And only
he can declare the line proper to him, its metric, and its point of
ending—this
                    is where the work comes in, this is THE WORK, the
beating out, the hammering
. . .

I have a hunch that, emotion being what it is, its control on our
breathing is such, that any of us, who will stay out in the open, in
the OPEN FIELD, will, unknown to ourselves
. . .

                                            declare, every so often,
unawares, a base beat and flow which will, order is such a part of the
law of rhythm, also declare itself.
                                And I hunch, that, when a poem
works, in the OPEN, it is just for this reason, of a controlling constant
against which all variants break and play. (*O & C Cor,* 1:127)

Recalling Creeley's description of Parker's genius for creating the "only
FORM," for "that which breaks out," Olson here formulates "all variants"
as a parallel "break and play" of the individual's *"breath"* in determining the
poetic line (*O & C Cor,* 1:39). As Creeley adds in the same letter, it is Miles
Davis's breathing, "his own wind," that marks the "NECESSARY: dissonance"
that distinguishes his work from the derivative playing of his peers (*O & C
Cor,* 1:39). Attempting to voice such dissonance, therefore, links the breath of
the jazz horn player to that of the composing poet. Though Allen Ginsberg's
discussion of this correspondence in his 1959 liner notes for the audio recording
of "Howl" are often cited as the critical source for such a poetics, it should
be noted that Olson's and Creeley's exploration of the analogy predates this
by nine years, and to quite a different, projective effect (Ginsberg, "Notes
for *Howl,*" 416). For Olson, then, this move amounts to a radical openness
toward the compositional process that a writer pursuing closed or traditional
forms could not abide. To "stay out in the open" means, among other things,
remaining open to the contours of the moment as they develop and affect
the poet, both intellectually and emotionally, as represented physiologically
by the heart and subsequent breathing that shape the "metric" of each line.
It involves, in other words, a reorientation of the compositional process

away from the demands of the tradition of inherited forms and toward the possibilities of bodies attuned to the improvised moment. The art or craft of such a method lies in the writer's ability to syncopate, to recognize, in other words, the "base beat" establishing itself, and so voice variations upon it in a manner akin to, say, Billie Holiday's vocal delivery. As Creeley saw, Olson's description effectively parallels a musician's approach to performing improvised jazz.

In his reply a few days later, Creeley again refers Olson to jazz insurgents, dwelling on the lessons to be learned from Parker. After joining the two Charlies—Olson with Parker—as his major influences, "[t]he Bird (also Chas)," he describes the saxophonist's extension of form:

> [he] has strung his way thru abt (now) 30 variations (on wax) of the one I GOT RHYTHM (agreed)—where we have, as you will know, a series of (basick) [sic] chords which can be extended in a strict (gripped) manner, inverted, wound, pitched, & heaved, or let's just—go. So we go, like: la do de da : becomes oo oo de la oo/ (oo) da ee oo/ . (*O & C Cor*, 1:155–56)

Here, the parenthetical asides tell almost as much as the rest of the text. For instance, Creeley clearly views Parker as an artist in the midst of his creative prime, as someone who has "(now) 30 variations (on wax)," but who presumably has performed more and so will record even more yet. As a result, Creeley is "(agreed)" that Parker has "GOT RHYTHM" and so details his rhythmic achievements in hopes of persuading Olson to consider more deeply the parallel possibilities offered by his playing, even going so far as to offer an onomatopoetic transcription of Parker's breathing. The letter goes on to offer suggestions for further listening in order to help Olson to "orient" himself and his poetics in relation to the rhythmic breakthroughs of bebop (*O & C Cor*, 1:155–56).

As with the earlier letter expressing his enthusiasm for Parker, Creeley adds a handwritten postscript "later," in which he begins to walk back his claims for jazz. This time, though, instead of framing them as merely a "tangent," he persists in arguing for Parker's importance:

> you will know/ that what makes the LINE in any of this, IS, most obviously, the breath—it is a profitable analogy, for the problems of

poesy, or—just so/ the bird/ within the limit of his sounds/ breath/ is attempting to reach to: form/ from content: just so/ you/I: with our sound/ sense: and TIME. It is interesting, as document, to cite his KNOWING of the problem. Tho it is assumed that all jazz (uh huh) has a (uh huh) beat . . . (uh huh). Hmmm . . . Well, so has mary had er has: a little lamb: I look to EXTENSIONS. (Creeley, *O & C Cor*, 1:157)

If the projective line focuses on "breath" as the source of its metric, then, Creeley, insists, Parker's manipulation of breath is instructive; it exhibits the attempt to "reach . . . form," while remaining "within the limit of his sounds," within, that is, the base beat of the rhythm section. As such, Parker's recordings offer evidence of the possible extensions of form within a given measure. This, in turn, complicates the sense of time beyond merely the repetition of a base beat. As Creeley notes, everything from jazz to poetry to nursery rhymes, "mary has er has: a little lamb," possesses a beat; the point, however, of advancing a postmodern or simply new poetic of any kind is to provide "EXTENSIONS," some variation on the known and given.

In subsequent letters, Creeley's insistence on the importance of jazz, and on Parker's example in particular, would continue. The day after penning the letter just cited, Creeley wrote to Olson on the value of sound in poetry. In it, he names a range of poets, from the Provençal troubadours to Gerard Manley Hopkins, as evidence against a tendency in the work of late-modern formalists like William Empson to "cut out too much of the potential for poetry, by this over-balanced emphasis on the 'word'/ in a limited sense. It is: almost as strong as sense: a SOUND instrument" (*O & C Cor*, 2:14). Without denying the logical import of poetry, Creeley is at pains here to reestablish "SOUND" as equal to sense. As earlier, such concerns stem from his larger preoccupation with jazz:

the matter (analogical) of the Bird again . . . let's assume that the Bird is 1/ trying to "say" something and that 2/ he is trying to say it against this background (a) sounds possible (b) base beat. Now: we can take as the base beat like 1/2/3/4, not only that so-called "base" stress, but, as well, its variants, or the emphases possible within its frame: so, when looking at a base beat/ in poetry, too: we must not only tag the main stress, but also, what can be played upon it, as variant, & still keep to the outline, of its stresses. Okay, so we got now the drums, bass, and say: chords (simple) going on the piano. Nice sounds already: you see, already we are building the "main" pattern: AGAINST which/ comes Bird & his instrument (mind, breath & tenor): well—there is the base beat, moving, so/ he starts. What he does, is to pit, there, against the base beat, his particular sound, and like words moving against base pattern (stress) he is able to invert, delay, push back & forward, the PARTICULAR sound, each, that he can make: what this does, is to push meaning into such as are so used. Well, listening to some records cd clear the logos for you in abt 5 minutes. (Creeley, *O & C Cor*, 2:14–15)

Again, Creeley pursues the analogy in the hopes of persuading Olson to listen, even if only for "5 minutes," to the possibilities for poetry inherent in Parker's playing. Outlining them here, he emphasizes Parker's playing "AGAINST" the main pattern established by the rhythm section ("drums," "bass," and "piano"). However, his stance is not simply a matter of sound, it is the breaking out of sound and sense, "mind, breath & tenor," through his saxophone. In Creeley's understanding, then, such signature sounds are only audible in the context of a contrasting "base beat"; this pattern allows for inversions and delays, for the pushing and pulling that exhausts the moment's possibilities. In a similar analogy, Creeley's short lyrics from this period manage a metaphorical movement, establishing patterns of expectation only to invert, expand, and contract them, all on the way to some fuller, more precise voicing. Though Olson's immediate responses to these letters are not always among the surviving correspondence, his later remarks show that he would come to see jazz as a "profitable analogy" for projective verse, even if his relationship to the music was quite different from Creeley's (Olson, *O & C Cor*, 1:157).

MAYAN DRUMS

In January 1951, Olson and his wife Connie moved temporarily to Mexico, occupying a house shared previously by Black Mountain colleagues, ostensibly to write and to allow him to pursue his interest in Mayan culture. Much of his ensuing correspondence with Creeley would be collected and published by the latter as the *Mayan Letters*.[14] Once in Mexico, Olson's appreciation for Creeley's jazz analogy becomes apparent in his newfound interest in the drum. Again, Creeley's enthusiasms seem to lead the way. In one of his first letters to Olson in Mexico, he reflects on his own desire to move, to live an itinerant life akin to his experiences before marrying (Creeley, *O & C Cor*, 4:138–40). His envy for Olson's situation leads him to reflect on Chano Pozo, the Cuban bongo and conga drummer who, along with Dizzy Gillespie, helped to pioneer Afro-Cuban rhythms in jazz: "Listening/ just now to drums/ bongo: Channo [sic] / dead now" (Creeley, *O & C Cor*, 4:140). As an aside from his nostalgia for youthful travel, Creeley frames Pozo's music as representative of a sense of possibility that is just out of reach. By addressing Olson in Mexico, Creeley sets a wider Latin American context for the reference, as though he were suggesting a larger, cross-cultural movement implicit in their shared understanding of projectivist poetics. In this vein, Creeley added to the bottom of the letter, in pencil, "Channo [sic]—fantastic *Voice* against the drums" (Creeley, *O & C Cor*, 4:140). Here, like an arrow pointing Olson onward, Creeley offers a Latin American corollary for Charlie Parker, whose own extension of form was phrased as part of a larger discussion of "'voice'" or breath and its positioning "AGAINST" a base beat (*O & C Cor*, 1:39, 2:15). Once again, it is this counter rhythm that so interests Creeley and that he recommends to Olson. The latter's Mayan adventure would offer an answer for this.

In his early letters from Mexico, Olson finds himself wondering at the various cultural advances left behind by Mayan civilization. This leads him to contrast their cultural achievements with those, in his estimation, of mid-century Mexico. Consequently, he associates the situation of contemporary Mexicans with that of African Americans:

> The point is, the arrestment, is deceptive: it is not what fancy outsiders have seen it as, seeking, as they were, I guess, some alternative to themselves. . . . Yet, they should not have misled us (which is the same as harming these Injuns [sic]: they have so fucking much future, & no present, no present at all. . . . What graces they have are traces only, of what was & of what, I'd guess, can be (to be a colored people today is something! Yah? (Olson, *O & C Cor*, 5:37–38)

By "a colored people" Olson appears to link his Mexican neighbors with African Americans through a term then contemporary for both. Though acceptable and even considered respectful at the time, the colorism implicit in this and Olson's other term of choice, "Negro," belies a blind faith in the pseudoscience of biological race. Though his study ranges more widely than my concerns here, Heriberto Yépez has argued that there are good reasons for suspecting Olson's entire project in Mexico and for reading it as an instance of hegemonic imperialism.[15] While there is clearly an anti-imperialist and anti-racist vein in Olson's writing that counters this interpretation, his language in the passage cited nonetheless supports it. After all, his perception that these "colored people" are also "Injuns [sic]" suggests the need for white Americans to delineate the significance of their cultural history. That said, Olson's desire not to be "misled" and to avoid "harming" them, coupled with his admiration for their "graces" and potential "future" is, to be sure, progressive for the time and a sign of his good intentions. It is also evidence of his clear break from the social and cultural programs of Pound and Eliot. However, such intentions do little to redress the racism that he seeks to move past; in fact, as his language suggests, they perpetuate and reinforce it. The following excerpt, with its praise for African American and Mayan drumming, witnesses much the same in this regard:

But the Negro in the States is way ahead of these 400 yr slept people! . . . for ex: jesus, the only thing you hear here, any place, when they make music (which is little) is the *drum*. But stacked up against [the Negro *crossed out*] Baby Dodds or whoever, pigeon shit—*or, what is most important,* stacked abt [i.e., up] against these old Mayan drums I've worked out on—five, so far, cut out of trees—you wld hear them, lad, hear 'em. (Olson, *O & C Cor*, 5:38)

The passage indulges further in the exoticism of the previous one, but here it invokes the jazz drummer Warren "Baby" Dodds as an example. For Olson, his Mexican contemporaries appeared to be merely beaten "Injuns [sic]," a "slept people," compared to the cultural vitality of the American "Negro," the greatest example of which, for him in this passage, was the inventive rhythms of jazz drumming and its suggestive potential for poetic voicing. The praise, of course, is undercut by Olson's blindness to his own patronizing racism. As Amiri Baraka argued, citing white critics of jazz who ignore the cultural situation out of which the music arose, "[t]he disparaging 'all you folks got rhythm' is no less a stereotype, simply because it is proposed as a positive trait" (*Black Music*, 13–14). That both groups could learn from the Mayan example—as played by Olson—is telling. The implication is that it takes a white American to reveal to these various Others the vitality of their cultural traditions. Scholars like Yépez have begun to grapple with this problem in Olson's thinking about Mayan and Mexican cultures; however, his problematic stance toward African American culture deserves further comment as well. In fact, earlier in the Mexican correspondence Olson engaged in even uglier language concerning the two groups: "I remain unconvinced that these archeologistas (lacking any prime taste) have caught hold of this nigger by his toe propre" (O & C Cor, 5:13). The use of "nigger," the linguistic token of white racism par excellence, to describe the Mayans clearly connects their situation in his thinking with that of African Americans. While there may be some question as to whether he is performing the speech of racist archeologists or engaging in it in the first person, regardless, Olson's nonchalant usage is indicative of his larger inability to confront, in any meaningful way, the racism that he frequently criticizes in others—in historical figures like John Hawkins, in *The Maximus Poems*, or in his letters to Creeley on the antisemitism of Ezra Pound, for example. As in the earlier instances cited, Olson positions himself in the passage as a kind of savior, recovering the civilization of a people lost to history. Partly, this is the result of his distrust of governments and institutions, those funding the "archeologistas"; partly, also, this is the result of his habit of seeing Mexicans as exotic others in need of his assistance. He cannot believe, for instance, that the local children in Mexico should disparage him: "these kids . . . stare in windows, walk in doors, climb over walls, lean out of the school windows and yell, in chorus: griing-GO, grrrriiing-GO" (Olson, O & C Cor, 5:14). Dennis Tedlock notes that while Olson could have simply recorded "gringo," he was instead "extending the writing of projective verse to the transcription of words already spoken" (*Olson Codex,* xxiii). While this is true, the cultural conflict at the heart of the passage should not be overlooked. The two go hand in hand here, and although the term "gringo" could be taken as a simple identification of Olson as a U.S. citizen, he hears it as "griing-GO," as an exclamation to go home to his own country. Hence his surprise, "unbelievable, the underground hate for Americans (all over)" (O & C Cor, 5:14). The offense, for Olson, is not in their perceived hatred of America (they, of course, are North Americans too), but in their unwillingness to recognize him as an anti-imperialist, as, in other words, one of them: "Am with them, of course, all the way, only it makes you sore, they don't (the mass) let you extricate yrself fr the antagonism" (O & C Cor, 5:14). While, again, his anti-imperialist intentions may be laudable, his writing tells a more complicated story. It is a little absurd to claim fellowship with impoverished schoolchildren in Mexico when you are vacationing in a beach house and provided with all the advantages that come with being a white American. His use of the term itself marks a clear division in his thinking: the United States, after all, is no more "America" than Mexico is, however Olson construed the slight. While at times he appears to be aware of this, it is remarkable how often he falls into stereotypical and racist patterns of thought, even while denying their import.

These tensions carry through his time in Mexico and are evident in his thinking on race throughout his writing career. Consequently, his praise of and support for the victims of imperialism are voiced as frequently as his clumsy attempts to extricate himself from complicity. Though he often confuses the U.S. with America, for instance, on other occasions he addresses such distinctions powerfully:

> we are confronted, as men forever are, by the LAG. Our fellow cits are, I take it, quite easily thrown off by any noun which contains Z's and X's . . . what I am saying is, that, to use X's and Z's makes for difficulties John Adams, or Kung Fu Sze, or even Omeros, don't. (Olson, *O & C Cor*, 5:52)

Here, Olson labors to show Creeley that the cultural "LAG" in regard to U.S. attitudes toward Latin American cultures comes from the inability of predominantly white, English-speaking Americans to recognize nouns with "Z's and X's" as the embodiment of concepts passed down from a shared, dignified civilization, as they more readily do for the works and thought of European colonials, or even those of ancient China and Greece. In looking to "Z's and X's" for parallels, then, Olson imagines that he and Creeley will have to overcome the challenges of racist imperialism in ways that their predecessors didn't. As he suggests later, Pound suffered from the same "disease" as "Columbus" (Olson, *O & C Cor*, 5:62). Though flawed, Olson's attempts to incorporate Creeley's jazz inspiration can be seen as a strategy in the struggle against this "LAG." For instance, the letter cited ends with Olson reflecting that Mayan astronomy is "hot," borrowing a usage from early jazz that will reappear throughout his time in Mexico and be enshrined in the famous closing to "Human Universe": "O, they were hot for the world they lived in, these Maya, hot to get it down the way it was—the way it is, my fellow citizens" ("Human Universe," 166). This sense of "hot," akin to the "Hot Jazz" of Louis Armstrong and others in the 1920s, implies the precise mix of excitement, enthusiasm, and arousal for the materiality of human experience that Olson sees as essential to the formation of any truly post-modern culture. The invitation to join him as "citizens" of such a "Human Universe"—one extended, by implication, to whites only—therefore, involves not just a willingness to engage with the "Z's and X's" of a previous culture, but with the African American popular culture of his present as well.

As though in response to Creeley's earlier note on Pozo, Olson's interest in drums while in Mexico shows that he took his friend's comments seriously and attempted to return the favor. Baby Dodds was primarily a Dixieland drummer who achieved recognition in the 1920s for playing with pioneering New Orleans acts led by Joe "King" Oliver and Louis Armstrong. As such, Olson's reference to him reveals a personal knowledge of and appreciation for pre-swing-era jazz, a music often alluded to and complicated by bebop. His later comments on art and rhythm draw upon this knowledge. After his return to Black Mountain College in the fall of 1951, Olson sought to extrapolate his Mexican experience in the form of laws or principles. Pronouncing on art and rhythm, Olson insisted that "man" hungers to "act, not to know," and goes on to claim that his primary action "is ART," adding that the essence of such action is rhythm: "art depends upon rhythm maximally. Its 'forms' are only accomplishable to the degree that they are completely rhythmical" (*O & C Cor*, 7:240). In the following letter, he traces this train of thought back to the importance of the drum, noting that for the Sumerians and other ancient civilizations—like the Mayans—the drum "was the prime & proper accompaniment for song" (*O & C Cor*, 7:246). This, just as did his Mayan rumination in Mexico, leads Olson to modern America and the example of jazz:

> STICKS & DRUMS. Of course all it means to me is IMAGES of the instrument I am most interested in, the human VOICE (fascinating thing, Harrison tells me, that, there is some evidence that the speaking voice, in different periods, comes to behave like the dominant instruments of the time: now, then, the sax, trumpet, and such as Durante & Armstrong, the washboard. (*O & C Cor*, 7:246–47)

His interest in Jimmy Durante and Louis Armstrong in the passage refers to their ability to vary rhythm in their vocal deliveries, as well as to scat sing, both hallmarks of the type of early jazz that Armstrong is usually credited with pioneering. It is a way of playing the voice as though it were a drum, using pauses and alterations of delivery to expand the rhythm established by the base beat, a skill at which Billie Holiday later excelled.[16] Olson's recognition of this once again demonstrates his desire to link "hot" cultures of the past with the possibilities inherent in the present, while also revealing his considerable knowledge of early jazz and his willingness to offer it as a complement to Creeley's enthusiasm for bebop.

ALL THAT IS LOVELY IN JAZZ[17]

Much of Creeley's early poetry embodies the form of jazz-inspired projectivism evident in his correspondence with Olson. As Keller has noted, Parker's influence manifests itself as "something comparable to counterpoint" in Creeley's approach to jazz rhythms (*Re-Making It New*, 145). As Sascha Feinstein has noted, Creeley's sense of the poetic line was directly informed by Parker's music (Feinstein, *Jazz Poetry, from the 1920s to the Present*, 90). *All That Is Lovely in Men*, a collaborative book of poetry and illustrations done at Black Mountain with the painter and trumpeter Dan Rice, marks one of the clearest examples of this. There, Creeley's introductory note for the collection frames the work that follows. In it, he argues for a "complementary sense" between the improvised rhythms of "Charlie Parker . . . and Miles Davis" and that of the poems gathered for the collection (Creeley, Introduction to *All That Is Lovely in Men*, n.p.). The bebop, or jazz, source for such choices may be less evident at first, but have been subsequently emphasized by Creeley, as a closer look will show.

Among the poems selected by Creeley for the collection, "The Whip" best demonstrates the jazz parallel he draws in the preface. Having appeared a year earlier, in *The Black Mountain Review*'s fall 1954 issue, and reprinted here without revision, "The Whip" may seem an unlikely candidate. A poem that appears to explore guilt, infidelity, and the power relations within a couple at the time of Creeley's separation from his first wife, Ann, and his competition with Dan Rice for Cynthia Homire's affection, "The Whip" certainly appears to be an odd fit in an examination of his jazz-inspired poetic.[18] Robert Duncan, for instance, read the poem as an extension of the troubadour tradition, a modern update where the other woman is the Dark Lady of Dante and Cavalcanti (Duncan, "After *For Love*," 99–100). An essential part of that update, however, is Creeley's approach to rhythm. He seemed to feel that by getting the timing right an authentic poetry would follow. As he explains in his *Paris Review* interview with Linda Wagner, "I felt that the way a thing was said would intimately declare *what* was being said, and so therefore, form was never more than an extension of what it was saying. . . . It's the attempt to find the intimate form of what's being stated as it is being stated" (Creeley, "[Creeley] Interviewed by Linda Wagner," 30). When read in the context of his analogy with jazz in the short, prefatory remarks, it would seem that all of Creeley's poetry from the collection could be shown to exhibit his jazz-inflected approach to rhythm. While not untrue, Creeley took special care in insisting upon the jazz inspiration at work in "The Whip."

In fact, as opposed to other writings from the period, Creeley himself later glossed the poem's jazz influences explicitly. In "Form," a short piece published in 1987, he elaborates on the poem's relation to Charlie Parker:

"The Whip" was written in the middle fifties . . . [and] it is music, specifically jazz, that informs the poem's manner in large part. Not that it's jazzy, or about jazz—rather, it's trying to use a rhythmic base much as jazz of this time would—or what was especially characteristic of Charlie Parker's playing, or Miles Davis', Thelonious Monk's, or Milt Jackson's. That is, the beat is used to delay, detail, prompt, define the content of the statement or, more aptly, the emotional field of the statement. It's trying to do this while moving in time to a set periodicity—durational units, call them. It will say as much as it can, or as little, in the "time" given. So each line is figured as taking the same time, like they say, and each line ending works as a distinct pause. I used to listen to Parker's endless variations on "I Got Rhythm" and all the various times in which he'd play it, all the tempi, up, down, you name it. What fascinated me was that he'd write silences as actively as sounds, which of course they were. Just so in poetry. (Creeley, "Form," 492–93)

Creeley's description of Parker's influence can be better understood in the light of his halting reading of the poem. Recordings, such as the one collected as part of the seminar "Rock Drill #3," which exhibits well his habit of pausing at the line ends, famously, in imitation of his mistaken assumption about William Carlos Williams's reading performance, make this clear.[19] Although the poem is not concerned in any obvious way with jazz, its execution bears a clear resemblance to jazz in its enfranchising of silence. In moving from one line to the next, the speaker appears to search for, and dramatically find, words to continue, to give voice to his emotional confusion. In a similar way, Parker or, more pointedly, Miles Davis in his *Birth of the Cool* recordings, then newly compiled and released, would employ silence while searching through an improvisation.[20]

Like Parker and Davis, who commonly worked both with and against a driving rhythmic pulse, Creeley's speaker works with and against what he terms a "set periodicity" ("Form," 492). While this can be understood as the couplets that predominate the poem, it is even more apparent in the syntactical thrust of the language and the tetrameter rhythm the opening line introduces. Creeley returns to this rhythm regularly—regularly enough, that is, to cause the shorter lines to fill the seemingly missing space with a pointed silence, as the speaker searches for the next line to continue. Consequently, the line breaks create a pattern of dramatic changes. Just as Parker's improvisations can move in small steps one moment, then, say, leap over flatted fifths the next, so, too, with Creeley's line breaks. As a result, syntactical breaks become more meaningful, with the resulting pauses necessitated by his intention that "each line is figured as taking the same time" creating pregnant pauses, Parkeresque uses of "silences as sounds" ("Form," 492–93). At this point, it may also be helpful to recall that Parker's music is instrumental—i.e., its content is its method. Creeley's notes on the jazz poetic at work in "The Whip" seem to take a similar approach toward words; it's as though they are notes or chords whose meaning comes from the various combinations in which they can be manipulated. Hence, also, the importance of line breaks and rhythmic variety in creating meaning by complicating the syntactical relations of common prose and speech, revealing the layers of possibility implicit in their typically one-dimensional referentiality, bringing them, in other words, into a fuller, three-dimensional reality.

"The Whip" can be shown to exhibit these methodological aims in a number of ways. The breaks at lines two, three, four, eleven, and seventeen, for instance, separate modifiers from the nouns and phrases they modify: "my love . . . a flat // sleeping thing," "She was / very white // and quiet," "I was / lonely," and "I think to say this / wrongly" (Creeley, "The Whip," n.p.). The resultant pauses suspend identity, forcing the reader to understand these characters as fractured and out of tune, both syntactically, in terms of the line, and emotionally, as befits the drama of the poem. More dramatic suspensions of sense come with more severe syntactical breaks, such as in lines six, nine, and ten, where subjects are separated from their predicates: "I / / also loved," "she / returned," "That / / encompasses it" ("The Whip," n.p.). The effect here is more extreme, causing the reader to recalibrate the syntax of multiple lines in the course of piecing together a meaning that wanders, much like the man's affections, and can only partially, on occasion, be contained in end-stopped lines. In all of these ways the syntactical complexity created by the varying line lengths works to develop the sound and sense of the poem in a way parallel to the meandering solos of an improvised jazz performance.

Such deftness in the handling of line-breaks affects the poem's rhythm as well. In examining rhythmic patterns in his work, it should be noted that although projective verse seeks to make a decided break from the rhythms of closed verse, asserting, in its place, the seemingly natural rhythms of the poet's breathing, Creeley and Olson continued using traditional terminology for feet and meter in discussing their work.[21] For Creeley, this makes sense, given his approach to free verse in short forms. As Marjorie Perloff has shown in scanning Creeley's work from this period, "[t]o call such poetry 'free verse' is not quite accurate," because whether it is the number of words per line, or the shifting rhythmic patterns of jazz, "something is certainly being counted" (Perloff, "After Free Verse," 155). In the opening stanza, the poem's rhythm is mimetic. For instance, in line one, the iambic rhythm of "I spent a night" is inverted, fittingly, with "turning," which substitutes a trochee for an iamb ("The Whip," n.p.). Line two, similarly, could be said to intersperse a pyrrhic and a trochee, in the middle four syllables of the line, varying from the iambs and trochees that open and close, to give the effect of the lightness of a "feather" ("The Whip," n.p.). However, these traditional lines provide merely the base beat or rhythm section for Creeley's syncopated variations. In doing so, the approach to rhythm here resembles closely his understanding of jazz's influence on the "hearing or thinking" of poets associated with Black Mountain, where he notes in a later lecture that they shared an appreciation for bebop's ability to rework standard melodies:

This music is coming, almost without exception, from . . . what they call old standards, songs that are immensely familiar. The chordal base and/or the melodic line is cliché—usefully cliché . . . the chords are kept as the ground; [but] the rhythm, the time can shift, and will shift dramatically. (Creeley, "Walking the Dog," 00:01:42–00:02:13)

The perception here of using an "old standard" as the basis for new variations presents well Creeley's approach to poetic rhythm in this period. As
he goes on to explain in the same lecture, bebop or jazz sparked "what the
imagination was then of prosody . . . what a particular cluster of poets were
then trying to work with," in terms of projecting the voice ("Walking the
Dog," 00:02:45–00:03:01). In keeping with this, the following lines contract
and expand, employing the silences heard in absence of the remembered
beats introduced in lines one and two to convey the shifting of a ponderous
weight, as the speaker works out of the conventional opening and sighs
through the "whip" of conscience.[22] As with the use of syntax already mentioned, the rhythmic breaks here probe the subject, rather than merely imitate it, as the opening lines appear to do. Time and again an iambic rhythm
reappears, only to be broken, shifted, and complicated, much as Charlie
Parker in the midst of a solo might return to an early melody as a pivot or
bridge to discover an unexplored note in the scale or a shift to a relative or an
alternative key altogether. Line six, for instance, appears in a rough iambic
pentameter, "the roof, there was another woman I," only to pivot, in the
next line, into a passage that doesn't accord with traditional meter at all,
"also loved, had" ("The Whip," n.p.). A four-syllable line with three stresses,
its rhythm is largely trochaic and so reverses the direction of the previous
line. This way of changing course, of darting back and forth, while turning
the subject over and over again, is characteristic of the poem. Rather than
mimic the sense of the words, it plays them as sounds whose weight advances
the larger conflict introduced by the opening, just as Parker fathoms the
full possibilities of a melody by playing it in as many different directions as
possible. Creeley continues to improvise over the top of the iambic beat of
the poem throughout, ending abruptly with the trochaic "wrongly" ("The
Whip," n.p.). Like a snare hit or trumpet flare, the poem's rhythm doesn't fade
out: it halts. In this way, the ending bears something of the mimetic quality
of the opening, whipping the speaker with a line that possesses a fittingly
"feminine" ending. The woman's gesture at the turn of the poem, patting
the man's back as he awakes from his dream about another lover, exhibits
a mix of sincere, even gentle concern, coupled with a bracing assertion of
power. Given Creeley's own marital problems at the time, it is difficult not
to read the poem biographically.

At roughly the same time as the composition of *All That Is Lovely in Men*,
Creeley reiterated to Olson in a letter that didn't make it into the ten-volume

correspondence the importance of jazz for projective verse. Next to a long section on poetic rhythm, Creeley wrote by hand in the margin *"P(ound) or P(arker): constant + variant"* as a way of drawing attention to his larger concerns for a poetry of syncopated breath beats (*Selected Letters of Robert Creeley*, 110–11). The note sums up nicely his contribution to the ongoing discussion of rhythm and poetic form that he and Olson continued throughout these years. Later in the letter, he spells it out plainly:

> Bird, and few others equal, are almost the only present relevance, in rhythmic structure, available . . . a poet can look to this usage for an analogy to his own—and, if he is not a literal goof, etc., can comprehend that Bird's premise for structure in terms of the musical (or harmonic) line, is or can be, his own. (Creeley, *Selected Letters*, 112)

While this reiterates comments made earlier in the correspondence, the persistence of Creeley's interest in jazz, and his dedication to Parker's example in this period, cannot be overstated. As though sensing that Olson's responsive interest in Armstrong and New Orleans jazz still misses the crucial development of bebop, Creeley makes plain his seriousness in offering the analogy:

> I am dead serious, and want sometime to do a gig on this whole area. . . . For example, I am more influenced by Charley [*sic*] Parker, in my acts, than by any other man, living or dead. IF you will listen to five records, say, you will see how the whole biz ties in. . . . Well, I am not at all joking, etc. Bird makes Ez look like a school-boy, in point of rhythms. And his <u>sense</u>, of how one rhythm can activate the premise for, another. Viz, how a can lead to b, in all that multiplicity of the possible. It is a fact, for one thing, that Bird, in his early records, damn rarely ever comes in on the so-called beat. And, as well, that what point he does come in on, is not at all "gratuitous," but is, in fact, involved in a figure of rhythm which is as dominant in what it leaves out, as what it leaves in. This, is the point. (Creeley, *Selected Letters*, 112–13)

Not only is Creeley "dead serious" about Parker's technical influence on his work, but he is also sincere about his influence on his life in general. This, of course, echoes the hero-worship of Parker characteristic of hipsters in the period, but it also marks an attempt to turn the enthusiasms of the moment into art, and in a way distinct from the expansive lines and greater accessibility of the Beats, as discussed earlier.

As opposed to their work, the lesson Creeley learned from bebop was to take Pound's—"Ez's"—poetic and marry it to Parker's rhythmic breakthrough, foregrounding the latter in the development of content. After all, the "point" of his repeated references to this analogy was itself not "'gratuitous,'" but deadly "serious." Parker's lesson, translated into poetics, constituted for Creeley the guiding principle and prime arena of projective verse. In a time of neo-formalism, the battle for rhythmic innovation was primary:

> [R]hythm is where the most work now comes in, that, if we can manage the declaration of rhythms more exact than those now in use—the iamb, etc.—we clean up. Likewise that rhythm is a means to "going on" far more active than any "thot," etc. And that sound is rhythm in another dimension. (Creeley, *Selected Letters*, 113)

The description here fits Creeley's work well. His sounds, like Parker's, often strike their audiences as being from "another dimension"; both artists open up space by expanding and contracting time through the expansion and contraction of the lungs, extending the form in the process. That he conceived the battle over projective verse, over the poetics of breath and voice that he forged with Olson, as essentially a fight for more various and nuanced rhythms, marks their difference from other jazz-inspired writers of the period. It also speaks to the perceived dominance of academic formalism at the time, whether the practice of American poets like Ransom, Tate, and the young Robert Lowell, of British poets like Auden, Philip Larkin, Donald Davie, and others involved in what would be termed the Movement, or simply the traditionalism presiding over midcentury literature and literary studies that resulted from the overwhelming influence of T. S. Eliot. In this context, a postmodern, open field poetics needed, in Creeley's mind, to begin with opening poetry to the syncopated breathing inherent in jazz rhythms.

Chapter Two

OUTSIDE BOSTON

STEPHEN JONAS IN THE POETRY OF

JOHN WIENERS AND JACK SPICER

Like Creeley, a host of younger writers would look to various ways of extending Olson's projectivist approach to breath and voice. In Olson and Creeley's native New England, in fact, a burgeoning group of writers were interacting with Cid Corman and developing distinctive poetic practices of their own. Corman, initially through his radio program *This Is Poetry* on Boston's WMEX and later by collaborating with them on the publication of his important little magazine *Origin*, knew of and supported Olson's and Creeley's early efforts. In fact, as Alan Golding has shown, Olson, Creeley, and the group of writers involved in *Origin* shared a common commitment to a distinctively "oral poetics" (*From Outlaw to Classic*, 132). In the early 1950s Corman was one of the few people in the poetry world willing to pursue such an agenda, and so had an intimate, if somewhat embattled, understanding of their work. As Olson wrote to him after being converted to Creeley's interest in Charlie Parker, "[h]ow does—or is there—an analogy to (as i'd gather any of us do) to jazz?" ("Memorial Letter," 42). The question frames their collaboration on the early issues of *Origin* as equivalent to a Parker improvisation. In a related way, then, the poets who joined Corman in Boston in the mid-1950s shared similar instincts, making Olson's jazz-inspired poetics their own in diverse ways.

Jack Spicer arrived in Boston in November of 1955. He left his native San Francisco for the East Coast, landing first in New York and then moving north, where he would befriend fellow poets John Wieners, Stephen Jonas, and Joe Dunn. Robin Blaser, then working at Harvard's Widener Library, had arranged a position for Spicer at the Boston Public Library, which, though short-lived, would prove crucial to his poetic development (Katz, *Poetry of Jack Spicer*, 7). In fact, during his twelve months there, he wrote the significant early poem "Song for Bird and Myself," as well as an important review of Emily Dickinson's poetry, forging an enduring friendship with Jonas and forming a crush on Dunn that would settle into an all-important publishing relationship later in San Francisco (Ellingham and Killian, *Poet Be Like God*, 74). As Spicer would later recall, his brief stay in Boston left a lasting impression on his poetry, thanks largely to Jonas, who taught him "how to use anger (as opposed to angry irony) in a poem" (Spicer, "Letters to Robin Blaser," 37). Such "anger" is apparent in the ferocity with which he would go on to pursue his unique approach to the projectivist poetics of breath and voice in mature collections like *After Lorca*. In fact, as that title suggests, Spicer's subsequent poetry would, thanks to Jonas, also be consonant with the angry passion of the flamenco singer Pastora Pavón, often referred to as La Niña de Los Peines. As Federico García Lorca writes in his now well-known lecture "Theory and Function of the *Duende*," Pavón got "rid of the scaffolding of song" in order to "make way for a furious and fiery *duende*" (95). *Duende*, of course, appears also in the form of the spritely, daemonic intruder, akin to, yet somewhat different from, the " 'mysterious power' " (91) cited by Lorca in the same work. Above all else, in Boston Spicer gained insight into this "daemon," reimagining it as Martian and outsider, embodying this voice "without voice" in various ways (Lorca, 95). Through his friendship with Jonas, Spicer would braid this sense of *duende* with jazz and projectivism to formulate his own unique, developing poetic.

Like Spicer, John Wieners, too, valued Jonas for playing a central role in his poetic development. Writing in an early journal, he credited Jonas with providing the "paradise" of Boston poets with "orders" (Wieners, *Stars Seen in Person,* 52, 126). The two had attended an Olson lecture at the Charles Street Meeting House in 1954 and, after Wieners had studied with Olson at Black Mountain College for two terms in 1955 and 1956, they joined with Spicer, Blaser, and Dunn to pursue their shared interests in a jazz-inflected projectivism that could incorporate their own distinctive Boston experiences. As a self-styled poète maudit, cruising parks and gay bars, Wieners demonstrates an allegiance to what Maria Damon has described as the "matrix of institutions and streets" that shaped his experience of working-class Boston (Damon, "John Wieners," 72). At the same time, his writing from this period reveals the degree to which Jonas's blending of projectivist principles and *duende* had influenced the "scorched throat" of his poetry (Lorca, "Duende," 92). In many ways, in fact, Wieners's exploration of this blending expands the possibilities of a poetics of breath by performing a lyric voice that is not confessional, but broken, in a sense parallel to the *duende* of Pavón or, to borrow an analogy closer to Wieners's own heart, to the syncopated delivery and heartsick longing of Billie Holiday.

Though his influence on better-known poets like Spicer and Wieners was pivotal, Stephen Jonas's work has largely eluded scholarly attention. Apart from an astute introductory essay by Joseph Torra and critical analysis of major works by Aldon Lynn Nielsen, little of note has been written on this important figure.[1] These two essays aside, Jonas's work has received little more than passing mention since his death in 1970, despite the high praise he received from well-regarded poets like Spicer and Wieners, and the appearance of two posthumous collections of his poetry: Torra's edition of *The Selected Poems of Stephen Jonas* in 1994, and his work with Garret Caples, Derek Fenner, and David Rich in editing *Arcana: A Stephen Jonas Reader* in 2019. In part, this may be due to the lack of factual biographical information on the poet, as well as to the occasional antisemitic remarks that appear throughout his work, remarks compounded by his ambivalence concerning his own racial identity. Certainly, these factors have complicated his reception. Nonetheless, Jonas was a key influence on both Spicer's and Wieners's thought during their formative periods in the mid-1950s and continued to attract the admiration of others involved in the New American Poetry throughout the succeeding decade. Having participated in poetry workshops with Corman in the early 1950s, Jonas evolved from a discipleship to T. S. Eliot and Ezra Pound to a projectivist poetics that drew heavily on Charlie Parker's jazz and Lorca's theory of *duende*. The blending of these influences would make for a compelling, and clearly influential, body of poetry. Tracing that influence through his friendships with Spicer and Wieners will therefore be a central concern here.

For all of these reasons, then, the poetics of breath formulated in the opening of this study becomes increasingly complicated in the work of these three poets. In their writing from this period, voice or breath, in a projectivist sense, can be seen as performing, in a form of *duende*, gay male experiences that had up until this time remained closeted. Drawing on jazz as an aesthetic resource intensifies this complication by adding both musical analogies and racial tensions to an already fraught situation. The result is a textual body scored with intersecting lines, improvising its affiliations with both earlier and then contemporary poetic practices through its negotiation of various fault lines within each poet's complicated understanding of identity. It is, in other words, a poetry animated by a voice made audible through the very suffering that leads to its dissolution.

Exploring these voices in greater detail, this chapter examines an important extension of the projectivist poetics founded at Black Mountain. While the previous chapter observed the intertwining of race, jazz, and open field poetics, gender performativity enters the conversation here as a fourth term. Of course, Olson's and Creeley's works perform gender as well, albeit in a largely heteronormative sense; however, the masculinist discourse through which they pursue their poetics of force varies little, if at all, from the conventional understandings assumed by more mainstream and academic poetry communities in the period. As Michael Davidson has shown, the homosocial poetics of "Projective Verse" exemplifies this in one way, while Spicer's circle in San Francisco witnesses a very different instance of it (Davidson, *Guys Like Us*, 33–34). If polis is, as Olson argued in *The Special View of History*, enriched by the incorporation of the marginal, then the campy and homoerotic performances found in the poetry of Spicer, Jonas, and Wieners effect precisely that enrichment, expanding the scope of projective verse and of the jazz analogy at the heart of it. As Nielsen has written, like other African American poets of the period, Jonas rooted the postmodernity of his work in a "struggle of usurpation over the corpus and the corpse of Euro-American modernism" (*Integral Music,* 68). The impulse to locate the African American experience as essential to the modern and, by extension, the postmodern as well, appears time and again in his recourse to jazz aesthetics. These musical concepts played a similar role for Wieners and Spicer. In their cases, however, and for Jonas as well, the fragmented self of homosexual experience in midcentury America, what Damon has described, in reference to W. E. B. Du Bois, as the "'double consciousness'" of gay identity in that era, plays an equally important role in their exploration of *duende* (Du Bois, *Souls of Black Folk,* 3; Damon, *Postliterary America,* 171, 179–80). As a closer look will show, these concerns combine to create a powerful expansion of the principles of projective verse, a kind of syncopation of the New American Poetry's poetics of breath and voice.

BLUE TEARS

A half century after his death, Stephen Jonas's life remains largely a mystery. As Joseph Torra writes, the poet's beginnings are inaccessible to scholars:

> Tracing Jonas' ancestry has proven futile. This is due in large part to his own efforts to erase certain aspects of his life and remain elusive about his past. His place and date of birth are unknown, though it has been reported that he was born somewhere in Georgia. . . . He was probably raised by adoptive parents and eventually he changed his name (though never legally) from Rufus S. Jones to Stephen Jonas. Over the years he used a number of other aliases as well. (Introduction, *Arcana,* 17)

Such ambiguity over the essential facts of the poet's biography appears to be intentional. As Jonas reported in a letter to Raffael De Gruttola, he had been adopted, and his birth parents were Spanish "I think Creole i.e. French-Spanish" and Portuguese (quoted in Torra, Introduction, *Arcana,* 17). On the other hand, friends like Wieners and Spicer—and, indeed, Jonas himself in his own poetry—identified him as African American. In the segregated America of the time, such obfuscation is understandable; Jonas clearly shaped his identity to suit his audience from one moment to the next. In the absence of additional biographical information, then, it would seem best to attribute such evasiveness not to deception, but to Jonas's struggle, like those of many other members of minority groups in the period, both African American and homosexual, to come to terms with an identity not recognized as American. As Nielsen has written, his work forms "a site from which to survey the continually intersecting lines of race and culture that so troubles the politics of American identities" (*Integral Music,* 62). However, for Jonas, writing these fault lines involved graphing not only the crisscrossing of race and politics, but of sexuality as well. In doing so, he engaged in an imaginative interplay with the parallel work of fellow gay friends and collaborators like Wieners and Spicer. In this way, his poetry can be seen as enriching the center of Olson's polis by speaking to it through the *duende* of voices rent by marginal subjectivities.

These concerns can be seen in Jonas's "Gloucester," a poem set in Olson's mythic hometown and subtitled "Impressions for J[ohn] W[ieners]" ("Gloucester," 75). The piece begins with a "trumpet blast" in a moment that is figured as an apocalyptic awakening, with the suggestion also of an introductory solo, akin, say, to Louis Armstrong's opening in "West End Blues" ("Gloucester," 75). Fittingly, much like Olson's Maximus, Jonas wrestles throughout with the judgment of history, of "former knowledge" ("Gloucester," 75). In this context, "Jazz at Storyville," itself a phrase resonant with both the New Orleans neighborhood where Armstrong began his musical career and the aptly named Boston nightclub where Jonas discovered jazz, becomes an escape from suburban life, from respectable family and "fine old house[s]" where "horrors" are "conceald [sic] in every closet" ("Gloucester," 75). Escaping such horrors involves an initiation into mysticism, sex, and poetry ("Gloucester," 75–76). "Our Lady," referring to Our Lady of Good Voyage church, whose Marian statue figures in both *Maximus* and *Four Quartets*, appears then as a kind of divine premonition of Jonas's poetic vocation ("Gloucester," 75). In fact, after a reading of Eliot's poem, Jonas recalls, "I was brought to my knees / and so it was that I decided for Poetry" ("Gloucester," 76). This autobiographical journey into his poetic origins is thus figured as a kind of divine calling, a ritualistic taking of vows; however, the acolyte here joins a cult of "Poetry" with a capital letter, inspired not by Eliotic notions of holiness, but by a counter tradition, a subterranean community of jazz, gay sex, and mystical spirituality. The poem's closing emphasizes this, with the "Judgment" of the poem's opening softened into "flowers reawakened to delect us" ("Gloucester," 76). Consequently, the piece ends with Jonas addressing Wieners directly, inviting him to join in the same calling: "My friend, / shall we partake further / of that mortal odor?" ("Gloucester," 76). The invitation here stretches a hand to Wieners in Whitmanian camaraderie, encouraging him to collaborate in the same project, turning or converting a poetic lineage founded by Eliot and Olson into a means of awakening their own marginal experiences. In this way, the poem acts as an apt introduction to the larger aims and ambitions of Jonas's poetic project, as well as to its overlapping concerns with Wieners's work.

These ideas are developed further in early poems such as the "manifesto-like" "Word on Measure," featured in the first issue of Wieners's magazine of the same name (see Torra, Introduction, *Arcana*, 21). As the opening of the piece declares, the little magazine should be a forum for "the Poem of the Fairy" (Jonas, "Word on Measure," 89). Replete with puns on "queen" and the "fairydust" that "rubs off the word," the manifesto practices a spritely form of *duende* in imagining poetic composition as "a sort of long handjob" where the exploration of language moves in tune with the punning humor and homoeroticism of Jonas's poetic circle ("Word on Measure," 89–91). Like "Gloucester," "Word on Measure" enacts a speech-based poetics that follow Olson's use of breath, and yet it pushes his practice into new territory by performing alternative approaches to working "in the open," writing a poetry that is, in other words, openly and unapologetically gay (Olson, "Projective Verse," 239). At the same time, however, such determinations link their poetic practices with the work of other African American writers who sought "to begin to begin again," as Nielsen has termed it, rooting postmodernism in an anterior tradition of Black artistry and folklore (*Integral Music*, 84). In Jonas's words, "the Poem of the Fairy" stands alongside "uncle Remus and little black sambo" as "home products," "like the thin man who's on junk" ("Word on Measure," 90). At once a "racial remaking," conflating the Native American Sambo with African American imagery, these lines also declare, in their breadth, an embrace of an alternative, homosexual tradition in American culture, an underground knowledge shared by the marginalized, as the colloquial source of "fairy" art (Nielsen, *Integral Music*, 84; Jonas, "Word on Measure," 90).

With Jack Spicer, Jonas would explore this poetic in greater detail. In fact, Jonas composed three poems for Spicer, each sharing the concern for an openly gay poetics aligned with Black music. Two—". . . An Ear Injured by Hearing Things (after a Statement of Jack Spicer's)" and "Morphogenesis (being a conventionalization 'Morphemes' of Jack Spicer)"—respond directly to Spicer's work, with Jonas exploring the grounds of their shared poetic principles and techniques. "An Ear Injured" broaches the jagged, asymmetrical rhythms of their approach to lineation, a technique also shared with Robert Creeley:

thoughts march
across the page
orderly
the mind
hems & haws
de-
    fining the line a
metrical dance (Jonas, "An Ear Injured" 32)

Here, the poem opens with a kind of statement and counterstatement, the "orderly" "march" of ideas interrupted by the staggering *duende* of second thoughts, the kind of limping discrepancies theorized by Nathaniel Mackey when he locates the concept in the "black aesthetic of Spain" ("Cante Moro" 195).[2] For instance, lines one through three each contain two heavy accents, directing a steady pace; however, they are succeeded in lines four and six by others with one accent and no accents, causing extended pauses where the change of pace creates openings for "hems & haws," for a kind of doubting dance of the mind. Troubling the line in this way borrows an angular rhythmical device common to jazz, as Creeley and Olson noted in the previous chapter. As the rest of the poem has it, such gaps "violat[e]" "the law" of poetic meter and so render it pliable, creating a "flexibility" necessary for new growth ("An Ear Injured," 32). Consequently, the poem clears the ground for the "what / have you" of everyday experience to flourish ("An Ear Injured," 33). Though somewhat abstract, the poetic pursued here shares much in common with the ambitions stated in "Word on Measure," as a look at "Morphogenesis" shows.

There, the building blocks of language are compared to biological cells and understood almost like arpeggiated chords, revealing in the process a musical inspiration at the heart of the two poets' shared understanding of bodily performance. Once again, "The Law" is troubled by rhythmic interruption and the uncertainty of "syntactical connections" (Jonas, "Morphogenesis," 81). This time, however, such discrepant engagement formulates an awakening via jazz performance. The poem's sought-after "place" of lively, awakened action is figured as the space surrounding a reed section:

The place we shall
come to know

is clearly stated
    in certain musical
    statements of
        horns upendings. ("Morphogenesis," 82)

As before, the orderly procession of equally weighted, if alternately accent-
ed, lines is interrupted, first by the hesitation created through the passage's
indentation, and then by the shortened line "statements of," which only
bears one stress. The hitch in the rhythm, along with the space effected by
the following line's additional indentation, creates a recalibration in the reading, an "upending" of the established form, akin to the rhythmic reversals
characteristic of bop and theorized by Lorca. That the typography intends
such recognitions is made plain in the subsequent passage:

(I take it that Jack Spicer's "phonemes" carry
    the printed circuitry that upon utterance
        reproduces the visual impression) ("Morphogenesis," 82)

Such "circuitry" is apparent in the manipulation of "'phonemes'" into ac-
centual patterns that lend a visual analogue, or score, for "utterance," for
verbal performance. In this way, the poem is analogous to the musician's
chart. The poetry itself, for Jonas, occurs in the act of reading. As the closing
has it, such technique leads, like the previous poem, to a recognition of the
vibrancy of the moment: "So instantly we reawaken / This is the first day
of our lives!" ("Morphogenesis," 83).

    While the two previous poems remain largely abstract explorations of
technique, their concerns are brought to bear in a much fuller way in the
longer piece, "Cante Jondo for Soul Brother Jack Spicer, His Beloved California & Andalusia of Lorca." *Cante jondo*, of course, is the "deep song" that
Lorca identifies with *duende*. Here, then, the "anger" or passion noted is
foregrounded. Stylistically, this is apparent in the various ways in which the
poem's shifting margins trouble the voice, as does the frequent use of Spanish
and African American Vernacular English. As for Spicer, for Jonas the beauty
and immediacy of this tradition of "deep song" is communicated through
jazz, and particularly through the playing of Charlie Parker, Horace Silver,
and other bop performers. In fact, as Jonas frames it, Spicer's engagement
with *duende* comes via his encounter with Parker's blues-inflected music:

Heard 'Bird's' playing & for three years

> > didn't know the taste of meat. sd. he didn't know
> >
> > music had attained to it. A tear & one blue note upon yr brow, baby.
> >
> > ("Cante Jondo for Soul Brother Jack Spicer," 70)

In this passage the changing indentation and shifting register affects a poly-vocal texture that is heightened and repeated throughout. This continues a few lines down where a very American form of Christianity is wedded to homoeroticism:

> The 'amen corner' is as close as we can come to cuadro flamenco.
> Walt Whitman's butterflys w/ singed wings, all silver white
>
> > star spangled the milky-way w/ their gissem.
> >
> > ("Cante Jondo for Soul Brother Jack Spicer,"
> >
> > 70)

Satirizing the charismatic tradition of many Protestant churches in the U.S., Jonas presents such conformity as the closest that the average American ever gets to the passion of a flamenco troupe. Such fiery rhetoric singes the wings of "Whitman's butterflys," his own version of the homosexual as "fairy," and leads to a pun on the patriotic "Star-Spangled Banner," where the stars of the American flag morph into the "gissem" of homoerotic encounter. Opposed to both legal codes and social mores of the period, and despite—or perhaps because of—its raunchiness, the image lays claim to an African-derived, homosexual identity that is nonetheless authentically American. Such playfulness also demonstrates one of Jonas's sharpest uses of *duende*, doubling the voice's blues with a humor that also nods toward jazz expressivism. Not only do the indentations suggest the angular rhythms of the bop performers mentioned throughout, but so does the potential pun on "gissem," a vernacular term for semen, itself thought to be the linguistic root, after all, for "jazz."

As an extension of this trope, the poem entreats Spicer to pursue, in a phrase that once again mixes Black music with flamenco, "their cante jondo blues of sounds / —bad sounds / from the ballin' bad fartin' fuck sounds" (Jonas, "Cante Jondo for Soul Brother Jack Spicer" 71). Such a poetry would thus mix high and low culture as part of a larger attempt to shift registers and so rend or syncopate the vocal performance. The "anger" or violence implicit in this action is apparent in Jonas's direct address to Spicer:

Spicer, we want a big round sound in poetry
                              like Ammons gets from a horn,
              or Picasso's high voltage line
                              execution of a picador. ("Cante
                              Jondo for Soul Brother Jack Spicer,"
                              71)

Combining jazz, high modernist art, and bullfighting through tripping margins and metaphor cloaked in the shifting registers of language, the passage epitomizes the poetics of *cante jondo* that Jonas pursued. Joining him in this pursuit, Spicer appears as a part of Jonas's complex racial imagination, from his antisemitic taunting of "money-changers" and New York "jews" to his own fraught sense of Blackness:

All over America the little magazines conspired
              to board Jack Spicer up in a California Street rooming house,
        for lack of space.
                            "duende"
                              "duende"
                                        —elbow nudged ribs & a wink:
                    "yeah, he's got it"
                    "aw *man*, he's black with it" ("Cante Jondo for
                    Soul Brother Jack Spicer," 73)

Here, the adoption of "space," of the use of typography common to open field poetics, is aligned with a performance of Blackness that borders on minstrelsy. Though clearly meant as high praise, the declaration of Spicer's Blackness itself troubles Jonas's song. Coupled with the poets' antisemitism, there is a sense in Jonas's work, one that he clearly shared with Spicer and Wieners, that figures the *duende* as releasing the "'dark song'" from within. While this typically takes the shape of illicit sex or jazz music, racism, also, was clearly a part of it. While there will be more to say concerning this aspect of Spicer's work as well, for now it is important to note that these elements are interwoven in Jonas's poetics. Consequently, his celebration of the "fairy poem," and of its various techniques, should be understood in this context as well.

Jonas's later poetry embodies many of the same aspirations and contradictions. Some of the most powerful instances of this appear in the serial poem *Exercises for Ear*. These "exercises" in close listening explore the interconnections between *duende*, Black music, and the homoeroticism apparent in the Spicer and Wieners poems. There, "scapulas" and "novenas" are juxtaposed with "*dir- / ty*" blues and sadomasochistic entreaties to S.S. officers (*Exercises for Ear*, 141–42). In this way, the opening of section XLV sums up the attitude of the poem well: ". . . blues ain't nuthin' / but which gender you / makin' it w'th" (*Exercises for Ear*, 143). Rending the voice, thus makes for various couplings throughout, whose encounters, moreover, bend blue notes over gendered and racial conventions. In this way, the resulting song sounds the discrepancies of a poetic in the open, of an embodied breathing whose voices syncopate any clear projective lineage with the questions and contradictions inherent in Jonas's troubled music. His white friends were clearly inspired by this.

PASSIONATE CONCENTRATION

The poetry of John Wieners would embrace the same world of troubles, though in slightly different ways. Curiously, his engagement with projective verse seems both more direct and more ambiguous. As Michael Seth Stewart has asked, "how could a student of Olson and his historical-political poetic project write personal, lyric verse" (Stewart, Introduction, *Yours Presently*, xvi)? In "Hanging On for Dear Life," a 1974 commemoration of Olson, Wieners speaks to both his friendship with the elder poet, and his recognition of clear differences in his own mature poetry. More than anything else, Olson appears in the piece as a larger-than-life exemplar. As Wieners recalls, "I know he was the world of literature for me" ("Hanging On for Dear Life," 23). Trite as this praise may seem, "literature," for Olson, meant something unique to those initiated into his thinking. As Wieners attests, Olson's poetry "resists" the attempt to register "'experience'" ("Hanging On," 23). In this way, it resists the traditional lyric and the confessional "I," both very much in vogue during the period. Mapping the self in a field of force, Olson's poetic didn't so much offer "content" to explore, but a methodology to use, an attention not to the meaning *in* words, but to what is affected "by words" ("Hanging On," 22). As Stewart explains, "[f]or Wieners, the personal was not the *matter* of the poem . . . it was a vantage to occupy, a center from which to understand, to call out to, the world beyond the self" (Introduction, *Yours Presently*, xvii). Wieners's praise, therefore, should be read as crediting the mentor who initiated him into the discipline of a poetic vocation. As he writes in an early letter to Olson, echoing the title of the essay, projective verse had become for him "a law one learns like walking . . . till finally you get to the knees on the other side of the room, AND HANG ON" (Wieners, *Yours Presently*, 61).

The major insight to be gained from this experience, as the title of the piece suggests, is the "perseverance to style" that can be achieved by allowing oneself to "get away from one's condition and see it, for the bizarre oddity it is to other persons" (Wieners, "Hanging On," 23, 22). Certainly, on many occasions, Wieners presents the speaker of his poetry as just such a "bizarre oddity," navigating struggles unknown to the average straight, or simply unhip, reader. This attempt to play witness to the self as stranger, however, while sharing some commonalities with Olson's approach, also marks a clear divergence in what would otherwise be called content. The method itself assures a certain measure of uniqueness and idiosyncrasy. As Wieners notes, he couldn't go to Olson for "content" ("Hanging On," 22). After his death, however—and somewhat ironically—Wieners does hear the vitality of Olson's "voice": "There is no hollow place in my life, now. There is just a missing voice, a lost person who might not be alive, but is" ("Hanging On," 23). The apparent contradiction here reaches for a paradox at the heart of Olson's poetics: that charting one's breath is both an intimately affirming and an ultimately alienating experience. As Wieners writes in "A poem for the dead I know": "We are all Lazarus, / And carry our dead friends with us" ("Poem for the dead I know," 31). Like Spicer's Orpheus, Wieners's use of Lazarus figures the poet as a character capable of bringing the dead back to life. In this sense, Olson's voice is, but isn't, dead. Surely, there is a hint of the supernatural here. Though Wieners doesn't attribute it to him, the *duende* practiced by Jonas assures, by rending the voice, that it is never more than synonymous with "the breathing of the man who writes" (Olson, "Projective Verse," 239). As Wieners himself insists in the short poem addressed to Olson, "[w]e have a flame within us I told Charles" ("We have a flame within us I told Charles," 84). The commonality of this "flame" justifies the comma splice, the universality of its "electricity," as the closing of the piece imagines it, guarantees that it is both impersonal and yet, through each individual witness, unique ("We have a flame," 84). As the recurrence of these concerns in his writing shows, their ambiguity resides at the heart of Wieners's poetic.

While in the piece he credits Olson with this recognition, he writes in a similar way concerning both Jonas's and Billie Holiday's influence on him in the 1965 journal titled, "Blaauwildebeestefontein" (Wieners, *Stars Seen in Person*, 102–3). As Stewart notes, Wieners's praises for Jonas and other mentors here "are especially important contributions to the emergent histories of the New American Poets and the poets they loved, and the only time within Wieners' corpus of poems, journals, and letters in which he explicitly addresses their shared history and legacies" (Stewart, Introduction, *Stars Seen in Person*, xxii). As such, his writings on Jonas and Holiday can be read as having an added value, referencing not only his own enthusiasms but clarifying, by extension, those of Jonas and Spicer as well. The passages on Jonas appear in a long poem titled, "Road of Straw," where he is given prominence, alongside Olson, Allen Ginsberg, Robert Creeley, Ed Marshall, William Carlos Williams, Ezra Pound, and others (Wieners, *Stars Seen in Person*, 124–29). Certainly, Marshall and Jonas have not received the subsequent attention given to these other poets, and yet they appear in the piece as the greater influences on Wieners. Marshall's "Leave the Word Alone" is cited by Wieners as the "only long spontaneous continuous poem of the 20th century" and is praised above the work of Olson, Ginsberg, and several others (*Stars Seen in Person*, 124, 126). "Leave the Word Alone," in fact, contains many similarities with Wieners's poetry, particularly the passionate insistence that poetry itself "is a painful process but it is a process I must go   through / to stay out of the asylum" (Marshall, "Leave the Word Alone," 333). Like Wieners, Marshall's stare into the dark self appears both necessary and tragic. Both, however, seem to have learned from Jonas the trick of surviving such gambits. As Wieners writes, Marshall was "directly influenced by Steve Jonas" (*Stars Seen in Person*, 124). Jonas's influence, moreover, consists of not only his writing, but of the interdependence between his poetry and his life:

> It was Steve Jonas who first presented
> to me, and Steve Jonas himself who
> first presented to Ed Marshall the
> world of Steve Jonas; ~~mental~~
> ~~hospitals, jails~~ go   the words (*Stars Seen in Person*, 125)

Here, like Olson, Jonas makes present—"who first presented / to me . . . who / first presented to Ed Marshall"—the experiences of Wieners and Marshall through the "present," or gift, of the "world of Steve Jonas." In other words, through his example, Jonas taught Wieners and Marshall how their own worlds could be enlivened in a poetry that voices suffering only to negate it: "~~mental~~ / ~~hospitals, jails.~~" This complexity provides a method for resolving two opposing concerns, the traditions of Williams, Pound, and others with their personal experience of the "madness" of Boston's streets, of their shared adventures in "the gutter" of the "Road of Straw" (*Stars Seen in Person*, 124–29). Though Black Mountain figures recur throughout, it is the combination of Olson and Jonas that inspires Wieners's unique swerve on the poetics of projective verse:

> Steve Jonas first presented
> orders to us in the early years of the decade
> preceding, the 1950's. And it was
> here on the streets of Boston
> we first heard Charles Olson, Marshall
> received his stimulus, Steve reached
> his maturity, and I renamed them
> all. (*Stars Seen in Person*, 126)

This brief, anecdotal history provides a helpful frame for understanding both Jonas and Wieners. While their encounter with Olson appears to have clarified and galvanized their work, its primary influence echoes from "the streets of Boston." In fact, as the close of the poem insists, though it is "madness," the inspiration of these poets is to write these streets, to accept it as the city's calling, "[d]ictated to against its will. / by Steve Jonas, again in 1952 and onwards. Love, John" (*Stars Seen in Person*, 129). As Wieners wrote to Robert Duncan, despite great suffering, Jonas found in Boston street life "'the mystical recurrence of things'" (Wieners, *Yours Presently*, 62). Why, or how, this might be so, and what Jonas's "orders" may themselves have been, however, remains unclear.

Later in the same journal, as part of a passage titled, "The Anticipation of Youth," Wieners focuses on the influence of Billie Holiday's music. Lamenting that "imagination has worn out," and that he feels "like an old man," Wieners reminisces:

> Billie Holiday ushered in my youth, when I was 12, 1946—and she sang on Commodore Records, "Strange Fruit" and she ushered it out when she died in New York, July 19th 1959 thirteen years later. I met her once at the High Hat in Boston when I was 21. (*Stars Seen in Person*, 148)

Like Frank O'Hara in his well-known poem "The Day That Lady Died," Wieners marked the occasion of Holiday's death as a crucial moment in his own life.[3] That his youth should be interwoven with Holiday's life and death, however, remains something of a mystery. As he adds later on, "Anyway she was 25 when I was first born on earth, and I was 25 when she left it. Strange coincidence" (*Stars Seen in Person*, 149). The inversion of the numbers in the passage—12 and 21—coupled with the repetition of 25 here create a mirror effect, as though his fascination with Holiday was the result of seeing himself refracted in her songs. In fact, this fractured, broken quality is precisely what he praises in her performance. As he describes it, "I have become of her, enamored of her ashes on the voice" (*Stars Seen in Person*, 149). This burnt or singed quality is apparent in many of Wieners's poems, as is the inward concentration, the total absorption, that he finds so inspiring in her singing:

> She had a great quality to her voice in that she never seemed
>   aware of what the audience was thinking of her, tho I
>   remember, was totally absorbed in what she was doing,
>   a passion for
> concentration, derived or gained, probably from the junk she
>   was using. (*Stars Seen in Person*, 148)

The passage thus breaks into projective lines to render Holiday's art. Like Wieners's poetry, her music confronts the audience with a kind of "deep song" or *cante jondo*. In this regard, her performance also resembles Lorca's description of *duende*, alluding, as it does, to his comments on Pastora Pavón, who also ignored the audience and sang with a scorched throat (Lorca, "Duende," 95). Pain and suffering thus go hand in hand with such eruptions of emotion. Holiday's drug use, in fact, led to her early demise. Meanwhile, Pavón's singing led her voice to become, similarly, a "jet of blood" ("Duende," 95).

Wieners no doubt understood this and so sought to make his own art out of the sincerity of his hard living. This aspect of Wieners's writing appears as another instance of his admiration for Holiday, as, in other words, an example in which such "concentration" reflects and refracts the self. The wear and tear of this process clearly weighed on him in this journal entry. Looking for a path forward, these reminiscences of Holiday's vocal performance return him to a sense of renewed commitment to recover in his own work the "compassion and wisdom" he found in her singing:

> The envy and drive she had to sing of love, I must speak, of her. My goddess of youth. Remembered of her now that youth is gone, is lost to me, I say, "as if all youth were gone. Credit Robert Duncan with maintaining what youth and love I have, gone with her
>
> Charles Olson with maintaining it. But I don't want this to be a paean of love to memory past. I want to go out and find it. And I will. (*Stars Seen in Person*, 149)

Wieners's ardent memory pivots here on a determination to avoid nostalgia, to pursue future writing. Taking the "love" Holiday expressed toward the inconstant and wounded characters of her songs, Wieners vows to renew his own attempts to sing the madness of Boston's streets. Significantly, her performance of *duende* becomes a gift, much like Jonas's "present," and it is similarly wedded to Black Mountain poetics through the incorporation of Robert Duncan and Charles Olson. As he noted in discovering Olson's "Projective Verse" in William Carlos Williams's *Autobiography*, its connection to passionate performance—"a line should run according to a man's breathing, and this is determined by the emotion of the poem"—reaffirms Jonas's primacy: "This is open verse, and mind-music, as Steve Jonas is constantly spouting" (*Stars Seen in Person*, 44). Taken together, then, Wieners constructs his own poetic origins in these passages, weaving projective verse, jazz, and *duende*, as passed down by Jonas and embodied by Holiday in these recollections of intense inspiration.

Throughout Wieners's early poetry, in fact, Holiday's "fiery *duende*" is apparent in burning images of hell associated with the pains of fraught and repressed homosexual desire in 1950s and 1960s America ("Duende," 95). "A poem for record players," for instance, conjures such music as distraction or cover for an illicit autoeroticism, "[t]he scratches I itch" (Wieners, "Poem for record players," 6). These sounds later become transformed into car engines, igniting and "turning over / all over town" in an act of Promethean theft, "taking away / from God his sound" ("Poem for record players," 7, 6). A similar act of compensation occurs in "Cocaine." There, the "artificial paradise" that is "Hell" can only be countered with drugs that "reduce misery" precisely by confusing "the sensations" and thus fading "the flesh that fires the night, / with dreams and infinite longing" ("Cocaine," 60). These themes find further elaboration in Wieners's meditation on the painter Edvard Munch in "A poem for museum goers." Here, the museum goers are "enveloped / in pain" ("Poem for museum goers," 24). In this regard, Munch's art appears as an analogue to Wieners's poetic, involving the viewer/reader in a world of imaginative suffering:

> . . . Munch
> knew it. Put the
> Shriek in their ears
> to remove it from his own. ("Poem for museum goers," 24)

Such "Hell," as the poem has it, becomes the world of art; however, much like "A poem for record players," it effects this recognition through a projection of muffled sound. "Open thy mouth," the poem commands the artist, likely also with the suggestion of the gaping mouth in Munch's famous painting *The Scream*. Yet, as visual art, the imagined noise is countered by physical silence. This muted, virtual scream, much like the muted joy detailed elsewhere in Wieners's work—in other poems and, perhaps most painfully, in journal entries concerning his family[4]—transforms the gallery into a fiery hellscape:

> . . . Death
> death on every
> wall, guillotined
> and streaming in
> flames. ("Poem for museum goers" 26)

In this way, Munch's undulating lines appear as burning fire, guillotining the museum goers, as though they were traitors to the new republic. Of course, there is also a class antagonism running throughout, with the suggestion of bourgeois museum goers confronted by the revolutionary artist. Most of all, though, the paintings elicit an extended meditation on the suppressed anger and desire that burns throughout Wieners's work. The *duende* of projective breath in his poetry clearly pivots on just such moments of suppression and release.

As seen in Wieners's comments on Holiday and in "A poem for record players," such desire often goes hand in hand with music in his poetry. Together, they also broach questions of race. In fact, in the journal entry quoted, Wieners chides himself at one point, reasoning: "I should be out on the street, living her life, blowing some colored cock" (Wieners, *Stars Seen in Person*, 149). The interweaving here of race, music, and sexuality animates much of his early work. Damon, for instance, reads "A poem for tea heads" as a longing in one sense for "homoerotic miscegenation" (*Postliterary America*, 182). As Nielsen has written, white poets like Wieners—and Olson and Creeley, as seen in the previous chapter—yearn to inhabit "the image structure of the farthest outsider" and so appear akin to Mailer's "White Negro" (Nielsen, *Reading Race*, 157). Poems like "Stationary" demonstrate these concerns more fully. There, the piece opens with Wieners in bed, "dreaming of boys, / old poets, / Bob Kaufman" ("Stationary," 80). The longing for such encounters, meanwhile, leads him to complete the dream in flames: "his hair burning out of his head. / A cigarette smoking in my hand" ("Stationary," 80). Blackness and fire once again become symbols of infinite longing and frustrated desire, much like the unfinished cigarette. So too does music:

> Hearing voices of fresh lovers on the radio
> next door, their spirits rush, you must
> remember their kisses their soft murmurings
> in the dark, like fundamental things apply
> as transient storms return the centaurs. ("Stationary," 80)

Like much of Holiday's music, the "voices" "on the radio" play a troubled memory, a song of "soft murmurings" and "fundamental" desires that end in "transient storms." Beyond this, however, there is also the yoking of the lovers, Kaufman, and the poet himself with mythological "centaurs," half-man, half-horse creatures who functioned as symbols for unchecked desire. Again, as Nielsen has shown, such projections create the suggestion that both Wieners and the African American poet Kaufman share a marginal space, that homosexuality and Blackness go hand in hand. While the two certainly occupy marginalized positions in midcentury America, the mythical, and somewhat barbaric, association with centaurs here casts Kaufman's racial difference in terms strikingly similar to Mailer's "White Negro" or, as Ellison wrote in response to Mailer, "the same old primitivism crap" (Ellison and Murray, 198).

In related ways, the better-known "A poem for cock suckers" demonstrates Wieners's most bracing juxtaposition of sexuality and race. Oral sex, in fact, often becomes synonymous with the practice of projective verse in Wieners's early poetry. In "Memories of You," for instance, after cataloging a long list of such encounters, Wieners laments that writing these escapades "was supposed to be a verbal blowjob of a poem," not merely a self-satisfying journal of sexual exploits ("Memories of You," 74). Consequently, oral sex should be read as a poetic trope in his work, as a unifying figure, a moment of communion between the transcendence of high art and the transience of street life. As the speaker of "Act #2" figures it, "I blew him like a symphony" ("Act #2," 52). A similar conjunction between sex and music occurs in "A poem for cock suckers," a piece in which Wieners identifies wholly with the title characters. The poem opens in a "queer" bar, where "we sing our songs / of love like the black mama / on the juke box" ("Poem for cock suckers," 18). Similar to Wieners's writing on Holiday and Kaufman, there is once again here a scene of appropriation akin to Mailer's "White Negro," the putting on of Blackness as a way of associating the "we" of the poem with the "farthest outsider" (Nielsen, *Reading Race,* 157). Yet, the association also comes with a rhetorical distancing in the second stanza, one that seeks to reposition the relations between center and margin: "it's a nigger's world" ("Poem for cock suckers," 18). Of course, as Nielsen rightly notes, "that might be news indeed to the masses of black people trying to make their own worlds for themselves" (Nielsen, *Reading Race,* 158). The bracing racism of the passage, however, strategically positions African Americans at the center of this world of outsiders, therefore moving homosexuals even further away. The emotional effect is a kind of pathos that seeks to catch the uninitiated reader off guard by suggesting that, even in this "queer" space, homosexuals remain alienated. In this situation, sexual encounter appears as a brief respite, a momentary connection, alleviating the pain of isolation:

It is all here between
the powdered legs & painted
eyes of the fairy

Friends who do not fail us
Mary in our hour of
    despair. Take not
away from me the small fires
I burn in the memory of love. ("Poem for cock suckers," 18–19)

"Between / the powdered legs" the "we" of the poem find friendship and momentary community. Wieners is no idealist, however; his portrayal of gay community in this period lacks any clear sense of solidarity. Even the desire for political recognition remains a vague suggestion, an anger that cannot be remedied. So, too, the desire for "love." Here, the poet's prayer is to "burn," to be permitted the "small fires" of such fraught passion. It is in such burning, though, that his approach to the *duende* of homoerotic poetry, to the project of an openly gay projectivism, becomes clearest.

In another "verbal blowjob," Wieners addresses Stephen Jonas. As "Parking Lot" confesses, "I blew a guy today / for eight dollars" ("Parking Lot," 82). The reference to money (ultimately unpaid) links sex with survival in a different way here. Rather than satisfy desire, in this case, it provides the potential for momentary subsistence and so marks a slightly different poetic, a move away from the youthful longing of *The Hotel Wentley Poems* and *Ace of Pentacles* and toward the anguished maturity of the later trilogy, *Pressed Wafer*, *Asylum Poems*, and *Nerves*. Consequently, the act functions as a kind of betrayal, however momentary, of a key aspect of the poetics forged in Boston and apparent in the earlier work. It also consists of a kind of doubling-down on despair, with Wieners admitting, "I stole the money from Steve Jonas / 'bread from a poet'" ("Parking Lot," 82). As both money and poetics, taking Jonas's "'bread'" thus works as a second betrayal in the poem, one that alienates friends and rends the self. It is a rare moment in which a white artist faces up to the appropriative reach of his artistry. At around the same time, in the 1965 journal where he composed "Road of Straw," Wieners lamented that "Steve Jonas seems / totally unrecognized, and I / remain terribly alone" (*Stars Seen in Person*, 127). As a gloss on "Parking Lot," the passage adds to the poem's sense of guilt. By 1970, Jonas would be dead and Wieners would be teetering on the edge of the schizophrenia that came to plague his later years. Rather than change course, however, the poem closes on a note of determined suffering:

Damned and cursed before all the world
That is what I want to be. ("Parking Lot," 82)

Wieners's commitment to the pain of *duende*, to a marginality that conflates homosexual suffering with African American struggle, and the fiery despair it produces, remains the same. Like Jonas, Holiday, and even, to a certain degree, Olson, Wieners held fast to the margins throughout his career.

Along the margins of Boston cultural life, Jack Spicer discovered fellow travelers. Having arrived in the city after a long apprenticeship as part of Robert Duncan's circle in San Francisco and a brief stay in New York, Spicer had developed poetic principles that would come into focus through his friendships with Boston writers, most notably Stephen Jonas. As Jonas's poem for "Soul Brother Jack Spicer" has it, his initiation into the music of Charlie Parker offered a clear parallel for Lorca's theory of *duende*, one that would be adapted and developed into Spicer's Martian poetics in his more mature work (Jonas, "Cante Jondo for Soul Brother Jack Spicer," 70). Though, as Daniel Katz has written, references to the theory are "surprisingly sparse" in the poet's work, nonetheless, his collection *After Lorca* witnesses a "reworking of some of Lorca's thoughts on *duende*," thoughts that he would continue to develop throughout his career (*Poetry of Jack Spicer*, 59). Perhaps his best-known collection, *After Lorca* is in many ways the product of Spicer's Boston period and particularly his friendship with Jonas. While it is important not to overstate Jonas's influence, it remains an overlooked element in studies of Spicer's poetry. As he himself makes plain, Jonas taught him how to "use anger (as opposed to angry irony) in a poem" (Spicer, "Letters to Robin Blaser," 37). For Jonas, such "anger" is apparent in the rent voice of the singer, or the playing of an instrument like a "picador," balancing it between the bull's horns and so staggering, troubling its forward motion (Jonas, "Cante Jondo for Soul Brother Jack Spicer," 71). As his lectures and other writings show, Spicer came to understand this quality well and frequently related it to his practice of "Outside": of transmitting the various dictations voiced to him.

In comments from the late-1940s that appeared as part of "The Poet and Poetry—A Symposium," which included Robert Duncan, William Everson, Rosalie Moore, and Leonard Woolf, Spicer makes plain his intention that poetry keep a close kinship with song. From this perspective, he criticizes the "New Critics" for removing poetry "from its main source of interest—the human voice" (Spicer, "Poet and Poetry," 230). Admittedly, no hint appears here of his later understanding of voice as coming from outside, as the voices of aliens or of the dead. However, as an early take on the subject, it does frame his abiding interest in a poetics of breath. As he insists, "[p]oetry demands a human voice to sing it and demands an audience to hear it. Without these it is naked, pure, and incomplete—a bore" ("Poet and Poetry," 230). Without voice, without its crucial "complexity of stress and intonation," poetry becomes for Spicer indistinguishable from nonfiction prose ("Poet and Poetry," 230). To enliven it, he holds up the example of Vachel Lindsay's performance poetry: "Thirty years ago Vachel Lindsay saw that poetry must connect itself to vaudeville if it was to regain its voice. . . . Our problem today is to make this connection, to regain our voices" ("Poet and Poetry," 230). Though the intention of this last statement would evolve and change during his time in Boston and immediately thereafter, Spicer's concern for countering boring poetry with an art sourced in popular expression and experience would remain. The lack of a relationship to popular song is lamented throughout. As he notes in the conclusion to his brief remarks, in poking fun at New Critical seriousness, "[t]here is more of Orpheus in Sophie Tucker than in R. P. Blackmur" ("Poet and Poetry," 230). Both serious and humorous at once, his preference for popular music situates the primacy of voice in Spicer's poetics, while looking ahead to the spritely ghost at work in the poetry he would develop in the succeeding decade.

At the 1965 Vancouver Poetry Festival, Spicer's lectures reveal the poetic leap he made in the intervening period. In "Dictation and 'A Textbook of Poetry,'" he offers an extended meditation on the practice, with its attendant ghostly voices. As he understands it, the process descends from Yeats's automatic writing and involves forces from Outside, much like Olson's conception of force in "Projective Verse":

> Now what Outside is like is described differently by different poets.
> And some of them believe that there's a welling up of the subconscious
> or of the racial memory or the this or the that, and they try to put it
> inside the poet. Others take it from Outside. Olson's idea of energy
> and projective verse is something that comes from the Outside. (Spicer,
> "Dictation and 'A Textbook of Poetry,'" 5)

Though his relationship with Olson was tumultuous, an underlying sympathy with the elder poet is evident throughout Spicer's writings. By situating Olson's projective poet as, in a sense, open to dictation from Outside, he also positions his work as a variation on the poetics developed at Black Mountain by Olson, Creeley, and Spicer's early mentor, Robert Duncan. Just as writers like Jonas and Wieners perceive connections between projective verse and jazz or *duende*, so Spicer's understanding of dictation—itself a development of these connections—also comprehends such lines of descent. As he notes later in the same lecture:

> Olson says the poet is a poet when he says what he has to say. Now, you can read that in two ways: what he "has" to say, namely "I want to sleep with you honey," or "I think that the Vietnam crisis is terrible," or "some of my best friends are dying in loony bins," or whatever you want to say that you think is a particular message. That's the bad thing.
>
> But what you want to say—the business of the wanting coming from Outside, like it wants five dollars being ten dollars, that kind of want—is the real thing, the thing that you didn't *want* to say in terms of your own ego, in terms of your image, in terms of your life, in terms of everything. ("Dictation," 6)

In this passage, the Outside appears as *duende* in the form of the daemon, the "it" that transmits desires from beyond that then are enacted through the poet—"the wanting coming from Outside." It is a wanting cut with opposition, pierced like the bull by Jonas's poet-picador. The discipline of achieving this state is one of constant erasure: it is akin to the practice of the Lacanian analyst—or the psychic medium. Yet, as Spicer admits, "mediums always have to have the accents that they were born with" ("Dictation," 7). The problem, therefore, is to transmit the message with as little intention or noise as possible, realizing from the beginning that "the poem comes distorted through the things which are in you. . . . It's impossible for the source of the energy to come to you in Martian or North Korean or Tamil or any language you don't know" ("Dictation," 8). The daemonic voices work through the poet's voice, making the best of poems, to use Spicer's own metaphor, a kind of well-tuned radio, transmitting ghostly signals. Of course, as Lori Chamberlain and Daniel Katz have shown, in *After Lorca* the process rendering these voices appears as an extension of the multivocal task of the translator.[5] While questions of translation practice and theory go beyond the bounds of this study, it is clear that Spicer conceived the process in terms of other media, transferring their compositional concepts into poetry, much like Lorca, Olson, Creeley, and Jonas.

Five days later, in the discussion incorporated into his talk on the process of composing *A Book of Magazine Verse*, Spicer was asked about *duende*, and jazz quickly became a model for his compositional approach. Notably, two years earlier, Olson, Duncan, and Ginsberg had participated in a discussion on the subject that stumbled through several iterations of *duende*, without arriving at any consensus.[6] Spicer's response demonstrates a clearer grasp on the subject, though, in typical contrariness, he begins by denying any interest in Lorca's famous theory, only to go on to detail its application to jazz, with the implication of equal relevance for his own poetry. Like Lorca, he relates *duende* to song and, like Wieners, to the singing of Billie Holiday in particular:

> The way I understand *duende*, and the way I think Lorca means it, is more like singing a song. . . . Did you ever hear Billie Holiday sing when she was good? . . . [T]here wouldn't be one note which wasn't off, but she'd just exactly know where to go off and where never to go on, but it would always be the same thing . . . she could just go right between the bull's horns and hold them, and everything else, and still remain unscathed, and get this kind of balance. It's a marvelous thing to be able to do, and of course she died like Marilyn Monroe did. ("Poetry in Process and *Book of Magazine Verse*," 139–40)

Once again, Billie Holiday is presented as an American analogy for Pastora Pavón. For Spicer, as compared with Wieners, Holiday's *duende* is apparent not so much in her ability to go into the *cante jondo* of self, in the form of the poète maudit, but in her persistent syncopation of rhythm, in her ability to "get this kind of balance" from being "off." This ability to cut against the grain in such a way as to be both "off" and on time, simultaneously, likens her to Jonas's picador. As Wieners also foresaw, however, this battle to lose or erase the voice in deep song also destroys the person behind the art: "of course she died like Marilyn Monroe did." Here, the mention of Monroe suggests that this high-wire act is ultimately self-destructive. In a certain sense, Spicer's judgment here is also prophetic; the lecture took place exactly two months before his own death. Nevertheless, as his comments show, Spicer's understanding of *duende* finds its primary example in jazz syncopation, as Jonas in his own poem had detailed.

These theoretical perspectives appear in the major poetical composition Spicer completed during his time in Boston, "Song for Bird and Myself." In the poem, "Bird," the then recently deceased Charlie Parker becomes a figure of daemonic inspiration who himself appears to have been similarly inspired in life. In contrast to the more familiar "Coltrane Poem" made popular through figures associated with the Black Arts Movement, an earlier genre of what I'd call "Bird Poems" emerged in the 1950s and 1960s, with Spicer's marking one of the most significant entries.[7] As Ellingham and Killian note, the poem was composed at Spicer's apartment, across the hall from Joe and Carolyn Dunn's:

> On the anniversary of the death of Charlie "Bird" Parker, Joe and Carolyn played one of Parker's Dixieland records over and over in requiem. Hearing that music from the next apartment, Spicer wrote "Song for Bird and Myself." (Ellingham and Killian, *Poet Be Like God*, 76)

In this context, the poem emerges as a determined attempt to write the jazzy *cante jondo* that Jonas encouraged. To begin, Spicer declares, somewhat autobiographically, "I am dissatisfied with my poetry / I am dissatisfied with my sex life / I am dissatisfied with the angels I believe in" ("Song for Bird and Myself," 69). While these dissatisfactions can be sourced in his life at this period—his search for a new direction in his writing, his unrequited affection for the straight Dunn, etc.—the swerve away from self and toward the "neoclassical" Parker should be read instead as a turn against the Romantic or personal lyric and toward the impersonal, toward a syncopation of "every note" as a way of opening up a space for the daemonic spirits, the "chewing angels," to sound a counter music ("Song for Bird and Myself," 69). In this way, Parker's ghost engages in a dialogue with Spicer much like Lorca's will later, in the introduction and letters of *After Lorca*. Only this time, Spicer is clearly the student, learning at the foot of the master:

> "Listen, Bird, why do we have to sit here dying
> In a half-furnished room?
> The rest of the combo
> Is safe in houses
> Blowing bird-brained Dixieland,
> How warm and free they are. What right
> Music." (69)

Spicer's question gets at the heart of his practice of *cante jondo*. In order to arrive at the deep song, it is essential to be alone. One must become a ghost, "sit here dying," with the suggestion that such a vocation will result in the artist's death, as it did for Parker, Holiday, and Monroe. The singing, moreover, is purposely off, the question that should close the passage having been converted to an abrupt statement, with the falling rhythm of "Music" resolving into an extended pause, staggering the pace ahead of Bird's reply:

> "Man,
> We
> Can't stay away from the sounds.
> We're *crazy*, Jack
> We gotta stay here 'til
> They come and get us." (69)

The poet and saxophonist are thus driven mad by "the sounds," the alternation between staccato and flowing rhythms in the passage capturing this well. It is the music of such voices that the combo cannot hear, but that impel the speaker and ghost of "Bird and Myself" to transmit in their art. The setting of the piece is thus a kind of haunting: the poem as séance.

The struggle with such voices comprises the center of the piece. There, wings predominate—butterflies, birds, and angels. They are therefore figures for the daemonic spirit whispering in the artist's ear. They are also, notably, terms used by Jonas, Wieners, and their Beat counterparts for fellow gay men. As though addressing this audience directly, Spicer insists, "THE POEM ISN'T OVER. Butterflies," and goes on to describe them: "butterflies represent the lost soul / . . . Represent the bodies / We only clasp in the middle of a poem" ("Song for Bird and Myself," 70). The writing here walks a fine line between the "Fairy Poem" Jonas detailed, or even the hellish despair of a Wieners piece, and the erasure of self common to Spicer. The latter emerges when the reader is instructed to listen, to become like a medium: "Listen to / The terrible sound of their wings moving / Listen" (71). The command then pivots into a metapoetic moment, questioning the reader's capacity to hear the poem as the product of dictation:

> Have you ever wrestled with a bird,
> You idiotic reader?
> Jacob wrestled with an angel.
> (I remind you of the image)

Or a butterfly
Have you ever wrestled with a single butterfly?
Sex is no longer important.
Colors take the form of wings. Words
Have got to be said.
. . .
Let the wings say
What the wings mean
Terrible and pure. ("Song for Bird and Myself," 71)

Like Jacob wrestling with an angel—including, of course, the potential homoeroticism of such an image—so the poet wrestles with butterflies, with
the spirit of *duende*. In doing so, Spicer explains, "[s]ex is no longer important . . . Words / Have got to be said"; words, of course, which are not the
poet's, as his cited comments on Olson show, but which come from Outside—from birds, angels, or butterflies. Becoming a vehicle for transmission
means therefore letting "the wings say / What the wings mean," without
interfering. This absence of intention is understood also as the "[t]errible
and pure" death of the author.

The poem concludes on a similar note. Resuming the dialogue, Spicer
questions his and Parker's roles in the process:

"And are we angels, Bird?"
"That's what we're trying to tell 'em, Jack
There aren't any angels except when
You and me blow 'em." ("Song for Bird and Myself," 72)

Parker's ghostly reply encapsulates Spicer's take on Jonas's poetic. The process
of dictation, of *duende*, creates the voices on the page, the "angels" we hear.
In allowing other voices to speak through him, the artist becomes analogous to Parker's saxophone, his ghostly breath conveyed throughout; or, in
a daemonic pun, the artist is a man "blowing" an angel, akin to Wieners's
use of "cock sucking" as a trope. The process is not simply playful, as in, say,
Jonas's "Word on Measure," since it involves a kind of death:

So Bird and I sing
Outside your window

So Bird and I die
Outside your window. ("Song for Bird and Myself," 72)

The continual death of self that this form of art requires would certainly take its toll on Spicer, as it did on Jonas, Wieners, and Parker, whose sufferings in Jim Crow America, it must be noted, are once again presented as a parallel for homosexual marginalization. "Outside," therefore, becomes analogous with the liminal space of the poetic, a locus of jazz and the supernatural that would continue to enrich Spicer's more mature work, as though by a process of inversion. As the closing of a related piece, "A Poem without a Single Bird in It," advises:

Go mad. Commit suicide. There will be nothing left
After you die or go mad,
But the calmness of poetry. (73)

In returning to San Francisco, these concerns would bear fruit in Spicer's first volume of mature poetry, *After Lorca*. A book-length exploration and extension of the practice of *duende* learned from Jonas, the collection also shares an attitude toward letter writing that appears in his review of Emily Dickinson's work for the *Boston Public Library Quarterly*. As Peter Gizzi has written, the review reveals "Spicer's recognition of the literary importance of Dickinson's letters and the poetic possibility of letters as a form" ("Jack Spicer and the Practice of Reading," 206). This understanding is apparent in the way Spicer frames their status in Dickinson's manuscripts:

One of the most difficult problems of the editors has been the separation of the prose from poetry. This may come as a surprise to some readers. The only surviving prose Emily Dickinson wrote occurs in her letters, and, in their published form, the poetry in them is always neatly set off from the prose. In her manuscripts, however, things are not so simple. She would often spread out her poetry on the page as if it were prose and even, at times, indent her prose as poetry. (Spicer, "The Poems of Emily Dickinson," 232)

Blurring the lines between prose and poetry lends added significance to Dickinson's letters. In fact, as Spicer describes it, every line of every letter could have been intended as a poem and so must be given at least two readings: once as prose, and another as verse. He emphasizes this problem in highlighting the editor's dilemma:

> Assuming that what Emily meant as poetry must be taken out of her letters, how does one go about it? Should one only print variants of lines which she has used somewhere else in her poems? Should one set up a standard for indentation, rhyme, or meter? Or should one merely do again what Mrs. Todd [the editor of Dickinson's letters] tried to do and divide the poetry from the prose by guessing the poet's intentions? ("Poems of Emily Dickinson," 232)

Such questions branch and fork. Should we even attempt to separate the poetry from the prose? Are these writings to be considered "finished," or might they be something closer to drafts? Most importantly, should we assume that Dickinson knew "what Emily meant," i.e., had arrived at something like what we call intention, in composing these pieces? As Jerome McGann has stressed, "Dickinson's scripts cannot be read as if they were 'printer's copy' manuscripts, or as if they were composed with an eye toward some state beyond their handcrafted textual condition" (*Black Riders*, 38). In thus querying the editor's practice in preparing what, at that time, would be the most comprehensive edition of Dickinson's eccentric work, Spicer sets the stage for his own technique. After all, no single answer will satisfy these questions; there will always be reasons to suspect, despite the most meticulous textual scholarship, that the best answer consists of something closer to a both-and, rather than an either-or.

Consequently, Spicer's use of the letter in *After Lorca* exploits all of these possibilities and more, engaging the reader in the multiple possibilities provided by the form's shadow play of imagined community. As both ghostly cipher and Spicerian voice, Lorca embodies a fictional character, as well as—like all such characters—an instance of the author speaking to himself. Clearly, this is part of what Spicer meant in suggesting to Olson that *After Lorca* should be read "as though it were a novel" (Ellingham and Killian, *Poet Be Like God*, 129). Like Dante, however, "Jack" is also a character in the narrative, as are each of its addressees, a community of textual ghosts, according to Spicer's understanding, corresponding for the benefit of an overhearing reader. Spicer's theory of correspondence centers the book:

Things do not connect; they correspond . . . That tree you saw in Spain is a tree I could never have seen in California, that lemon has a different smell and a different taste, BUT the answer is this—every place and every time has a real object to *correspond* with your real object. . . . Even these letters. They *correspond* with something (I don't know what) that you have written . . . and, in turn, some future poet will write something which *corresponds* to them. That is how we dead men write to each other. (Spicer, *After Lorca*, 133–34)

It is important to emphasize here that the status of such "approaches" is complicated by the mode of address. Is it theoretical writing? Interpersonal address? Fictional monologue? Diary entry? Does the use of metaphor and the playfulness of the address elevate the passage to the level of poetry? As with Dickinson, the best answer may be all of the above, or at least a radical openness to each possibility coexisting simultaneously. Reading *After Lorca* like a novel, however, as Spicer instructs, brings many of these possibilities into play, effecting the crab-like progress that his work often demands of the reader. In doing so, they enact a ground of co-response, of imaginative interplay between members of a ghostly community who trade lemons, trees, "I don't know what." As such, their correspondence rends and forks the voice of Spicer's poet, just as the "branching voice" of the poem "Forest" is emblematic of the *cante jondo* made possible by such swerves away from projective or Beat expressiveness, from any notion of writerly intention ("Forest," 132). As Katz has written, "for Spicer poetry is less a question of *finding* one's voice than of letting it be *lost*" ("Jack Spicer's *After Lorca*," 86). It is not that Spicer's work lacks voice, but that it lacks any stable or conventional sense of the poet's voice beyond the mere fact that, as he admits, "mediums always have to have the accents that they were born with" (Spicer, "Dictation," 7). Slaying such intentions thus leaves a field of pure ciphers, "dead men" whose chatter awaits future readers and, ultimately, future poets to discover correspondences and so adumbrate their textual exchange.

Surely this has great importance also for Spicer's understanding of translation. Though, as Clayton Eshleman has shown, a considerable number of passages are largely literal, they respond to Lorca's originals in an essentially creative manner.[8] Given his approach to dictation and correspondence, it could hardly be otherwise. Spicer thus leaves the reader with the paradox that the translator has intervened only minimally, yet his translations greatly alter our sense of the original through the game of ghostly correspondence that frames the text. In this regard, "Ode for Walt Whitman" takes on special importance. As Eshleman has argued, the Whitman ode is the "toughest and most engaging" piece in the book ("The Lorca Working" 38). Katz, similarly, finds it to be the "centerpiece of Spicer's collection," adding that it mediates not only Lorca's interest in Whitman, but also Spicer's concern for Ezra Pound's practice of translation in *Homage to Sextus Propertius*: "Spicer 'receives' Lorca voicing Whitman while doubling Pound, inevitably raising the question of who is dictating to whom and who is translated by what" (Katz, "Jack Spicer's *After Lorca*," 86). While it is true that Spicer attempted to "establish a *tradition*" through such translations, as his letter to Robin Blaser makes plain, the key figure often left out of such discussions has long been Stephen Jonas (Spicer, "Letters to Robin Blaser," 48). Dedicating the piece to Jonas frames the translation in a significant way, adding a character to the book's narrative, one who held a key position in helping Spicer to achieve the mature poetic at work throughout the collection. In this way, his translation of "Ode for Walt Whitman" should also be read in terms of its addressee, so that Lorca's poem to Whitman is redoubled in Spicer's dedication to Jonas. For reasons more and less obvious, the poem's conflicted approach to a homoerotic poetics interests all four characters.

This conflict is apparent at the outset in nature imagery that Spicer translates dutifully. Surrealist metaphors that appear in the original as "ninguno quería ser el río, / ninguno amaba las hojas grandes" are rendered as "[n]o one wanted to be a river / No one loved the big leaves" (Lorca, "Oda a Walt Whitman," 124–26; Spicer, "Ode for Walt Whitman," 126).[9] Shortly after, "ninguno quería ser nube" appears similarly as "[n]o one wanted to be a cloud. No one," where the slightly altered lineation, bringing the "ninguno" that begins the following line into the ending of this one, heightens the sense of loneliness (Lorca, "Oda a Walt Whitman," 126; Spicer, "Ode for Walt Whitman," 127). Such metaphorical language requires little intervention in order to serve its purpose. In other words, by allowing Lorca to speak through him, that is, through his "accent" as medium, Spicer allows the contrast between country and city, between the hinterland of the imagination, with its shifting shapes—rivers, clouds, etc.—and the hard, urban landscape of "mud," "wire fences and death," to emerge in a new context ("Ode for Walt Whitman," 127). Here, if one listens closely, there is the effect of four voices singing in unison: Whitman, Lorca, Jonas, and Spicer. Essential to this new context, of course, is Spicer's California, particularly its ability to embody his sense of the American West as an uncharted territory that thus challenges the established order of East Coast cities like Boston and New York. The rivers and clouds therefore add not simply a romanticized approach to nature, as they often suggest in Whitman, but a regionalist argument folded within a poem conflicted over accepted gender conventions. In this sense, the mutability of clouds and rivers suggests both the open possibility of life in the West but also the fluidity of gender roles that accompany this experience. The denial of such possibilities thus characterizes Whitman's and Lorca's New York (and likely Spicer's experience of the city as well). In this confined and restricted setting, it is only, tellingly, the "perfect voice" who can "tell you the truth about wheat" ("Ode for Walt Whitman," 127).

What is the "perfect voice" in this scenario? Clearly, it is polyphonic, the medium's rendering of Lorca's ghostly echo. Its perfection, however, is more difficult to define. As the poem develops, Lorca infamously attempts to separate Whitman's "virginal" and "chaste" beauty from the "[m]uddy tears" of "los maricas," the "pansies" whom Spicer translates with the bracing "cocksuckers" (Lorca, "Oda a Walt Whitman," 128; Spicer, "Ode for Walt Whitman," 127–28). In a sense, these can be construed as both Wieners's "cocksuckers" and Jonas's "fairies," derogatory terms that both poets nonetheless reclaim as poetic metaphors; terms, in addition, that Spicer knew and so should certainly be read in the complexity of that context. While Lorca's ambivalence over this category, and the clear, even fascistic turn taken in his original, has been a subject of some debate, Spicer's design in translating the term is less clear and only becomes clearer if he is implicated in the violence Lorca seeks, if the translation itself were, in other words, a form of killing the author. On one hand, of course, as Davidson has written, Spicer in fact practiced a "tough guy stance" against fellow homosexuals he judged as "effeminate," and so likely sympathized in many ways with the dark turn in Lorca's original (Davidson, *Guys Like Us,* 42). On the other hand, Spicer's ambition to compose purely from dictation suggests that the "perfect voice" would be one that eliminates the translator as much as possible. The passage, in fact, attempts to have it both ways. As Katz has shown, despite the seeming impersonality of his poetics of dictation, *After Lorca,* by employing personal letters and dedications to friends, "seems to be addressed to a version of the 'personal' which wouldn't be a 'big lie'" (*Poetry of Jack Spicer,* 63). This version would embody not an impersonal poetic, such as, say,

Eliot's, but enact a collapse of the impersonal and personal extremes (Katz, *Poetry of Jack Spicer,* 64). In *After Lorca,* this collapse between the two creates a stage for performing such tensions. After all, it appears that the "perfect voice" of the poet conjured by both Lorca and Spicer comes from Outside. As Spicer writes in "Some Notes on Whitman for Allen Joyce," Whitman's world appears as one without "cruelty," as a "lost paradise," "a fairy story" ("Some Notes on Whitman," 55–56). Like Jonas's "Fairy Poem," Whitman's "fairy story" can be attributed to a lost world of presence, where authenticity could be brought into being by a pure, "perfect voice."

For Spicer, however, such perfection may remain desirable, but it is no longer accessible. The "cruelty" cleaving his world and Whitman's thus opens up a space where only the rent voice of *duende* can reflect its duplicity. Such doubleness embodies the sense of perfection at work in "Ode for Walt Whitman." When Spicer translates Lorca as "[a]gainst" the "Fairies of North America, / Pajaros of Havana," and so on, adding, through his act of creative translation, "Cocksuckers of all the world," he effects a kind of disappearing act ("Ode for Walt Whitman," 130). It is as though he calls for his own "[d]eath," for the death of the poet as "fairy" or "cocksucker," as he, and Wieners and Jonas, had framed it ("Ode for Walt Whitman," 130). In this regard, the "perfect voice" appears to be a ghost, at once both deeply personal and totally public, the cry of deep song and yet merely black marks on a white page. Hearing this play of voices comprises the poem's closing image, where "a little black boy" announces to "the white men of gold / The arrival of the reign of the ear of wheat" ("Ode for Walt Whitman," 130). Spicer's translation of "la espiga" here as wheat, rather than, say, "corn," creates an echo of the earlier passage, where the "perfect voice" tells "you the truth about wheat" ("voz perfecta dirá las verdades del trigo") (Lorca, "Oda a Walt Whitman," 126, 124; Spicer, "Ode for Walt Whitman," 130, 127). The "perfect voice" thus becomes a mirror for the voice of the "little black boy," while the reader is positioned among the "white men of gold" who must learn to hear the "ear of wheat." While the Lorca original clearly conjures Biblical imagery, separating the proverbial wheat from the chaff, the Whitmanian from the pansies, Spicer, in keeping with his larger practice in the poem, appears to collapse the two. In other words, in death, the "cocksuckers" correspond with the Whitmanian. As Spicer writes in the following letter, "[t]his is how we dead men write to each other" (*After Lorca,* 134). Of course, for a writer seeking to collapse the public and the private, this approach comes at a high price. According to Damon, suffering is inseparable from Spicer's poetry: "[t]he double-bind of Spicer's poetics is that in the name of love, they doom him to death . . . his outsiderhood and misery in some sense guarantee his authenticity as a poet" (*Dark End of the Street*, 176, 177). In a similar way, Jonas corresponds with the "little black boy" of the poem. In guiding Spicer to an understanding of such poetic anger as Lorca's original surely exhibits, Jonas provided him with a method for rending the voice, for effacing the self through the deep song of *cante jondo*. Ultimately, for the reader as for Spicer, one imagines, the first step to hearing such song is to listen, to allow its forkings to branch and augment through them.

Taken together, then, Jonas, Wieners, and Spicer forged a poetics that extended in related ways principles inherent in projective verse. What links these poets, above and beyond their shared time in Boston, is a common set of poetic influences and approaches to the "anger" or *duende* cited, ones that each, in fact, would add to, expand, and even swerve away from in their own distinctive approaches to the evolving poetics of breath and voice in the period. Though Spicer never had a formal connection to Black Mountain, his close associate Robert Duncan taught there, and through Duncan he was introduced to and intrigued by projectivist poetics. Despite quarrelling with Olson, Spicer was certainly influenced by his, and later Creeley's, work. As Ellingham and Killian have written, "[e]ven though he was hurt and puzzled by Duncan's increasing attention to the 'Black Mountain' circle, Jack couldn't deny the attraction of Olson's ambitious, Whitmanic, gestural poetics" (*Poet Be Like God*, 86). Jonas, meanwhile, didn't attend Black Mountain either, learning about it instead through his friendships with Wieners, Cid Corman, and, later, Olson himself. In all of these ways, then, Olson's and Creeley's poetics of breath became a template for each of the three to make their own.

In doing so, jazz would play as important a role in Boston as it had at Black Mountain. Jonas's poetry, of course, is heavily indebted to Black musical traditions, especially the jazz of Charlie Parker. Like Creeley and Olson, Jonas found an analogy between Parker's improvisational flights and the possibilities for new poetic rhythms (Torra, Introduction, *Arcana*, 24). Similarly, Wieners credited Billie Holiday's syncopated voicings as the inspiration that led him to understand his own complex identity as a poet (*Stars Seen in Person*, 148–49). From Jonas, Olson, and Creeley, Wieners would learn to articulate this complexity through a speech-based poetry that, by turns, syncopates traditional lyric content and readerly expectations. Spicer's poetry, meanwhile, confronts readers with related challenges, yet it is rarely considered in relation to jazz. Apart from his Boston poem "Song for Bird and Myself," jazz itself rarely enters his poetic world. Still, parallels abound. His understandings of both dictation and translation bear resemblances to compositional concepts native to jazz, as does his larger approach to seriality, despite the apparent reference to European music of the period. All three poets pursue their projects from within communities where jazz held a privileged place, presiding over the beatnik aesthetic that informed hipster enclaves from New York to Black Mountain, and from San Francisco to Boston.

Consequently, their relationships demonstrate an abiding, and ambivalent, concern with racial difference that bears revealing parallels with their own emerging awareness of a burgeoning gay liberation movement. As the unabashed approach to homoerotic content in the work of all three poets attests, a newfound determination to make public the most closeted details of gay experience appears in their writings at the same time as gay communities in the United States began to see themselves as a minority group, much like African Americans—a group, moreover, engaged in its own long march toward civil rights (Damon, *Postliterary America,* 161). For Jonas, this awareness seems also to have been a burden. The avatar of a hip, jazz poetic for white friends like Wieners and Spicer, he nonetheless shifted his racial identity to fit the poetic occasion. As Nielsen has written, Jonas "cast aesthetic questions and his own poetic in racial terms," despite the fact that his antisemitism and ambivalence over his own racial identity provide "a virtual casebook for the study of multiply directed racisms" (*Integral Music,* 66, 62). These ambiguities are drawn out in different ways by Wieners and Spicer. Both associate homosexuality with Blackness in terms of political and social marginalization, and both, at times, appropriate that positionality for rhetorical gain. Such appropriations appear in poetry that often gives primacy to Black male beauty, while embracing, in stereotypical language similar to that of Olson and Mailer discussed in the previous chapter, racist assumptions about Black experiences. As is evident in his later encounters with the African American poet Bob Kaufman, Spicer's appreciation for the artistry of jazz, of Black music, did not prevent him from engaging in threatening and deplorable forms of racism, including sharing in Jonas's paranoid invocations of antisemitism. In fact, after his lover, Russell FitzGerald, left him for Kaufman, Spicer reportedly wrote the epithet "nigger" on

FitzGerald's copy of the latter's 1959 "Abomunist Manifesto" (Ellingham and Killian, *Poet Be Like God*, 138). Such complications make for difficult reading; however, they also broach the difficulties and cross-purposes inherent in foregrounding breath and, with it, the body, as Olson, Ginsberg, and others involved the New American Poetry insistently do.

Chapter Three

HOWLING PARKER

JAZZ, RACE, AND BEAT PERFORMANCE

Bob Kaufman's encounter with Jack Spicer brings to the surface an under-current of racial tension that many innovative poets in midcentury America worked hard to ignore. While it is true that many New American poets drew inspiration from African American culture and from fellow Black authors, as Olson's and Creeley's enthusiasms for jazz and John Wieners's and Jack Spicer's friendships with Stephen Jonas demonstrate, those encounters also reveal a perpetuation of common racist attitudes and assumptions, often despite the better intentions of white writers. Of course, this situation was not unique to Boston and Black Mountain. In San Francisco, New York, and even further afield, similar conflicts arose. While it should be reiterated that such tensions are endemic to American culture in general and not the special problem of innovative poets; nonetheless, they pose especially poignant questions in the context of an avant-garde that saw itself as both aesthetically and culturally progressive. As the Kaufman-Spicer encounter demonstrates, marginal identities can both cross and double-cross in unpredictable and somewhat surprising ways.

Though this aspect of the Beat hipscape has been a research interest for some time, scholars continue to unearth new discoveries. As A. Robert Lee has recently asked, "Can the African American seams in Beat writing, etymologies and music ever be doubted?" (*The Beats: Authorships, Legacies,* 152). Similarly, scholars like Nancy McCampbell Grace have explored the ambivalent approach to racial difference apparent in essential Beat works, like Jack Kerouac's *On the Road* and *The Subterraneans*.[1] Though Kerouac's fiction falls outside the scope of this study, his influential example deserves some consideration. Leo Percepied, the thinly veiled, autobiographical protagonist of *The Subterraneans*, for example, critiques at times the "white ambition" and "white daydream" of his origins, while he nonetheless falls into predictable racial stereotypes when he imagines that his African American lover, Mardou Fox, evinces a preternatural understanding of jazz: "she is the only girl I've ever known who could really understand bop" (*Subterraneans*, 45, 67). Of course, the implications here surface elsewhere in Kerouac's work as well. For instance, Sal Paradise, that other famously autobiographical protagonist in *On the Road*, proclaims his wish to "exchange worlds with the happy, true-hearted, ecstatic Negroes of America" (*On the Road*, 180). Though, admittedly, there is clearly an air of appreciation and deeply felt respect in such passages, there is also a stereotypical, counterfeit representation of African American experience rendered in these scenes that is part of a larger pattern of cultural appropriation. Jon Panish, whose *The Color of Jazz* helped to inaugurate this line of investigation, frames these tensions well:

> The notion of "respect" in these characterizations is particularly interesting because it implies the exact opposite of what actually happened in the contest between black and white culture in the 1950s and 1960s. If we understand "respect" to connote not only esteem but also the kind of deference that prevents one from interfering with the object of esteem, then we cannot say that white youth and outsiders respected African American culture. It was precisely because these Euro Americans stood in a superior social and political position vis-à-vis African American culture that they could appropriate or exploit these resources. (Panish, *Color of Jazz*, 18)

The enthusiasm of Kerouac's protagonists aside, such passages in Beat writing manifest another side as well, one perhaps beyond the perception of authorial intention, but nonetheless real for Black and white alike in the era's hipster subculture. In fact, while Panish here focuses on "white youth" in a general sense, such youth included, and often were inspired by, Beat writers like Kerouac.

More specifically, scholars have examined the unique situation of Black authors within Beat circles, with special attention to Bob Kaufman. Maria Damon, for instance, has explored the ways in which countercultural communities like that of the Beats failed "minoritized subjects" like Kaufman by presenting "an oppositional subculture that claims to provide conditions for an unalienated life but cannot make good on its claims because of its ambiguously complicit relation to the mainstream" (*Postliterary America*, 162). Aldon Lynn Nielsen, meanwhile, has written of the "occluded" role Kaufman plays in both popular and academic histories of the Beat movement (*Integral Music*, 150–51). As Nielsen notes, "Kaufman had seen the public bleaching out of the artistic movement whose major works, including both 'Howl' and *On the Road*, were inconceivable without the influence and models of black arts" (*Integral Music*, 150). In addition to these, Amor Kohli has written on the omission of Kaufman from Beat histories, unearthing the "revolutionary potential" that he found in jazz music and sought to embody in his own poetic performances ("Saxophones and Smothered Rage," 166). More recently, Jimmy Fazzino has shown how Kaufman, Ted Joans, and Amiri Baraka imbued Beat writing with a "commitment to avant-garde aesthetics and politics" that expanded their community to incorporate like-minded poets across the globe (*World Beats*, 65).

As each of these scholars have shown, Kaufman and Baraka typically appear as the most prominent "Black Beats," African American writers whose works both are, and are not, part of the accepted Beat canon. While Baraka's work aligns with several different avant-garde poetic communities, and so will be addressed directly in the succeeding chapter, the poetry of Kaufman, in its essential Beat-ness, will be the focus here. In fact, in exploring his relationship to Beat poetics, I want to consider his writing in the context of the white Beat par excellence, Allen Ginsberg. Ginsberg's friendships with both poets were significant, and his influence upon both played a pivotal role in their careers and in the subsequent reception of their work. While other aesthetic traditions can be traced in Baraka's writing, Ginsberg's poetics of breath and voice proved an abiding influence for Kaufman, shaping his overall preoccupation with embodied performance, while, at the same time being reimagined and refashioned by his practice of it. In this way, Kaufman's work prefigures Black Arts Movement responses to the New American Poetry, locating that movement's relationship to white Beats like Ginsberg in the future anterior of African American expressivity. While Ginsberg's "Howl" made visible a generation of marginal, disaffected white youth, his early poetry's apolitical approach and adoption by mainstream America also effectively muffled the politicized screams, cries, and shouts of Black poets like Kaufman. For his part, Ginsberg worked to overcome this dilemma in both his poetry and his activism throughout the later 1960s and the 1970s. The problem, however, in his earlier work can be viewed clearly in the divergence between white and Black responses to the music of Charlie Parker. What Parker in particular, and bebop in general, meant for Ginsberg, Kerouac, and other white Beats was markedly different than what they meant for Kaufman. Exploring these differences, then, will aid in the ongoing effort to restore the racial and po-litical contexts of Beat writing by tracing a manner of performativity that develops at an inverse ratio for white and Black poets. That is, while white writers like Ginsberg tempered their performative "Howl" as their fame grew, replacing it often with somber elegy and guilt-ridden regret, Afro-Beats like Kaufman increasingly deployed a host of shouts, screams, and cries as their careers developed into the later 1960s and beyond, both in response to earlier white appropriations of Parker's jazz and, paradoxically, as a testament to their own increasing marginality. The goal of this chapter, then, will be to situate these cries in the fullness of the Black music and racial politics that did so much to shape the era's poetics.

NEGRO VOICES CRYING

Allen Ginsberg was more forthright than many New American poets concern-ing the African American inspiration at the heart of his poetics. Throughout his career, he deferred to Jack Kerouac in attempting to explain his own approach to jazz. As his recently published lecture notes detail, not only was Kerouac's style set by his perception of the breath notes of bop musicians, but Ginsberg's, too, was shaped by the rhythms of jazz: "When I use the phrase 'spontaneous bop prosody,' I'm thinking of 'salt peanuts, salt pea-nuts,' or some squiggle of rhythm in Kerouac's head that follows that odd accenting, the irregular accenting, the noniambic accenting of Gillespie" (*Best Minds of My Generation*, 35). The angular rhythms and spoken refrain of Dizzy Gillespie's signature song create here the possibility for an improvised poetic—and this even though Gillespie's fame drew in part from the studied, almost professorial persona he cultivated in popular media. While more could certainly be said concerning white misrepresentations of jazz musicians, what requires further attention here is the figuration of "breath" as the vehicle for a quasi-mystical expression. In "Notes for *Howl*," for instance, Ginsberg elaborates on this:

> I thought I wouldn't write a *poem*, but just write what I wanted to without fear, let my imagination go . . . write for my own soul's ear and a few other golden ears. So the first line of *Howl*, "I saw the best minds," etc. the whole first section typed out madly in one afternoon, a huge sad comedy of wild phrasing, meaningless images for the beauty of abstract poetry of mind running along making awkward combinations like Charlie Chaplin's walk, long saxophone-like chorus lines I knew Kerouac would hear *sound* of—taking off from his own inspired prose line really a new poetry. ("Notes for *Howl*," 415)

The entire passage takes off from Kerouac's famous essay "Essentials of Spontaneous Prose," from the breathing of "long saxophone-like chorus lines" to the intention to "write for my own soul's ear," which responds clearly to the advice in Kerouac's essay to "tap from yourself the song of yourself" ("Spontaneous Prose," 226–27). In building upon Kerouac's method of jazz writing, breath becomes the central figure of Ginsberg's poetics as well. As he explains later in the same piece, "[i]deally each line of *Howl* is a single breath unit . . . mental inspiration of thought contained in the elastic of a breath" ("Notes for *Howl*," 416). Yet, as he admits, the line's convergence with the poet's breathing varies from reading to reading, and so cannot, literally, be notated once and for all (416). Nathaniel Mackey has found this admission particularly telling, noting that it in fact creates other possibilities:

> So the breathing of the poet changes from occasion to occasion, breath length and breathing pattern change from occasion to occasion. What, then, is the value of notating, if that's in fact possible, the dictates of breath peculiar to one occasion, of appearing to fix those dictates for all time, for all future readings? . . . The "New American" poetics of breath, offering no consistent or comprehensive practicum, was

primarily a figurative, theoretical discourse, a symbolically and symptomatically telling discourse. Taken literally, it merely states or restates the self-evident: verbal enunciation has to accommodate the speaker's need to breathe. Taken otherwise, it animates thought, encourages thought to unbind what's bound up in the self-evident. ("Breath and Precarity," 5–6)

In this case, such unbinding reveals the inevitability of improvising, both in the obvious sense of varying one's delivery to fit different reading occasions and in the somewhat less obvious sense of allowing the unconscious to chance upon the unexpected, to find its shape in the act of composing, as opposed to writing for a set or inherited design. While such ambitions echo modernist descriptions and exhibitions of free verse, they advance upon it in a fashion parallel to that of Olson's and Creeley's recognition of the analogy to be found between the syncopated rhythms of bop musicians like Parker and Monk and the possibilities they offered to postwar poets. In "Meditation and Poetics," Ginsberg in fact credits Olson with inspiring this openness when he compares the principle of constant movement in "Projective Verse" to the "dharmic principle of letting go of thoughts" ("Meditation and Poetics," 270, 271). By focusing this process on the exhalation of breath, Ginsberg's poetic, like that of Black Mountain writers, also revisits the well-worn subject of poetic voice.

His approach to this subject, however, differs from traditional discussions of authorial attitude or sincerity of character. Instead, Ginsberg, like Olson, figures voice as the echo of the poet's body, as the link to a haunted physicality:

In 1948 I had a vision and heard William Blake's voice reciting "Ah! Sunflower": deep, earthen, tender, suffused with the feeling of the ancient of days. . . . Subsequent composition . . . brought me to my native New Jersey voice issuing from throat and breast and mind. ("Poet's 'Voice,'" 257–58)

Voice appears here as both ghostly cipher and regional dialect, hearkening from the distant past and locating itself in the stubbornly physical, material body. As Adriana Cavarero has shown, conceptions of voice that attend to the "fleshliness of the body," to its seductiveness in the "hot rhythms of its emission, the pleasure of the throat and saliva," attunes to a politics of relationality, one that seeks not only to sound its uniqueness, but also to listen to the plurality of bodies comprising a polis (*For More Than One Voice*, 11–16). In his own writing on voice, Ginsberg expresses a parallel understanding, insisting, for instance, that the poet's voice must be read in the context of the whole body: "Feeling, and rhythm, which is concomitant bodily potential of feeling, take place in the whole body, not just the larynx. The voice cometh from the whole body" ("Poet's 'Voice'" 258). As though rehearsing ancient wisdom, he employs the archaic form of the verb here to emphasize the fact that such insight is at once age-old and shockingly contemporary. Written in 1965, the essay marks a pivotal period during which Ginsberg's political activities increased as his poetics began to turn toward the more engaged work of *The Fall of America: Journals 1965–1971*. Consequently, he concludes the piece by revealing the subversiveness of such an approach to poetic voice: "[i]deological consequences follow naturally—revolution and eternity and death" (258). As both he and Cavarero attest, then, to realize the material uniqueness of voices challenges the very basis of Eurocentric conceptions of order; in place of Plato's republic, in fact, it offers the poet's vision of a radical democracy. African American poets like Baraka and Kaufman no doubt took inspiration from this vision, even if Ginsberg's poetry did not always live up to its lofty ambitions.

Though his essay on voice appeared almost a decade later, his most exemplary uses of this new poetic were well-known by the time he first encountered Black poets. *Howl and Other Poems* appeared first in Lawrence Ferlinghetti's City Lights edition in 1956. The sensation caused by the title poem, of course, predated even this and would catapult Ginsberg into the national spotlight, where he would remain for the rest of his life. In the poem, and indeed in the collection as a whole, the concerns later described in his writing on breath and voice can be observed, particularly his interest in jazz music. Of course, scholars have frequently discussed the jazz influence apparent in "Howl"; however, little has been written concerning Ginsberg's attitude toward racial difference there and in related poems. In fact, African Americans play a central and recurrent role in his work during this period, which thus reveals a great deal regarding his friendships with African American writers like Baraka and Kaufman. "Howl" appears as the single text most responsible for drawing Baraka and Kaufman into the Beat scene. As Amiri Baraka recalls, even on an air force base in mid-1950s Puerto Rico, the piece caught his attention and drew him into Ginsberg's orbit ("'Howl' and Hail," 8). More than anything else, though, Baraka emphasizes the anti-imperialist critique in "Howl," what Benjamin Lee has chronicled as the marriage of Old and New Left politics in the poem ("'Howl' and Hail," 9; Lee, *Poetics of Emergence,* 102–3). In this regard, Baraka's memory of Ginsberg's work reflects also his recollection of Charles Olson's *Maximus,* where its anti-imperialist call to "take the way of / the lowest," and "go / contrary" fired his imagination ("Olson and Sun Ra," 00:15:17–53; *Maximus Poems,* I.15).

In "Howl," though, while an imperialist critique is implied throughout, it is clearest and most pronounced in section two. There, the repressive, consumerist culture of 1950s America takes on biblical proportions through the guise of Moloch. As Ginsberg notes, the name was taken from Leviticus, from "the Canaanite fire god, whose worship was marked by parents burning their children as propitiatory sacrifice" (*Collected Poems, 1947–1980,* 760). Readers thus find themselves as the Beat children sacrificed to "war" and "banks," for "Filth! Ugliness! Ashcans and unobtainable dollars" ("Howl," 131). The imperialist violence depicted in the section, with its capitalist hellscape supported by endless war, clearly resounded with Baraka throughout his career, from his earliest beginnings to his Marxist later stage. However, the mental and emotional violence of the passage no doubt appealed to him also, and to Kaufman as well. Like the speaker of "An Agony. As Now," the "I" of section two addresses the reader from within the prison house of the soul, as though updating for postmodern America the "mind-forged manacles" of Ginsberg's beloved Blake ("London," l.8):

Moloch, in whom I sit lonely! Moloch in whom I dream Angels! Crazy in
    Moloch! Cocksucker in Moloch! Lacklove and manless in Moloch!
Moloch who entered my soul early! Moloch in whom I am a consciousness
    without a body! Moloch who frightened me out of my natural ec-
    stasy! Moloch whom I abandon! Wake up in Moloch! Light stream-
    ing out of the sky! ("Howl" 131)

The poet appears in this section as a mere projection of, or voice within, Moloch. Identity has been stolen and renamed "Crazy," "Cocksucker." As John Wieners's poetry from this period has shown in the previous chapter, while both terms could be inverted and redeployed with positive connotations, they emanate from a regime determined to pathologize homosexual encounter and, as many New American poets regardless of race or gender attest, the very imaginative life at the heart of avant-garde experiment. Though the poet would abandon this regime, its hegemony is in fact inescapable: "Moloch whom I abandon! Wake up in Moloch!" Most dehumanizing of all, in absorbing his identity Moloch robs him of any physical uniqueness: "Moloch in whom I am a consciousness / without a body!" If, in Ginsberg's poetics, the breath's significance hinges on its capacity to anchor textual performances in their various physical contexts, then Moloch's body snatching effectually steals one's voice. Like a vampire, it feeds upon the living and leaves only a ghostly cipher to complain. For African American poets like Baraka and Kaufman, who resisted such imperialism in their military and merchant marine experiences, this political critique of American society's pathological pursuit of imperial dominance would have expressed a host of sympathetic concerns.

Yet, when African Americans appear in Ginsberg's poetry, they are similarly abstracted, their individuality replaced by stereotype. In "Howl," where jazz recurs throughout, the African Americans performing the music are largely absent, relegated to the anonymous "negro streets" of the opening, the sad elsewhere of the hipster's exile ("Howl," 126). Later, in "Kaddish," for instance, Ginsberg's brother Eugene is described as pathetic, living "near Negro whorehouses" ("Kaddish," 216). Meanwhile, the conjunction of systemic poverty and religious illumination appears in poems like "In the Baggage Room at Greyhound," where a "mustached negro Operating Clerk" happens to be named "Spade," a common racial slur. Ginsberg employs the term throughout the 1950s and 1960s in poems and letters. Yet, in the midst of applying an offensive stereotype, the speaker of the poem elevates this counterfeit image to the level of divinity: "Spade reminded me of Angel, unloading bus, / dressed in blue overalls black face official Angel's workman cap" ("In the Baggage Room," 153). Here, the co-worker's angelic appearance is woven into the stereotypical performance of Black servitude. Such humble dedication is more a projection of white fantasies than any sense of solidarity with or a realization of the plight of Black workers.

More often than not, when Ginsberg does attempt to voice some form of solidarity, it comes in a mode of blackface performance. In "Seabattle of Salamis Took Place off Perama," for instance, the anthropomorphic "Jukebox of Perama" becomes "Mr Jukebox," who has a "white brain revolving / black disks" ("Seabattle of Salamis," 288). The image appears as though it is meant to conjure the racial complexity of Mailer's "White Negro," of the white hipster subculture that Ginsberg emerged from and clearly addresses here. Through the figure of "Mr Jukebox," the ancient Greeks of the battle of Salamis now transform into a Black stereotype:

> Negro voices scream back 1000 years striped pants pink shirts patent leather
>   shoes on their lean dog feet
> exaggerated sneakers green pullovers, long hair, hips & eyes!
> They're jumping & joying this minute over the bones of Persian sailors—
> Echoes of Harlem in Athens! . . .
> The Muses are loose in the world again with the big black voice bazooky
>   blues,
> Muses with bongo guitars electric flutes on microphones . . .
> Tin Clarinet prophesying in Delphos, Crete jumping again!
> ("Seabattle of Salamis," 288)

The ancient Greeks imagined here are, in fact, contemporary white Europeans engaging in dancing and singing meant to evoke stereotypes of Black performers. Granted, there is a not-so-subtle argument in the passage; namely, the ancient battle in which the outnumbered Greeks defeated the Persians has been rewritten. In other words, the poem imagines the growing hegemony of American culture as exporting African American and, presumably, non-western cultural values to Europe. In a sense, the tables have been turned. In the long history since the sea battle, the Persians have returned in a new form, syncopating and subverting the arc of history. As the poem's closing has it, the end of western history resounds with the cultural triumph of African American music, with performances by Dusty Fletcher, Screaming Jay Hawkins, and others: "Open the Door Richard, I'm Casting a Spell on You, Apocalypse Rock, End of History Rag!" ("Seabattle of Salamis," 288). Still, Ginsberg's ragging of history is made possible here by his blindness to his own appropriations and misrepresentations in the poem. Like Olson in Mexico, Ginsberg abroad often engages in a similar struggle with his relationship to American empire, just as at home he attempts to transcend whiteness, as though it were possible to stand outside of the power play that racial distinctions entail.

In his early work, as, again, with Olson, part of the problem may well come from a lack of experience. As he wrote to Gary Snyder after returning to New York in 1958, "Meeting a lot of Negroes here, first time, thru LeRoi

Jones [Amiri Baraka]" (*Selected Letters of Allen Ginsberg and Gary Snyder,* 29).
Read in the light of his lecture notes on Beat history, such encounters only
occurred ten to fifteen years after he and Kerouac enthusiastically adopted
Black music and culture as the central inspiration of their writing. While
it may be tempting to describe such meetings, from this historical vantage,
as ten to fifteen years too late, it is perhaps impossible to underestimate the
barrier posed by legal segregation in the period. Whatever the cause, once
Ginsberg did have occasion to meet African American poets, he quickly
forged close bonds, particularly with Baraka. Unfortunately, however, even
these are tainted with occasional racist epithets and stereotypes. Writing to
Lawrence Ferlinghetti, for instance, Ginsberg describes in multiple letters
his trip with Baraka to read "to the shades" at "Howard Spade University"
(Ferlinghetti and Ginsberg, *I Greet You at the Beginning of a Great Career,* 87, 89).
Despite the fact of Ginsberg's long friendship with Baraka, such references
are wincing. Certainly, their growing political differences only added to this.
A few years later, for example, writing to Gary Snyder on a proposed book
voicing support for the revolution in Cuba, Ginsberg struggled to defend his
opposition to Baraka's newly found political intensity: "LeRoi began such a
project but I think it tended to bog down in his own intellectualism. Knopf
wants such a book. But LeRoi gets too polemical-materialist" (Ginsberg and
Snyder, *Selected Letters,* 34). Here, his judgment appears to contradict itself.
After criticizing Baraka's approach first as too "intellectual," he then pivots
to critiquing its "polemical-materialist" approach, as though it were both
too abstract and too concrete at the same time. Such responses suggest that
a deeper problem may well have been Ginsberg's own discomfort with the
ways in which Baraka's politics forced white writers to face up to their own
complicity. Struggling with this, he wrote to Ferlinghetti that although Baraka
had written for his support, he ultimately felt torn and couldn't bring himself
to "believe" in Castro's revolutionary politics (Ferlinghetti and Ginsberg, *I Greet
You,* 131). Such angst appears in Ginsberg's poetry from this period as well.

Most notably, passages in the long poem "Angkor Wat" voice some measure
of repentance and regret. A Buddhist temple, the monumental complex in
Cambodia stands as the largest religious site in the world, originally dedicated to the Hindu deity Vishnu, God of preservation, karma restoration,
and moksha, all of which appear in need of rescue throughout the poem.
Consequently, it takes aim at American imperialism in a number of ways, with
Ginsberg asserting, at one turn, that "the whole of white folks' universe . . .

should be owned by Negroes" ("Angkor Wat," 321). That the poet implicates himself in this "universe" of injustice is clearer earlier in the piece, where Baraka, then LeRoi Jones, is addressed directly:

> Nothing but a false Buddha afraid of
>   my own annihilation, Leroi Moi—
> afraid to fail you yet terror those Men
>   their tiger pictures and uniforms ("Angkor Wat," 310)

A practicing Buddhist, Ginsberg's self-criticism here should be taken quite seriously. The fear that prevents him from making a more heroic sacrifice is, however, strangely phrased in this passage. "Leroi Moi" emphasizes the "I" that Ginsberg fears to lose, while also suggesting a blending of the two. In fact, after admitting here his failure to take up the fight against injustice, his hiding behind a Buddhist rhetoric of peace, he addresses Baraka once again in AAVE, in other words, in a form of blackface:

> Leroi I been done you wrong
> I'm just an old Uncle Tom in disguise all along
>   afraid of physical tanks. ("Angkor Wat," 310)

On one level, the passage reiterates the confession Ginsberg made in the previous stanza, admitting that his pacifism may in fact be mere cowardice. Of course, this is commendably honest, more forthright, certainly, than most white poets of the period could be. Yet, on another level, the "Uncle Tom" mask distances the confession from Ginsberg himself. The dialect of the opening line enables the poet to speak a stereotypical version of AAVE, much like a blackface performer, while the donning of an "old Uncle Tom" "disguise" allows Ginsberg to assume a metaphorical blackness. Growing out of subsequent interpretations of the title character in Harriet Beecher Stowe's abolitionist novel, an "Uncle Tom" is presented here as a kind of traitor, as someone who was cowardly and subservient toward whites. While Ginsberg's acknowledged privilege in the order of American empire aligns in some ways with this, his assumption of a form of Blackness as the mode in which to present this confession cuts against the grain. It suggests that while he is somewhat complicit, he also shares the experience of Blackness and so is not as guilty as other whites. This essential misreading of racial politics would cloud his subsequent relationship with Baraka and other African American friends. Though Ginsberg would continue to attempt to come to terms with his own racial positioning, his frustration and confusion would only grow after Baraka and others relocated to Harlem and took up central roles in the Black Arts Movement.

During this period, Ginsberg would travel across the country, haunted by Black voices and memories of his strained friendship with Baraka. Composing on an Uher tape recorder given to him by Bob Dylan, the poems of this period develop into an attempt to fathom the uniqueness of voices in ways that his previous work obscured or occluded.[2] In "Beginning of a Poem on These States," "Continuation of a Long Poem on These States," and "These States: into L.A.," the poet's own recordings are interrupted repeatedly by those of African Americans on the radio. In the first, Dylan, the Beach Boys, the Beatles, and even Frank Sinatra appear as the joyful soundtrack of a journey into the wilderness of America (Ginsberg, "Beginning of a Poem on These States," 369–72). Only in returning to San Francisco, to the city, however, are Black voices heard, presented anonymously as "negroes screaming over radio" ("Beginning of a Poem on These States," 372). As in his earlier poetry, African Americans are kept once again at an exotic distance, associated with the dangers of the hellish cityscape. Something similar happens in "Continuation of a Long Poem of These States," where "negro voices rejoice over radio" ("Continuation of a Long Poem of These States," 375). Though the connotation is positive here, the anonymity and cultural distance of his earlier work remains. The following piece, however, brings these passages into juxtaposition with the war in Vietnam. In "These States: into L.A.," a poem composed on the drive from San Francisco to Los Angeles on Christmas Eve 1965, Ginsberg balances news of the war abroad with that of the battles at home for civil rights. The closing, in fact, juxtaposes the words of Henry Cabot Lodge, the former Republican Senator and then ambassador to South Vietnam, with those of Medgar Evers, the civil rights leader murdered at his home two years earlier. The Lodge passage spins American exceptionalism into an ironic portrayal of hegemony:

> Lodge spoke from Saigon "We are morally right,
>   we are Morally Right,
>   serving the cause of freedom forever giving these people
>   an opportunity . . . almost like thinking"— ("These
>   States: into L.A.," 379)

As presented, Lodge's insistence on the moral superiority of capitalist democracy not only offers the possibility of "freedom," but also the potential of "forever" changing a nation's "thinking" in an eerie turn that, as Ginsberg frames it, suggests a Gramscian critique of U.S. postwar military operations in southeast Asia. Such bombast is countered and complicated by other "voices back of the brain":

> The voice of Lodge, all well, Moral—
> voice of a poor poverty worker,
> > "Well they dont know anybody dont
> > know anything about the poor all
> > the money's going to the politicians
> > in Syracuse, none of it's going to the poor."
> Evers' voice the black Christmas March
> > "We want to be treated like Men, like human . . ."
> > ("These States: into L.A.," 379)

Lodge's moral has now been undercut by the reflections of the "poverty worker" on corrupt politicians. Such a regime is clearly not moral. Heightening this challenge to the established order, Ginsberg hears the voice of Evers, the slain civil rights leader, pleading to be regarded as, "like human," with the ellipses directing the reader to associate this aspirational equality with "Men" such as Lodge. The resultant effect thus juxtaposes Evers's claim to full citizenship with an American exceptionalism whose official policy perpetuates racial violence at home and abroad. Evers's murder, then, stands as a stark reminder of the cost of American "thinking," while also haunting any thought of "freedom." In this way, such voices haunt Ginsberg in this period, framing his perspective on what appears, increasingly in these poems, as the asylum or prison that America had become. As the poem's closing has it, sirens light the police state:

> Aquamarine lights revolving along the highway,
> > night stars over L.A., exit trees,
> > turquoise brilliance shining on sidestreets— ("These States: into
> > L.A.," 379)

Similar juxtapositions and associations appear elsewhere in Ginsberg's writing from this period as well. "Wichita Vortex Sutra," for instance, similarly closes with the ironic admission that, "The war is over now— / Except for the souls / held prisoner in Niggertown," noting that the offensively named ghetto marked a section of Wichita between Hydraulic and Seventeen Streets ("Wichita Vortex Sutra," 411, with note at *Collected Poems,* 780). Once again, violence abroad is matched by violence at home. "Kansas City to St. Louis" features long quotes from pro-segregationist callers on talk radio, rendering them ironically, allowing them to fall on their own illogic ("Kansas City to St. Louis," 413–18). At one point early in the poem, a caller seems to pose a question directly to Ginsberg and his white readers:

> "for those agitators—
> Why dont they move in with the negroes? We've been separated all along,
> why change things now? But I'll hang up, some other Martian might want
> to call in, who has another thought." ("Kansas City to St. Louis" 413)

The caller in this passage appears oblivious to the contradiction suggested; after all, the very segregation he seeks to preserve would prevent white "agitators" from living with Blacks. While his self-identified "Martian" position may have been meant to offer some measure of humor—as part of a tacit awareness between the caller and the larger audience listening that they are seen by popular media as aliens voicing unpopular opinions amid what they perceive to be a domineering, ascendent Left—the power of such rhetoric to close the conversation in fact nullifies any possibility of "another thought." Ginsberg's reflection on the passage thus envisions the entire universe as a vast American prison, one where U.S. hegemony controls all aspects of reality: "The Voice of Leavenworth / echoing thru space to the car dashboard" ("Kansas City to St. Louis," 413).

Ginsberg's recently published journals from this period reveal a poet similarly haunted by racial discord and return frequently to his estrangement from Baraka. Fretting over his own potential death or imprisonment, he often links together Black and white artists, politicians, and writers whom Ginsberg admires as victims of an American police state. In a draft poem of 1968, for instance, one such journal entry draws together John and Robert Kennedy, Martin Luther King, Malcolm X, Che Guevara, Patrice Lumumba, and Andy Warhol as victims of American violence (*Fall of America,* 373). Later entries similarly lament the injustices suffered by Robert Williams, the president of a North Carolina NAACP chapter who advocated for self-defense strategies in Black communities and whose 1962 book, *Negroes with Guns*, impressed Baraka, leading Ginsberg to present Williams as the victim of CIA attempts to bar him from returning to America (*Fall of America*, 465). Meanwhile, a recollection of a 1970 dream about "Huey Newton, the supple chested Panther," the co-founder, that is, of the Black Panther Party, leaves Ginsberg dejected once again, meditating on whiteness and cowardice: "Huey Newton has a clearer path? At least can get up & speak from direct experience of prison guards' brutality & state folly & viciousness . . . remote & cowardly away from city I rot tied to my own karmic feebleness . . . loving no one" (*Fall of America*, 535–36). Such thoughts appear as both echoes of his earlier writings on the Black Panthers and harbingers of his later attempts in the early 1980s to commemorate John Sinclair's White Panther Party, a collective of whites who wished to work as allies of the Black Panther Party as part of the larger Rainbow Coalition (Ginsberg, "Outline of Un-American Activities," 32–44). In a 1970 letter to his father, Ginsberg defends the Black Panthers against accusations of racist violence, insisting that after spending time "smoking pot with Cleaver & Carmichael," he was convinced that they only "fight back when attacked" (*Letters of Allen Ginsberg*, 348). At the same time, however, in opposing the Black Panther's perceived essentialism, Ginsberg's own struggle with whiteness once again comes to the fore:

> As I would not see myself as Black if I were black, I don't see myself as a Jew as I am a Jew, & so don't identify with nation of Jews anymore than I would of nation of America or Russia. Down with all nations they are the enemies of mankind! (*Letters of Allen Ginsberg*, 349)

While there is not space here to address Ginsberg's complex identification of Jewishness as both a form of religious worship and a larger racial or ethnic grouping, clearly his perception of "Blackness" differs from the uppercase experience attested to by many African Americans. The power to choose whether or not to "see" oneself in racial terms is a privilege accorded only to whites. While Ginsberg's Jewishness certainly complicates this, it nonetheless does not prevent him from experiencing race as an unnecessary or additional part of identity—as a guise one can take off or put on, without consequence. Such luxuries, of course, are not afforded racial minorities in America. Despite this, Ginsberg nevertheless closes the letter by voicing solidarity with the Panthers, encouraging his father to do the same: "we are in no position to lecture Panthers. I once asked Carmichael what he'd do if he were me—he said sensibly, 'Pacify the white violence, calm the whites.' Obviously that's one thing we can do" (*Letters of Allen Ginsberg,* 350).

Such solidarity, in fact, becomes the focus of his recurrent dreams about, and efforts to rekindle his friendship with, Amiri Baraka. In the poem "Chicago to Salt Lake by Air," he imagines the "gray cloudmass over Nebraska" morphing into "Leroi Jones' deep scar brown skin at left temple" ("Chicago to Salt Lake by Air," 491). The poem, dated March 30, 1968, reflects on the injury Baraka received when he was arrested on weapons charges during the 1967 Newark riots. As a 1969 journal entry notes, Ginsberg admired Baraka's sacrifice and felt the sting of cowardice for his own fear of engagement:

> Leroi Jones' magnetism comes from his knowledge on his skull of police violence. Ultimately, I wake in morn afraid of violent dispersal of my possessions music books mss. and household—Retreat from fighting State for fear of being fought back by the state. And so feel guilty dreaming of the Crazies & motherfuckers who having no possessions and no material attachment are not compromised in sentimental friendship with the FBI, Local Police, Newspapers, TV Talk Show Hosts. . . . Leroi walked off the set on one half hour broadcast. (*Fall of America,* 453–54)

Ultimately, whether through pacifism or racial privilege—or some combination of the two—Ginsberg has avoided Baraka's knowledge. The fact of it, and of their continued estrangement, haunts Ginsberg in these journals, interrupting his sleep just as Black voices interrupt his travels in the poetry from this period. After all, he felt that Baraka had walked out on him much like the TV talk show host listed here, adding poignancy to Ginsberg's own self-reflections. Rather than appear as the righteous, countercultural poet, he instead appears to himself as nothing more than an absurd TV personality.

Similar frustrations surface elsewhere. After one such dream, Ginsberg records meeting Baraka in a sleazy nightclub as part of "some political Art History Convention," where he gazes on the latter's wounds:

> Saw Leroi with his nose bashed in, broken healed boneless scarred in mid-face—he lifted his eyeball to show me butchered corpse-face . . . the war wound—the folk I was part of—had shown him Iron force,

fist or heel—he pushed his nose aside with thumb and center of his face was flat except for scar tissue gleaming in Night Club light. (*Fall of America*, 483)

The grotesque display is, once again, interrupted by guilt. Here, "the folk I was part of" suggests that Ginsberg himself felt culpable for Baraka's beating. To this is added the cadaverous wounds that convey an extreme sense of subconscious guilt, while also dehumanizing Baraka, literally removing his face. The larger implication, that "Leroi," Ginsberg's friend in the downtown scene, is dead, also reverberates. The nightclub atmosphere contributes to the passage's lurid fascination, augmented by the subsequent shift in scene to another room where Baraka performs "sexual magic, reciting an African Summons Prayer," a prayer described bizarrely as a form of magic ritual intended to move a pair of red boots across the room (*Fall of America*, 483–84). These scenes lead Ginsberg to recall that in his dream he was convinced Baraka "must be right be right in every way" (*Fall of America* 483–84). While the passage exhibits a mix of repulsion and attraction, figuring Baraka at once as grotesque cadaver and then as exotic sexual partner, trading, thereby, in common Black male stereotypes, its conclusion reveals Ginsberg once again missing his friend, "brooding over his lost love," and howling in frustration:

& if I'm enfeebling the Honkie, why doesn't he encourage me for it instead of putting me down like that? Asserting his manhood romantically over mine or [?]? Anyway, Carmichael told me in London "pacify all whites," which I'm doing. (*Fall of America*, 484–85)

Ginsberg had organized the Committee on Poetry to gather signatures and prepare a defense fund for Baraka in anticipation of his trial. As his letters to Snyder show, he had raised nearly $10,000 on Baraka's behalf, though the latter still wouldn't return Ginsberg's calls (Ginsberg and Snyder, *Selected Letters*, 101). While Ginsberg was far from the only white poet to feel abandoned by Baraka in the mid-1960s, he clearly went further than most in attempting to repair the breach, despite their political differences. As Baraka would later recall, "I wanted to make War, Allen to make peace," yet, "[f]or all our endless contention . . . we remained, in many ways, comrades in and of the word, partisans of consciousness" ("'Howl' and Hail," 9).

In "Crossing Nation," written at roughly the same time as these journal entries, Ginsberg lists various frustrations as a measure of the country's pathological attitude toward violence: "LeRoi on bum gun rap, $7,000 / lawyer fees, years' negotiations . . . Cleaver shot at, jail'd, maddened, parole revoked" ("Crossing Nation," 499). Baraka here is joined with Eldridge Cleaver, among others, in a catalogue of America's victims. Though he chastises Bob Dylan's *Nashville Skyline*–era embrace of country music and hetero-normative pieties in the passage, "Dylan silent on politics, & safe— / having a baby, a man," critiquing his seemingly reactionary turn, the poem concludes with the speaker questioning his own motives: "What do I have to lose if America falls? / my body? My neck? My personality?" ("Crossing Nation," 500). The rhetorical questions pile up here to challenge the very voice of the poem. The speaker's uniqueness, his "personality" is rendered incoherent in the wake of such violence. Such identity as America guarantees can no longer be inhabited by the poet. Facing this head on, Ginsberg discovered that, as many white poets and other would-be allies in the period found, resisting the violence of American empire means confronting a white identity that is inseparable from it.

SPITTING ANTI-POETRY

As Neeli Cherkovsky recalls, at a 1979 benefit for *Beatitude*, Bob Kaufman held a place of reverence even late in his life for Allen Ginsberg: "[H]e said, 'Allen Ginsberg is the President of Poetry. He's our Pope. We're going to install him in Rome. First, we'll have to buy him a cappuccino at the Trieste and then fly to Rome on a chartered biplane. In Rome, we will all learn Sanskrit and write a new version of the Mass'" ("Remembering Bob," 211). Recalling his poem, "Ginsberg (for Allen)," Kaufman here reveals the degree to which his example, as both a political and a spiritual leader, clearly influenced him over the course of his entire career. Though this has been assumed by scholars investigating Kaufman's role as one of the three "Afro-Beats," little has been written on his friendship with Ginsberg. Less, in fact, exists in the poetry and correspondence of Ginsberg, Kerouac, Ferlinghetti, and other white Beats. Aside from a few letters noting concern over his 1959 arrest in New York, Kaufman is largely absent from their published records. In part, this is due to the dearth of reliable biographical information on Kaufman. As Mel Clay admits in the introduction to his "impressionistic biography" of the poet, the sources for almost all details concerning his life derive ultimately from personal anecdotes and the memory of his wife, Eileen Kaufman (Clay, *Jazz, Jail, and God*, 7–11). The quotes from Ginsberg and Kerouac that adorn the cover of Clay's book reveal as much as any biography could. As Ginsberg recalled, "[w]e're blessed by the ghost of Bob Kaufman whose spirit exists ever breathing in the earth" (quoted on the front cover to *Jazz, Jail, and God*). Meanwhile, Kerouac attests that "Bob Kaufman's life is written on mirrors in smoke" (quoted on the front cover to *Jazz, Jail, and God*). Both present the dispersed, nebulous figure of Kaufman as an otherworldly character, a specter haunting their scene from a world apart, steaming the mirror of Beat self-reflection. In fact, this ability to blur, in hindsight, the image of white Beats, to alter contemporary revisions of racial discourse in their works, borders on the hauntological and is perhaps Kaufman's signature power.

Kaufman's ghostly presence has clearly affected his reception. As Jacques Derrida has written, in respect to Hamlet's haunted observation on time's injustice, spectral characters such as Hamlet's murdered father recall the living to larger meditations on the nature of justice (*Specters of Marx*, 18). Such calls to remember the fugitive past can only issue from "an elusive specter," from one who "engineers [s'ingénie] a habitation without proper inhabiting" (18). Like the ghost of the elder Hamlet, Kaufman's spirit thus inhabits Beat history while at the same time being largely occluded from it. Though this paradoxical relationship to his white peers was unavoidable, as Ginsberg's interactions with Baraka have shown, Kaufman's situation is nonetheless unique. From his years of self-imposed silence to his itinerant wanderings around San Francisco's North Beach neighborhood, he similarly appears to have "engineered," in Derrida's terms, a marginal existence. As Harryette Mullen insists, Kaufman "deliberately chose a marginal life rather than have marginality imposed upon him" ("Harryette Mullen on Bob Kaufman," 00:04:36–42). In a similar way, Raymond Foye has observed that "Kaufman was more of an apparition than someone real. He was an otherworldly but not unnoticed specter of the bohemian quarter known as North Beach. I have never known anyone whose *presence* was so defined by *absence*" ("Rain Unraveled Tales," 217). All of these circumstances have thus given rise to Kaufman's posthumous standing as the obscure, silent Beat, at once the avatar of the century's most popular performance poetic and the unrecognized inspiration, the absent presence at the heart of the era's most celebrated poetic history.

For these reasons, Foye may have summed up Kaufman's career best by crediting him, in the words of Ezra Pound, with having "gathered a live tradition from the air" ("Rain Unraveled Tales," 220). This performance tradition, bending back to Pound's troubadours and reaching forward through Olson's projectivism and Kerouac's spontaneous bop prosody, offers a kind of anti-poetry, a noisy counter to the relative silence others have heard. As Foye and devorah major have noted, Kaufman rarely oversaw the typescripts of his own poetry, trusting others to transcribe his drafts and bardic performances for publishers and posterity (Foye, Editorial Note, vii, "Rain Unraveled Tales," 221–22; major, Foreword, *Collected Poems of Bob Kaufman*, ix). Eileen Kaufman also attests to this, as does his late companion Lynn Wildey. As David Henderson has written, "[i]t was Eileen who insisted her husband help her write them down. Kaufman was really into being a quintessential Beat who cared nothing for publication and who cared everything about spontaneity—about literal beatitude" (Introduction, *Cranial Guitar*, 11). Similarly, Kaufman's compositional process centered on orality: "Wildey said Kaufman saw sound as sculpture, and often referred to him as a sound poet. He would lie in bed and talk to himself in mantra-like rhythms. He would sound out a poem over and over" (D. Henderson, Introduction, *Cranial Guitar*, 26). This commitment to sound and performance was married, in fact, to a larger concern for the anonymity of the poet, for a perspective akin to Spicer's sense of tradition, of "generations of different poets in different countries patiently telling the same story, writing the same poem" (*After Lorca*, 110–11). Henderson quotes Foye's recollections of Kaufman's spontaneous readings as apprehending poetic tradition in a similar way:

> His approach to poetry was really in keeping with poetry as an oral art. I mean, it doesn't come out of writing, it comes out of speech and recitation. . . . Bob had this knowledge of American poetry he could call on at will and endlessly recite from Eliot, Charles Olson, Stephen Spender, Claude McKay, or Langston Hughes for hours on end. And he would often times mix these poems in with his own poems so you didn't know where Eliot left off and where Bob Kaufman began. And that was not an egotistical way of putting himself on that level, it simply had to do with the fact that for Bob all poetry was one. (Introduction, *Cranial Guitar*, 24)

This approach, coupled with a poetics of breath and voice inspired by jazz, marks Kaufman's work as the prime example of Beat performance, with its commitment to an artless sincerity evident in its spontaneity. Such remixing of voices, in fact, aligns well with both Kaufman's and Ginsberg's Buddhist understandings of the self, where subjectivity—to say nothing of property rights—is merely a fiction. Clearly, it accords also with the poetics drawn from Kerouac and popularized by Ginsberg in the "Notes for *Howl*," which, of course, originated as liner notes for his own bardic performance, the first pressing of his Fantasy Records album. Kaufman's work, however, as will be seen, took on a more consciously political inspiration than did that of either Kerouac or Ginsberg, at least in his early phase, as scholars like Kholi and James Smethurst have shown.[3] In many ways, like Olson, Kaufman never abandoned his work as a labor organizer and activist in popular front politics, instead transforming these passions into his own form of protest poetry. These concerns can be seen as a response to his position as the self-proclaimed "silent beat" ("October 5th, 1963," 119–20). As though in anticipation of and response to the whitewashing of Beat history, Kaufman's poems bear a preoccupation with physical presence. Most often this appears via his syncopation of Ginsberg's howling poetics through the anti-poetry of his responsive screams, cries, and shouts. Like his spontaneous coffeehouse performances, this element of his poetics insists that readers attend to the physicality of the body, to the racial indexing that he did not have the luxury of denying or ignoring, as many of his white peers clearly did. This, too, can be seen in his affection for jazz, both in his understanding of Black music as inherently political and in his adaptation of improvisatory methods, used in his spontaneous compositions and incessant versioning or reworking of previously published lines and phrases to revise earlier material or create new poems. In reading these aspects of his work here, then, I want to explore Kaufman's poetry as a response to Ginsberg's guilty conscience and to the stereotypical descriptions of "negroes" in Kerouac and other white Beats, a response that foregrounds the body's physicality by seeking out the ghostly ephemerality of vocal performance as the fullest realization of the Beats' jazz poetics.

Kaufman's early poetry demonstrates a studied ambivalence in his response to the work of white peers. In fact, several of the poems appearing in his 1965 collection *Solitudes Crowded with Loneliness* reflect this aspect of his engagement with them. "West Coast Sounds—1956," for instance, records his early encounters with well-known Beats. Among the "Jazz sounds," "wig sounds," and "Earthquake sounds" of San Francisco, the poem also catalogues "Allen ... Giving poetry to squares," "Corso ... pleading," "Rexroth, Ferlinghetti / Swinging," "Kerouac ... Writing," and "Neal, booting a choo-choo" ("West Coast Sounds" 8). The soundscape thus captured resounds with a predictable hipness, which even Kaufman at this stage was eager to escape. The poem, in fact, turns on "Now, many cats ... Too many cats" and looks ahead to a future escape he would make with his wife Eileen a couple of years later: "Sardines splitting / For Mexico. / Me too" ("West Coast Sounds," 8–9). On one level, the poem finds relief through imagining a version of the collection's titular "Solitudes"; yet, its speaker's silent flight responds to the "sounds" of an all-white subculture. Ginsberg, Corso, Rexroth, Ferlinghetti, Kerouac, and Cassady: all writers whose art was rooted in Black music, but who, none-theless, could only understand Black Beats like Kaufman as ghostly figures haunting their own self-images. As Ginsberg recalled, because of his race Kaufman was something of a novelty among white poets in San Francisco:

> Bob Kaufman was there on the mimeograph machine doing the actual work of putting out *Beatitude*. I think that was the first time I met him and it was wonderful because I hadn't seen anybody black so much involved in the North Beach poetry scene, adding a kind of enlight-ened sociability and generosity and contact with all the poets around. (Quoted in D. Henderson, Introduction, *Cranial Guitar*, 10–11)

Though Ginsberg's praise is clear, so too is Kaufman's marginality, his awk-ward relationship to others in the almost exclusively white scene.

For his part, Kaufman would return the favor. "Ginsberg (for Allen)," for instance, praises Kaufman's peer for his oppositional poetics. As the title suggests, the poem is a "Ginsberg," a take on a familiar Ginsberg subject, done in a form of homage. The opening, in fact, appears to allude to "The Lion for Real," a poem that appeared in Ginsberg's 1963 collection *Reality Sandwiches*, though it is dated 1958. In that piece, "stenographers," a "Reichian analyst," an "old boyfriend," and a "novelist friend" all manage to ignore the lion's Harlem reality, while the author reconciles himself to the symbolic beast that, in the end, becomes an "ancient Presence" and "Lord" (Ginsberg, "Lion for Real," 174–75). Throughout, the lion's menacing reality—intertwined with the exotic predator's African origins and implicitly African American address in Harlem—appears intended to frighten and confuse a white audience. Kaufman's poem, meanwhile, begins with Ginsberg, ironically, "tossing lions to the martyrs," a move that has led to great defections away from "The Church," but, somewhat surprisingly, toward "God" (Kaufman, "Ginsberg (for Allen)," 17). The irony here positions non-Christians as the faithful attuned to God, while the Catholic Church appears godless and perverse, with the "Holy Intelligence Àgency" and the "holy stepfather" pursuing government action against the poet for such subversive behavior (17). Insofar as Ginsberg's lion offers the stark challenge of a reality that readers perversely avoid, Kaufman's opening incorporates the figure humorously, in a form of praise for Ginsberg's insistence on forcing his audience to contend with it.

Kaufman's poem then pivots into the speaker's imaginative flight. As he insists, the "I" of such writing is manifold:

> I am not not an I, secret wick, I do nothing,
>   light myself, burn. ("Ginsberg (for Allen)," 17)

Here, the double negative creates an echo, the self rippling out into reverberations that both are, and are not, the "I" of Bob Kaufman. To be sure, the notion at the heart of the passage echoes a key tenet of both Kaufman's and Ginsberg's Buddhism: that the self is no-self. Having been raised in a (reportedly) African American, Jewish-Catholic family in New Orleans, Kaufman's movement in the poem, from subversive Catholicism to Buddhist enlightenment, mimics perhaps his own biographical journey. While more research is needed on the religious aspect of Kaufman's poetics, for my purposes here, I want to focus on the polyvocal approach to poetic voice that emerges from denying the western, autonomous "I." Looked at more closely, the speaker, rather than being an individual, is transformed into the fire of the imagination, the textual "I" that both creates and destroys identities. From this vantage, the poem's "Ginsberg," too, is changed, becoming instead a character "behind my eyes," a figure of the mind ("Ginsberg (for Allen)," 18). Consequently, the voice of the poem resounds with an ambivalence characteristic of both Kaufman's and Ginsberg's signature sounds. As homage, then, it attests to Ginsberg's influence on Kaufman's writing, to his central place in the latter's imaginative realm and to the polyvocal texture now apparent in his work. Such influence is rendered "equatorially sound," a music, in other words, that harmonizes the hemispheres of an imagined world through its sincerely human pathos: "I love him because his eyes leak" ("Ginsberg (for Allen)," 18). Such imaginative sympathy, then, avoids any simple faith in voice's capacity to reveal presence, while still corresponding with the world of the flesh. In this way, rather than reference Ginsberg as a merely poetic or cerebral influence, it is in his felt tears that Kaufman recognizes their genuine affection and solidarity. Kaufman finds Ginsberg's compassionate humanity at the heart of his embodied poetics, an almost divine compassion rooted in an awareness of the dissonance posed by fleshly resistance to the abstract, monolithic version of humanity enforced by church and state.

The force of such state power is apparent in Kaufman's "Jail Poems." The series was written at the San Francisco City Jail, Cell 3, 1959, as the author makes plain ("Jail Poems," 47). Kaufman's incarceration likely occurred in August of that year, resulting, perhaps, from one of his spontaneous performances or from possession of marijuana, as Ginsberg's frustration in a letter to Ferlinghetti, dated August 13, suggests:

> Dear Larry: Fast note:
> I got on the phone . . . a little unsure what the situation exactly is with [Bob] Kaufman—and sent you a telegram today—here's the text in case it never gets thru . . .
>   "Cops arresting poets they don't like and stepping on their toes ridiculous soon they'll be beating up people near bookstores and coffee shops and demanding kickbacks at poetry readings. Call out the spiritual fuzz and put cops back where they belong on level of streetcar conductors and public servants. Who wants to pay dues to a nasty illiterate gestapo? Stop and down with police state laws against the holy weed marijuana." (Ferlinghetti and Ginsberg, *I Greet You at the Beginning,* 93)

Though Kaufman's troubles with the police would recur, they rarely appear in the journals and correspondence of white Beats. As a result, Ginsberg's note of solidarity marks an important exception to the relative silence on the part of other white Beats regarding Kaufman and offers a further rationale for Kaufman's poem. It's not implausible that Kaufman saw Ginsberg's telegram after his release. A similar critique, at least, of America's fascistic criminal justice system appears in Kaufman's "Jail Poems" as well, where, for instance, number fourteen adapts lines from a Bill Margolis poem to imagine an alternate history, one where a bored "Adolf Hitler" moved to San Francisco, "became an ordinary / Policeman," and "devoted himself to stamping out Beatniks" ("Jail Poems," 45).

In keeping with "Ginsberg (for Allen)," the "Jail Poems" also balance an impassioned physicality with a strategic dispersal of the conventional lyric "I" into the polyvocal wind. For example, the second poem searches for an escape from the poet's cell, from the "shrieks and private hells" that populate what the subsequent piece imagines as a distinctively American "universe of cells" ("Jail Poems," 42–43). Notably, Ginsberg's later poetry, for instance in "Kansas City to St. Louis," conjures a similar universe, one where "the Voice of Leavenworth" echoes "thru space" (Ginsberg, "Kansas City to St. Louis," 413). In Kaufman's second "Jail Poem," however, it is the dispersal of self, the voice on the wind, that enables an escape from the cell:

> Entrances and exits, in . . . out . . . up . . . down, the civic seesaw.
> Here—me—now—hear—me—now—always here somehow. ("Jail Poems," 43)

The elliptical syntax and emphatic use of dashes in these closing lines break open the poem, just as they break out the imprisoned self. The early poems in the series begin somewhat conventionally, with the appearance of a sonnet cycle (the first poem, in fact, has fourteen lines). The dissolution of such form here, along with conventional expectations of grammar, thus frees the poet to perceive himself riding the "civic seesaw," his fortunes rising and falling as arbitrarily as those of all African American citizens must in such a state. The imagined rise, therefore, offers new locations, textual "nows" where the "I" disperses "always," "somehow." At the same time, however, the poem's closing also voices a desperate, repetitive plea to be heard amidst a dour realization that it seems the speaker will be "always here" in this cell. As the opening poem has it, "I am sitting in a cell with a view of evil parallels, / Waiting thunder to splinter me into a thousand me's" ("Jail Poems," 42). Such longing for freedom, even through punishment, captures well the studied ambivalence of the series, as well as the determined patience of the nonviolent civil rights protests then increasing across the nation. Such patient struggle, in fact, abides throughout Kaufman's work.

In a related way, "Jail Poem" number seven broods on the absent, no-self hinted at earlier. While it may fall short of the longed-for "thousand me's" of the first piece, it nonetheless opens with a list of negations that effectively double the self:

> Someone whom I am is no one.
> Something I have done is nothing.
> Someplace I have been is nowhere.
> I am not me. ("Jail Poems," 44)

Here, the singularity of self is denied: "no one." However, it would be incorrect to read this denial as absence; after all, "[s]omeone," "[s]omething," and "[s]omeplace" remain, even if they've been crossed out. Like the "I" that is "not not an I" in "Ginsberg (for Allen)," the "I" that is "not me" refuses a unified, western subjectivity, opting instead for an open-ended, dispersed form of identity. It is, as the remainder of the poem details, a resistance to conventional logic, to the categorical thinking that finds "questions" for "answers" and organizes "streets" within "cities" ("Jail Poems," 44). In fact, the comma, rather than a period, at the end of the penultimate line, marks this resistance well. Like the labyrinthine streets of old city centers, the punctuation refuses to act as a stop sign, to clearly demarcate space. The closing line, "Thank God for Beatniks," thus functions as both comic relief and pun, revealing the itinerant, improvisatory jazz inspiration at the heart of his Buddhist resistance to the sureties of western subjectivity, while also saluting his sympathetic Beat, or "Beatnik," comrades, whose principles share the same origin ("Jail Poems," 44).

Elsewhere, Kaufman's more overt writing on jazz takes on a similarly political tone. "Walking Parker Home," also from *Solitudes Crowded with Loneliness* (1965), marks a fitting introduction to this aspect of his writing, characterizing Black music as a passionate witness to the suffering endured in the quest for freedom. As Kohli and others have similarly noted, jazz was a central interest running throughout Kaufman's work, inspiring both aesthetic celebration and political redress (Kohli, "Saxophones and Smothered Rage," 165–66). Kaufman's special affection for Charlie Parker accords with his ubiquitous influence among white Beats as well. In addition to naming his son Parker, Kaufman writes of Bird repeatedly throughout his early career, just as Kerouac and other Beat writers of the period do in their own work. The poem, therefore, is situated among a host of other celebrations of Parker's genius, be it enthralled descriptions of the saxophonist's improvisatory abandon or the studied poetics that resulted from such close listening. In celebrating Parker in this way, however, white Beats often missed the political implications at the heart of his playing, while also misapprehending his practiced virtuosity as a stereotypical form of unrepressed primitivism. For Kaufman, Parker's music repeatedly calls to mind a physical form of suffering. This can be seen in the opening line of "Walking Parker Home," where "[s]weet beats of jazz" are "impaled on slivers of wind" (4). As though the air itself were hostile, each beat becomes martyred sound. The poem thus positions Parker's music as a kind of victim, its sweetness attacked by the very air Americans breathe. As the poem continues, "[b]ronze fingers— brain extensions" seek out "trapped sounds," themselves a "[s]mothered rage" that recalls "[n]erve-wracked suspicions," "[p]anicked excursions," "black tears," and "remembered pain" ("Walking Parker Home," 4). From the outset, then, the poem reverses white appropriations of jazz, shifting the perspective away from the vague mysticism and ecstatic abandon that it often represents and toward an embodied suffering that reveals the racial tensions at the heart of such music.

In doing so, Kaufman focuses his understanding of Parker on the blues inspiration at the heart of the saxophonist's playing. While hearing "shadows" of Coleman Hawkins and Lester Young in Parker's music, Kaufman's attention goes to the back-slashed pauses of "Kansas Black Morning/First Horn Eyes/," and the saxophone's "[g]old belled pipe of stops and future Blues Times" predominates (4). In personifying the saxophone in this way, Kaufman's poem thus sounds the various hopes and disappointments, desires and sufferings, apparent in the blues, marking this tradition as a stubbornly embodied and defiantly Black music. In this way, the "[c]ool revelations / shrill hopes" of Parker's playing appear at odds with the predominantly white audience, the music's "beauty speared into greedy ears" ("Walking Parker Home," 4). Almost vindictively, jazz here attacks listeners, forcing them to experience a parallel sense of pain. In a similar way, Parker's "horn" is imagined as "pounding the soul," as though it were a physical thing (4). This sense of suffering, then, as well as its potential for catharsis, for the experience of a freedom yet to come, locates Parker's blues in the body, in "[d]eath and indestructible existence" (4). In fact, his perception of the latter becomes, in the concluding section of the poem, cause for hope and celebration. "Wailing his triumphs of oddly begotten dreams," Parker's music reveals the brainchild of an odd couple, a cross-cultural conception whose interracial suggestion is apparent in the imagined future of "[h]is legacy, our Jazz-tinted dawn" (5). While insisting on jazz as essentially Black music, Kaufman's metaphor nonetheless looks ahead to a multicolored "dawn," an image suggestive of a diverse, interracial America shaped by the experience of African American expressivity. Such tensions, of course, were personal for the poet. As Eileen Kaufman recalls, their status as one of the few interracial couples in North Beach was a source of constant struggle: "'They were against us from the git-go [*sic*]. We were one of the first blatant interracial couples in North Beach that stayed together and had children. So they were afraid of a pattern there. And they got so mad at Bob they would stop the elevators between floors and beat him up'" (quoted in D. Henderson, Introduction, *Cranial Guitar*, 13–14). The closing lines of the piece reinforce and extend these themes, giving "the nerveless" audience a body in which to feel the "raging," almost purgatorial "fires of Love" ("Walking Parker Home," 5). By attending to the physicality of Black music, Kaufman here offers a parallel blues, a music of suffering and redemption that effectively returns the body to Beat appropriations of Bird's artistry through an act of racial solidarity and accompaniment. As the title has it, the poem itself is a form of "Walking Parker Home."

These themes recur in Kaufman's various "War Memoir" poems. Despite their significant differences, each of the three opens with birthing imagery and "screams" that, like "Walking Parker Home," foreground the body's sonic resonance (Kaufman, *Collected Poems*, 39, 118, 140). These poems also figure jazz as the sound of physical suffering, "[c]rying above the pain," "[l]aughing blobs of blood & faith" (*Collected Poems*, 39, 118). While all three versions of the poem challenge the reader with "shouts," "screams," and grotesque imagery more akin to war than jazz, the first confesses that "(Jazz is an African traitor)" ("War Memoir," 39). In this way, the three poems position jazz as a subversive form of art, a protest against the typical white American, presented here as the "one-hundred-percent red-blooded savage" ("War Memoir" 140). In the second version of the poem, these savages, in fact, appear guilty of an especially bloody form of appropriation:

So they sat down in our blood soaked garments,
and listened to jazz
        lost, steeped in all our death dreams ("O-Jazz-O War Memoir,"
        118)

Again, the lines appear to depict white audiences appropriating Black music. The poem's "war" evokes the battles to end segregation, battles that take their place in the endless civil war of American culture. Here, then, whites wear Black suffering as fashion, exploring nightmarish "death dreams" as entertainment. The anger, therefore, is unmistakable, transforming jazz into a cultural battleground, a front in an ongoing domestic war.

Such readings are, admittedly, complicated by Kaufman's incessant rewriting, by his creative versioning of previous material. With each change to the poem, in fact, the anger remains but a very different perspective on jazz emerges. For instance, the first, and shortest, of the three, published in *Solitudes Crowded with Loneliness*, contrasts the life-affirming music of jazz with the deathly hegemony of mainstream American culture that opposes it. Meanwhile, the second version, which appeared a few years later in Kaufman's second collection, *Golden Sardine* (1967), greatly expands upon this, casting patriotic, mainstream Americans, those "[b]usy burning Japanese in atomicolorcinemascape," as racist vampires feeding upon the suffering apparent in Black music ("O-Jazz-O War Memoir" 118). Admittedly, the racial lines drawn by these poems are blurry; rarely, in fact, does Kaufman take the essentialist position that would become more common among Black Arts poets later in the decade. Yet, his work consistently returns to racial and political concerns, putting him ahead of his white peers in forging an engaged, interracial Beat ethic. The third take on this poem, in fact, printed in his late collection, *The Ancient Rain, Poems 1956–1978* (1981), witnesses such shifting perspectives by moving away from casting blame and instead embracing culpability through the collective, interracial "we" of Beat community. Kaufman alters the crucial "they" to "we sat down in our blood-soaked garments," thereby reversing the closing from a defiant statement of mainstream culture's death—"And listen, / And feel, & die"—to an affirmation of jazz's life-affirming potential: "And we listen / And we feel / And live" ("O-Jazz-O War Memoir," 119; "War Memoir," 141). In this revision, the anger of the two previous versions turns inward, directed at the "we" of Kaufman's circle, sounding much more like a regretful rereading of Beat attitudes toward jazz. Published almost two decades later, when the once outsider Beats had long since migrated inside the cultural mainstream, this third version of the poem would appear to address the changed situation. Of course, biographical reasons—lost to history, as often with Kaufman—could also be postulated. What is clear, however, is that while other, lesser changes appear as well, these crucial differences problematize any coherent reading of the poems. Clearly, all three foreground physical suffering as essential to the experience of jazz; however, the last two in particular do so in diametrically opposed ways. As a result, the "stereophonic screaming" that ends the first version of the piece may sum up Kaufman's take on the subject best ("War Memoir," 39). It is, at least, the most comprehensive statement to be made on them.

Such versioning, though, is not unique to the "War Memoir" poems. The well-known "Would You Wear My Eyes," for instance, originally appeared as "Out of It" in the *Umbra Anthology,* with the title and last line missing ("Would You Wear My Eyes," 184–85). By complicating, and problematizing, any attempt to critically assess the text of his poetry, Kaufman's approach moves closer to dramatic adaptations of Shakespeare or to the continual reappropriation of stock material in jazz, the blues, and in oral-formulaic poetry. For a poet who frequently performed his work from memory, often splicing his words with those of others, and who, for the sake of publication, trusted family and friends to transcribe his work, such strategies make perfect sense. Indeed, I want to suggest here that Kaufman's approach to jazz poetics necessarily entailed such recursive composition. After all, when "I am not me," all concern for unitary perspective and linear development no longer applies. Instead, Kaufman approaches already-existing work, including his own, as material for new poetic performances, much like a jazz musician might make use of popular standards or even previously recorded material when improvising. In this regard, what I have been calling his versioning, his reuse of whole poems or even individual lines, should be seen as akin to the refashioning of familiar melodies in jazz. This aspect of his work, with its complication for print circulation, creates a radical ephemerality consistent with jazz compositional practices, in terms of aesthetics but also in terms of the political positioning that such methodologies pose in resisting any fixed certainties or cultural conventions, even those of the predominately white publishing industry.

Kaufman's "Abomunist Manifesto," a 1959 broadside that predated his first collection of poems by six years, contains multiple instances of such resistance. The work has attracted many readers through its politicized deployment of nonsense. Amiri Baraka, for instance, has noted that "to me the Abomunist was sort of a full-service Beatnik. Let's say pre-commerce. From the real feelings of being opposed to society, and that that whole society had to be overthrown. That's what I got from the . . . *Abomunist Manifesto*" (quoted in

D. Henderson, Introduction, *Cranial Guitar*, 11–12). Baraka, of course, was not the only reader to find Kaufman's political commitment indicative of a "full-service" Beatitude. George Kaufman, the poet's brother, has also attested to an ongoing commitment to radical politics throughout his life; meanwhile, Jerry Stoll has suggested that Kaufman was always much more politically active than his white peers, voicing solidarity for Caryl Chessman and participating in civil rights protests, work that Stoll claims inspired Ginsberg's later involvement in protest movements of the 1960s (as noted in D. Henderson, Introduction, *Cranial Guitar*, 9, 11). The very appearance on the page of the text of "Abomunist Manifesto," often in all caps, shouting at the reader, would influence work by Ted Joans and later Black Arts poets. Kaufman himself would employ the technique increasingly as his career wore on, a textual shout to accompany a silent beat.

The manifesto's defiant comedy captures this irony well. The surreal logic of the piece is apparent in the second line: "ABOMUNISTS SPIT ANTI-POETRY FOR POETIC REASONS AND FRINK" (Kaufman, "Abomunist Manifesto," *Collected Poems*, 57). While the irony of pursuing "ANTI-POETRY FOR POETIC REASONS" is obvious, the neologism "FRINK" pushes the entire statement one step further into nonsense. As the "LEXICON ABOMUNON" has it, FRINK is a tough word to define: "FRINK: v. To (censored). n. (censored) and (censored)" (Kaufman, "Excerpts for the LEXICON ABOMUNON," *Collected Poems*, 60–61). Though the definition here is, in effect, crossed out, the meaning is nonetheless clear; the appearance of "censored" material, in addition to the orthographical parallels and obvious rhymes with "fuck" and "kink," suggest a mysterious—and therefore all the more devious—sexual activity. That such poetry is "SPIT" at the audience reinforces the aggressive, defiant mix of art, erotica, and politics at the heart of the manifesto, connecting its wordplay, in fact, with a surrealist lineage that similarly inspired contemporaries like Ted Joans. In this way, the shouts and screams of the manifesto explode like atomic bombs, suggesting a source for the title in the merger of A-Bomb and Communist, and marking, therefore, the ABO-MUNIST as the "full-service" postwar radical that Baraka imagined. In all of these ways, the manifesto itself provides a fitting response to Ginsberg's then ubiquitous "Howl."

In doing so, however, the manifesto also makes an oblique comment on race through the title's pun on the abominable snowman. The mythical, ape-like wild man of the Himalayas had been the subject of European expeditions for some time; however, the deployment of this imagery in Kaufman's North Beach context figures the similarly difficult-to-track-down poet, the silent, Black beat, as abominable in a parallel sense. The manifesto's declaration that "ABOMUNISTS DO NOT FEEL PAIN, NO MATTER HOW MUCH IT HURTS," appears as an ironic, defiant response to Kaufman's own rough treatment at the hands of police ("Abomunist Manifesto," 57). Yet, the piece points toward a larger community as well, no doubt the beatniks with whom Kaufman lived and proudly counted himself among. The very imagery of an abominable snowman, often represented as a white-haired, ape-like human, bears an equal resemblance to fantastical fears over the growing prevalence of Mailer's "White Negro." In this regard, the manifesto's call for a radical mixing of religious divisions points suggestively toward the larger interracial ambitions of the Beat scene: "ABOMUNISTS BELIEVE THAT THE SOLUTION TO THE PROBLEMS OF RELIGIOUS BIGOTRY IS, TO HAVE A CATHOLIC CANDIDATE FOR PRESIDENT AND A PROTESTANT CANDIDATE FOR POPE" ("Abomunist Manifesto," 57). The two offices traditionally held by Protestants and Catholics, respectively, are thus reversed, with the presumed conventions of each being reimagined in the process. While the joke would prove prophetic—John F. Kennedy would become the first Catholic to successfully run for president a year after the manifesto appeared—such notions would have seemed as abominable as an interracial relationship, or a Black poet, to many Americans at the time of its publication. Such tensions are woven throughout the piece alongside a larger affirmation of the importance and centrality of the imagination. While many, in fact, have focused on the manifesto's "REJECTIONARY PHILOSOPHY," it is equally committed to a belief in "DREAM," to a bohemian celebration of the fact that such poets "DO NOT WRITE FOR MONEY; THEY WRITE THE MONEY ITSELF" ("Abomunist Manifesto," 57–58). As the closing statement has it, "ABOMUNISTS REJECT EVERYTHING EXCEPT SNOWMEN," the last word reasserting their denial of mainstream or conventional values in favor of embracing their abominable, outcast state, while also suggesting a sly reference to the earlier "Snow Man" of that American poet equally touched by surrealism, Wallace Stevens ("Abomunist Manifesto," 58).

Though the manifesto manages to balance such rejection with celebration, the "ABOMUNIST RATIONAL ANTHEM" stages these ironies at an even further extreme. The schoolboy humor of the piece is evident throughout, from the epilogue's direction, "to be sung before and after frinking," to the closing note, "[m]usic composed by Schroeder" (Kaufman, *Collected Poems*, "ABOMUNIST RATIONAL ANTHEM," 64–65). Like the adult speech of the Peanuts comic strip, the anthem's warbling nonsense points to the irrationality of so-called common sense: "Derrat slegelations, flo goof babereo / Sorash sho dubies, wago, wailo, wailo" ("ABOMUNIST RATIONAL ANTHEM," 64). As with the use of "FRINK" earlier, a surrealist approach to the value of unconscious association, to the sense of nonsense, is also apparent here. Even more, however, the anthem revels in the physical pleasure of sound poetry, in the body's irrational articulation of air. In this sense, the poem does not pledge allegiance, so much as it mocks such patriotism through its flouting of linguistic conventions. Some passages, in fact, frame such resistance in a style reminiscent of scat singing: "Voometeyereepetiop, bop, bop, bop, whipop" ("ABOMUNIST RATIONAL ANTHEM," 65). The juxtaposition of greatly varied syllable counts here approximates the syncopated rhythm of bop drumming, while the repetition of the word "bop" itself recalls the origin of the subgenre's name in scatting. This musical element is matched by a number of false friends, words that either appear, or are pronounced, as familiar vocabulary—"goof," "dubies," "loco," "pot"—adding a layer of hipster jargon to an otherwise completely baffling piece. Some coinages reinforce this sense of almost connecting with a conventional meaning. For instance, "babereo" hints at both "babe" and "barbaric," while "boomedition" appears to describe the very style of the broadside's author, "BOMKAUF" ("ABO-MUNIST RATIONAL ANTHEM," 64–65). Of course, to assume anything more than a hint or suggestion would be overreading. As Maria Damon has written, "[t]hough it is possible to decode this poem to some degree . . . the point is not to do so, but to experience the disorientation of babble" (*Dark End of the Street*, 39–40). Taking together the instances, then, with others like "Dearat," which could be read as "Dear rat," or "mangi," which echoes "mangey," the rational irrationalism of the anthem creates an atmosphere of triumphant debasement, a grungy, bohemian takedown of conventional sound and sense ("ABOMUNIST RATIONAL ANTHEM," 65).

As such, Kaufman's Abomunist work extends the political critique observed in his other poetry, and it would continue to do so in future writing. In fact, the "ABOMUNIST RATIONAL ANTHEM," with its scat-like resistance to any recognizable form of patriotism, would reappear in the 1967 collection *Golden Sardine* as "CROOTEY SONGO." Though the baffling vocabulary would remain exactly the same, the appearance on the page is altered by the switch to all caps. Reimagining the anthem thus as a shout dramatically changes the delivery, shifting the tone from one of measured playfulness to baffling anger. Much, of course, had changed in the nearly ten years since the appearance of the original version, and it is tempting therefore to read the new version as responsive to Kaufman's own self-imposed silence, or to the altered tone of emerging Black Arts poets. Ultimately, however, as often in Kaufman's writing, the political consists more in the manner of its performance than in any overt content. In this regard, shouts and cries, by their very nature, embody a form of anti-poetry, an acoustic resistance to the racial politics implicit in mainstream poetic practice.

In all of these ways, then, the racial ambivalence at the heart of Beat poetics resounds through Black and white poets' engagement with Charlie Parker. Bird's playing, with its lightning-fast chord changes and expansive approach to improvisation clearly affected many in the midcentury American avant-garde. Like their Black Mountain peers, the Beats drew from this a dedication to perpetual movement, rhythmic innovation, and the signature importance of breath. The poetics of breath and voice that emerged from Olson's "Projective Verse" finds a clear parallel in the "Spontaneous Bop Prosody" of Kerouac and Ginsberg. Both approaches base their innovations on Parker's performance style, making the physicality of performance, and the uniqueness of embodied voices, central to their application. When taken up by African American poets, sympathetic friendships emerge alongside frustration and conflict. Like Olson and Creeley, what for Ginsberg and Kerouac was merely an aesthetic debate takes on a clear political salience in the interpretation and adaptation of their work by Bob Kaufman and others. In fact, Kaufman's poetry witnesses a clear response in the anguished politics of the body that his mode of jazz poetics performs.

As will be seen in the case of Amiri Baraka, Kaufman was not alone. Like Ginsberg, Olson and his disciple Ed Dorn sought to practice a form of allyship in their friendships with Baraka. As Kaufman's experience shows, however, the perpetuation of white privilege, even into the realm of interracial friendships in determinedly progressive communities, proved difficult to resist.

Chapter Four

BROADENING THE VOICE

AMIRI BARAKA AMONG THE HIPSTERS

Like Kaufman and Ginsberg, a young Amiri Baraka, then LeRoi Jones, arrived in New York eager to join a growing movement of hipster artists, writers, and musicians united by the culture of jazz.[1] As with Kaufman—but unlike many of his white peers—Baraka would come to interpret this movement as both a cultural and a political development, as a kind of " 'united front' " demanding action (*Autobiography of LeRoi Jones*, 232). What that action entailed, of course, remained somewhat vague until his visit to Cuba in 1959. During his early years in the Village, however, Baraka simply sought to establish himself as a writer and impresario in the growing hipster scene, eventually corresponding with Allen Ginsberg, who was then living in Paris (*Autobiography*, 220). Soon after, however, Baraka began making friends with the many Black Mountain alums who played important roles in the scene as well, connecting ultimately with Charles Olson. Even from his first association with Olson, Baraka understood the elder poet's work as revolutionary, as engaging with the world outside of the poem through its commitment to a haptic poetics. While Ginsberg's poetic example and friendship would remain important during these years, Olson's insistence in "Projective Verse" that adopting a poetics of breath and voice involved changing one's "stance toward reality" proved the deeper and more lasting influence on Baraka's writing (Olson, "Projective Verse," 239). Though his friendship with Olson would end as abruptly as that with Ginsberg, the poetic debate at the heart of it remains underexamined and largely unexplored. In order, therefore, to better understand Baraka's crucial role in broadening the poetics of breath and voice, I want to focus here on his reimagining of Olson's "Projective Verse." Throughout his career, in fact, Baraka returned to the essay, using it as a starting point for his evolving stances toward late-twentieth century poetics and politics.

Given his instinct for change, however, tracing any consistent influence on Baraka's writing poses unique challenges. Understandably, many early studies framed his subsequent turns toward cultural nationalism and third-world Marxism as complete and total abandonments of Beat–Black Mountain poetics.[2] While it is true that many friendships were broken in the middle 1960s, it is also the case that many were recovered and maintained throughout Baraka's later career. The same could be said concerning his poetics. In fact, much of the poetry written during his nationalist period and published in, say, *Black Magic*, continues to resemble stylistic approaches found in his earlier writings. Meanwhile, though avowedly Marxist collections like *Hard Facts* attempt a more direct, populist appeal, from *Poetry for the Advanced* onward, as Ben Hickman has shown, Baraka's method recovers a space for musical performance, one, I would add, that is best understood as an expansion or extension of the poetics of breath and voice that he discovered in the late 1950s (Hickman, *Crisis and the U.S. Avant-Garde,* 124–39). In this way, the long arc of Baraka's career could be described as another form of the "Changing Same," as Nathaniel Mackey has adapted that phrase, an abiding, though often reformulated, commitment to a poetics that could score the voice in a manner parallel to the experimentations of then-contemporary Black music.[3]

In navigating these concerns, I have also been guided by Fred Moten's observation that Baraka's career embodies a "break" in a more complicated or layered sense, one that pivots into "[s]yncopation," to borrow a musical use of the word, rather than abandonment or closure (*In the Break,* 85).[4] In this way, Moten presents Baraka's revisionary aesthetic, fittingly, in the very language of Olson's open field poetics: "Amiri Baraka's work is in the break, in the scene, in the music. . . . His work is situated *as* the opening of that field, as part of a critique immanent to the black radical tradition that constitutes its radicalism as a cutting and abundant refusal of closure" (85). In language echoing "Projective Verse," Moten reads Baraka's commitment to change, to a "cutting" radicalism, as marking the consistency of his poetic achievement. Similarly, I want to explore it here as a revision of the poetics of breath and voice, as an "opening of that field" to embrace a politics of practical engagement, of immanent critique. As Michael Magee notes, Black Mountain poetics also bear an allegiance to John Dewey's *Art and Experience*, and particularly to Dewey's insistence there that the life of art consists in its "active and alert commerce with the world" (Magee, *Emancipating Pragmatism*, 138–39; Dewey, *Later Works, 1925–1953*, 10:25). For Baraka, such commerce necessitated political engagement, a poetry of revolution, in other words, that neither Olson's prose nor Ginsberg's example seemed to make clear. Consequently, I will be arguing throughout this chapter that Baraka's work constitutes not so much an abandonment, but an intervention, a creative misreading of "Projective Verse" in particular and the New American Poetry in general, one inspired by his apprehension of the political commitment attendant upon Olson's and Ginsberg's interest in the analogous methodologies of jazz and the embodied dissonance of their postmodern approach to breath and voice.

THE HIPPEST THING

In "The Village," the sixth chapter in *The Autobiography of LeRoi Jones*, Baraka traced his earliest experiences associated with Black Mountain. Hanging out at the fabled Cedar Tavern in the late 1950s, he met former students like Dan Rice, Joel Oppenheimer, and Fielding Dawson, among others, and through them learned about the college and its growing legend:

> I learned about Charles Olson's work and began to read it. Also Robert Creeley and Robert Duncan. I got hold of copies of *The Black Mountain Review* and witnessed real excellence not only of content but design. One, a thick white-covered book, had a Dan Rice pre-minimalist abstraction that I thought was the hippest thing I'd ever seen . . . All these people had come out of Black Mountain or been there at various times and we upheld its memory and its aesthetic. (Baraka, *Autobiography*, 228–29)

In Baraka's remembrance of these early and influential encounters, the enthusiasm and sense of group identification he shared with an otherwise imposing list of names is notable; "*we* upheld," he asserts, Black Mountain's "memory and its aesthetic." Though his work has often been discussed as a form of jazz poetry that takes its cue from the Beats, there is here in his own words an equal, if not stronger, commitment to the poetical community forged at Black Mountain and transplanted to his own West Twentieth Street and Cooper Square apartments in New York. The two are not mutually exclusive. Baraka mentions Fielding Dawson and Michael Rumaker, among others, as introducing him to the poetry and poetics of Olson and Creeley. As has been discussed earlier, both dwell on the role of jazz and the importance of voice in their apprenticeships at Black Mountain (Rumaker, *Black Mountain Days*, 345; Dawson, *Black Mountain Book*, 78). Charlie Parker and open field poetics recur in their memoirs, twin enthusiasms for Baraka as well. His own recollection of his Greenwich Village days is full of references to Parker, Davis, Ornette Coleman, and visits to jazz clubs like the famed Five Spot with the likes of Dawson, Olson, and others.

In this context, Dan Rice would have been an important figure. His "hip" cover for *Black Mountain Review* 6 likely resounded with Baraka not only because of its pre-minimalism, but also because Rice's aesthetic was indebted in many ways to his early experiences as a jazz trumpeter playing with Stan Kenton and Woody Herman.[5] Rice, in fact, initially enrolled in Black Mountain in 1946 with the intention of studying music (B. E. Butler, *Dan Rice at Black Mountain College*, 12). After returning to study art, he shared "Stan Kenton, Woody Herman . . . [and] Miles Davis" records with faculty and students like Creeley and Dawson (Dawson, 191). Rice's cover drawing for the *Black Mountain Review*, as well as those for his collaboration with Creeley on the important early collection examined earlier, *All That Is Lovely in Men*, respond to jazz poetics with what Creeley terms in a blurb on the cover of that work, a "corresponding sense" of line, one parallel to that of "Charlie Parker and Miles Davis." For all of these reasons, Baraka's admiration for Rice, whose drawings also appeared at this time on the cover of a Joel Oppenheimer collection of poetry, *The Love Bit*, published by Baraka's Totem Press, marks yet another indication of Baraka's commitment to what he saw as the jazz-influenced example of Black Mountain.

His enthusiasm for Olson's aesthetic was born from these friendships. As Baraka recalls in his *Autobiography*, he soon fell under the elder poet's sway:

The Black Mountain people linked me to a kind of Anglo-Germanic school, more accessible than the academics, but still favoring hard-edged, structured forms. Olson and Creeley were its twin prophets, but Olson had the broader sword, the most "prophetic" stance. His concerns went further and touched me deeper. (232)

Even in retrospect, Baraka's affection for Olson here is clear. As Tom Clark writes in his biography of Olson, at this time he was "a figure of 'awe'" for Baraka (278). Such admiration is evident in the edition of "Projective Verse" he published through his Totem Press, and in the way he regularly featured Olson and other Black Mountain disciples in his influential little magazine *Yugen* and newsletter *The Floating Bear*.

For his part, Olson was certainly grateful. As he wrote to Robert Creeley in December 1959, he felt he would be lost without his new friend:

I go easily with LeRoi. . . . In fact the past year he has "saved" my life in publishing by just being scattered . . . as against the horrible managed biz it all has been since you and the Review. (T. Clark, *Charles Olson*, 278)

Despondent over the college's closure and the consequent end of the *Black Mountain Review*, Olson felt that such scattering kept his influence alive, spreading the seeds of Black Mountain far beyond the campus and its former faculty and students. As Aldon Lynn Nielsen has noted, in the postwar period Black writers in general, and Baraka in particular, often played pivotal roles in facilitating the careers of their white peers (*Black Chant*, 54). In a more intimate way, however, Baraka may have helped Olson too. The phrasing in the letter recalls the elder poet's oft-quoted anecdote concerning Ezra Pound, who claimed that, while he was in St. Elizabeths Hospital after the war, "Olson saved my life" (quoted in Cornell, *Trial of Ezra Pound*, 71). There is in this echo the suggestion of lineage, with "GrandPa" Pound, as Olson referred to him, helped by his stylistic inheritor and then, in turn, aided by Baraka, almost as a way of passing the torch (Olson, "GrandPa, Goodbye," 145). Whether intended or not, Olson's affection for his disciple, like Pound's before him, would soon sour.

In the late 1950s and early 1960s, however, Baraka and Olson shared a mutual admiration that is evident in the former's contributions to Donald Allen's groundbreaking anthology, *The New American Poetry*. The prose statement "How You Sound??" reveals much about Olson's importance in the anthology and, more pointedly, in Baraka's early interpretation of the poetics of breath and voice. The essay refers to Olson more than any other in articulating Baraka's poetics, nodding toward "Projective Verse" throughout. At the center of the piece, Baraka asserts that "[t]here must not be any preconceived notion or *design* for what the poem *ought* to be," referencing Olson as his guide on this point:

> "Who knows what a poem ought to sound like? Until it's thar." Says Charles Olson . . . & I follow closely with that. [. . .] The only "recognizable tradition" a poet need follow is himself . . . & with that, say, all those things out of tradition he can use, adapt, work over, into something for himself. To broaden his *own* voice with. (You have to start and finish there . . . your own voice . . . how you sound). (Baraka, "How You Sound??," 424–25)

Circling back to the piece's title, Baraka's statement describes his poetics as a broadening of the voice, grounding compositional practice in the spoken vernacular. For an African American writer, however, this paradigm would be complicated by vernacular usages, and political consequences, that Olson, in situating breath at the center of his poetics, did not anticipate. In "Projective Verse," for instance, Olson appears to skirt this issue in his conception of syllable and line—of the former as the child of the ear and the head, and its twin, the latter, as the product of the heart and the breath—ignoring the larger question of ethnic and regional dialect (Olson, "Projective Verse," 242). These elements, meanwhile, appear condensed and reworked in Baraka's statement, "[t]he only 'recognizable tradition' a poet need follow is himself." Yet, "himself" turns out to be less Romantic genius and more postmodern bricoleur. His "*own* voice," after all, is an amalgamation of "all those things" he has reworked from tradition. In this, too, his thoughts were directed by Olson's example. In the passage following his formulation of the importance of syllable and line, Olson alludes to Pound in claiming that "[t]he dance of the intellect is there [i.e., in the writer's handling of syllables], among them, prose or verse. Consider the best minds you know in this here business: where does the head show, is it not, precise, here, in the swift currents of the syllable?" ("Projective Verse," 242–43). In articulating the representative distinctiveness of each writer's artistry, Olson thus himself reworks Pound's "dance of the intellect among words," making it part of his own critical vocabulary (Pound, "How to Read," 25). He will go on to incorporate Cummings and Williams, as well, in advancing toward this poetics, just as Baraka will credit "Lorca, Pound, Williams, and Charles Olson," in constructing his own parallel project (Olson, "Projective Verse," 245; Baraka, "How You Sound??," 425). All of which is to say that the answer to "How You Sound??" was, for Baraka at this stage, a conscious reworking of "Projective Verse," though the implications of this stance remain unaddressed.

An early poem that can be heard in dialogue with this essay is "The Bridge." In fact, it is an excellent example of what Kimberly Benston has termed the "Barakan voice," a "[s]yncretic, disruptive, and dis-located" voice, one that "establishes itself in the very space of its perpetual undoing" (*Performing Blackness,* 192). Dedicated to John Wieners and Michael McClure, "The Bridge" seeks out a space for Baraka's unique sound. As Andrew Epstein has written, by dedicating the poem in this way, Baraka offers "a meditation on selfhood and community" in attempting to navigate contested ground (*Beautiful Enemies,* 191). In addition, though, as Mackey has noted, the poem can be read as a "descent into the black subconscious," paralleling, in its musical terminology, the explorations of avant-garde jazz in its determination to break free of structure, to forget the "head" of the tune (Mackey, "Changing Same," 38). Punning, therefore, on both the "bridge" that links two land masses and the "bridge" of a conventional, thirty-two bar pop song, the poem imagines a liminal space for Baraka's developing poetic:

I have forgotten the head
of where I am. Here at the bridge. 2
bars, down the street, seeming
to wrap themselves around my fingers, the day,
screams in me; pitiful like a little girl
you sense will be dead before the winter
is over. ("The Bridge," 25)

In the opening, Baraka imagines his speaker as lost, both in the music (the "head" of the tune) and on the map ("where I am"). Playing the map, the "bars" that "wrap themselves around my fingers," he converts the city into a scream, not unlike the screeching, distorted playing of the later John Coltrane, Ornette

Coleman, and other avant-garde musicians of the early 1960s. In their work, as in the poem, the breath of the saxophone player, and the distressed human body it emanates from, is emphasized. That the speaker, like the little girl, will be "dead before the winter / is over" suggests that the poem's adventure is doomed, is simply a part of the title's *Twenty Volume Suicide Note*. As the bridge disappears, "what / we wanted to call ourselves" becomes similarly lost ("The Bridge," 25). The question of selfhood here is woven into a concern for the vulnerability of Black voices, figured thus as the memory of a forgotten music, one that acts like a physical bridge, connecting the past to the present.

In the absence of such bridges, Baraka closes the poem on a rich and suggestive conception of Blackness. The penultimate stanza in the poem works toward this realization, confusing reader and writer, "you" and "me," in a swirling release from fixed identities:

> The bridge will be behind you, that music you know, that place,
> you feel when you look up to say, it is me, & I have forgotten,
> all the things, you told me to love, to try to understand, the
> bridge will stand, high up in the clouds & the light, & you. ("The
> Bridge" 26)

The commas in this passage work to complicate the mode of address, isolating phrases to reveal their capacity to mean apart from, as well as within, the larger grammar of the ongoing sentence. This complication of grammatical identity mimics the passage's attitude toward selfhood in general; rather than fixed phrases and clear logic, the lines' many possibilities reflect a loosening of the relations, of the bridges, that lead to and determine "ourselves." What's left after these connections are lost, after the song has ended, is an unnamable act: "sliding through / unmentionable black" ("The Bridge," 26). Blackness here offers a kind of photographic negative, an inversion of identity. Shorn of all connecting bridges, voice, in the sense of signature identity, is dispersed, the self approaching a space that can't be described, that is "unmentionable." In this way, it is a kind of death, as the title of the collection indicates. As the dedication suggests, in offering the poem to Black Mountain and Beat friends, respectively, "The Bridge" situates Baraka's poetics of sound in the space between these two camps. To describe that space as "unmentionable black" attests to the larger predicament that Baraka sought to work through. It would take a trip to Cuba to fully sound this realization.

As previous commentators have noted, the budding friendship between Olson and Baraka would be complicated by the latter's much-discussed trip to Cuba in 1959. While scholars have long noted its importance for inspiring Baraka's political idealism—the poet himself admits as much in his autobiography—its effect on his relationship with Black Mountain figures has not been sufficiently examined. In fact, his memoir of the trip, "Cuba Libre," focuses on his white friends' lack of political engagement ("Cuba Libre," 20). For his part, Olson understood Baraka's critique and crafted "The Hustings" in November of 1960 as a direct response. Dedicated "to LeRoi Jones / two days after the election / of John Fitzgerald Kennedy," the poem offers what Olson understood as a corrective to the perspectives broached in "Cuba Libre" by calling Baraka to return home to his poetic community: "Please come immediately. . . . We shall all eat   All is here" ("The Hustings," 532, 535). In this regard, Olson's mode of address assumes the poet-pedagogue role that Baraka would later criticize. In fact, the poem can be read as exploring the teacher-student relationship in more ways than one. Kennedy, famously, had been an unimpressive student of Olson's at Harvard—the "ice-box called John Fitzgerald Ken- / nedy," as he is described in the first version of the poem ("The Hustings," 529).[6] As Clark notes, Olson despaired over his growing isolation from social and political life in this period, missing his more idealist days in the Roosevelt administration and resenting the abandonment of New Deal commitments he perceived at the heart of the Kennedys' rise to power. Poetry, therefore, became for him a powerful means of creating alternative, imagined communities of shared interest. In this way, Olson responded to Baraka's growing impatience with a politics of personal engagement, realized through art.

Such disagreements, however, were not limited to Olson. Baraka's letters with Ed Dorn, another Black Mountain disciple of Olson and Creeley, chronicle a similar argument in October of 1961. At the time, Baraka had described Dorn's poem on the execution of Dr. Olga Herrara Marcos, "An Address for the First Woman to Face Death in Havana," as " 'counter-revolutionary' " (Baraka, *Amiri Baraka and Edward Dorn: The Collected Letters*, 53). In responding, Dorn sought to defend the poem on moral and aesthetic grounds, grounds that he projected, like Olson, somewhere above the concerns of contemporary politics:

Come on, back off. I'm not no fucking counter-anything. I'm as truly
gassed as anyone, but much more embarrassed than others, at the poor
prospects of fellow poets singing the praises of any thing so venal as
a State . . . you ought to know the very word Batista makes me puke.
. . . The only point I ever had is that when a picture, namely of Mrs.
Herrara, Marcos, is printed, showing her puckered up babyface tears,
brought forth by the lunatic braggart announcement of her death, it is
a matter of *public shame. Sides*, are a bigassed drag. The biggest small-
talk of all, like which one are you on? motherfucker. (Dorn, 53)

Dorn's complaint, similar to Olson's, is that Baraka fails to understand poetry's ability to enact the political without engaging in the "drag" of party of
politics. As he goes on to state, "there is no embarrassment for sympathy"
(Dorn, 54). Such humanistic concerns lay for Dorn above or separate from
ideology. "*Sides*," in this sense, represent the tribalist reduction toward which,
for him, all political action tends; hence, the "poor prospects" of a state
poetry. Yet, in casting the disagreement in such terms, Dorn, like Olson, is
also pressing Baraka to *side* with poetry over and above politics: "like which
one are you on?"

Baraka's reply insisted on the "Luxury" of moral or aesthetic concerns
divorced from politics, rejecting the "exquisite objectivity of circumstance"
(Baraka, 59). Such posturing is linked, for Baraka, with a relativism posing as
humanism, with a lack of commitment that he could not abide:

O.K., we are both *good* men, but I think, now, that mere goodness is a
limitation . . . just as Christians try to limit Christ to mere Goodness.
"Moral earnestness" (if there be such a thing) ought to be transformed
into action. (You name it). I know we can think that to write a poem,
and be Aristotle's God is sufficient. But I can't sleep. And I do not
believe in all this relative shit. There is a right and a wrong. A good and
a bad. And it's up to me, you, all of the so called minds, to find out.
(Baraka, 59)

Baraka's own form of earnestness here casts Dorn's—and, by extension,
Olson's—unwillingness to engage in contemporary politics as mere relativism. In his mind, good poems, of this sort, are insufficient and so need to
be "transformed into action," i.e., political action. Anything short of this, in

Baraka's post-Cuba understanding, risks "justifying evil" (Baraka, 59). Instead, as "Cuba Libre" suggests, he will seek out a poetics of impassioned politics. Divorcing poetry from politics was, at this point for Baraka, shameful: "I feel I am copping out, letting people down, if I say in the face of this ugliness 'I am a poet'" (Baraka, 59).

These concerns would come to a head in a later exchange with Olson concerning the publication of *Blues People* and the essay, "What Does Non-violence Mean?" While the former could, at times, celebrate Baraka's vision of the "aesthetic analogies" of jazz, literature, and the visual arts, the book is famous for insisting upon the importance of the historical and political realities shaping the music and the subsequent art it influenced (*Blues People*, 233). For instance, such analogies necessarily involved interracial collaboration and so were not without their own problems. As Baraka complained, a white hipster could always return to a middle-class America that was closed, from birth, to the African American musicians they imitated and revered:

> Certainly a white man wearing a zoot suit or talking bop talk cannot enter into the mainstream of American society. More important, that white man does not desire to enter the mainstream (because all he would have to do is change clothes and start "talking right," and he would be easily reinstated) . . . The white beboppers of the forties were as removed from the society as Negroes, but as a matter of choice. . . . [T]he Negro himself had no choice. (*Blues People*, 187–88)

The criticism, that white beboppers like Creeley, Dawson, and Rice, simply choose a rebellious style without the real-world experience attendant upon the African American musicians they admired, echoes a larger concern running throughout the book: namely, that the political realities of its "Blues People" have not simply been overlooked, but are at some level incomprehensible to whites. Notably, voice becomes the matrix by which such realities are revealed. By refusing to talk "right," whites choose to adopt Black vernacular. Black writers, of course, do not have such freedom to choose, especially if they attempt a poetics of breath and voice. Such a poetics situates a Black body, with dangerous vulnerability, on a white page.

"What Does Nonviolence Mean?" published in the same year as *Blues People*, questions the larger concerns motivating Martin Luther King, Jr.'s, nonviolent protest movement as a way of combating this vulnerability. For

Baraka, King's movement represented simply the alliance between white liberals and a Black middle-class who had little to offer to the vast majority of African Americans:

> The black middle class, and its spiritual forebears, the freedmen and house slaves, have always "fought" to maintain some hegemony and privilege, and as a privileged class within the American system as defined by the Liberal/Missionary class of American white men. And because of this they have always had to be pawns and tokens in the white class war that constantly goes on over the question of what to do with Negroes. The NAACP, SCLC, CORE, and any other group who advocate moral suasion as their weapon of change (reform) have been members of the Negro middle class, or at least bound by that class's social sentiments. These organizations, and others like them, are controlled by the Negro middle class and sponsored by white liberal monies. (Baraka, *Home*, 137)

Such talk of "reform," therefore, rang hollow. Like Hughes in "The Negro Artist and the Racial Mountain," Baraka continually critiqued what he termed the "black middle class" for, in his mind, seeking to escape the realities of racial difference through their access to a version of American affluence. In this way, they are, for Baraka, less reformers and more upholders of the very unequal status quo. While this group, and King in particular, are the focus of his writing here, white liberals are taken to task as well. Roosevelt, in particular, is chided for his administration's parallel complicity:

> It is the same kind of spurious and pragmatic realism that motivates most American "reformers," *e.g.*, most of the socio-economic policies of Roosevelt's New Deal were not meant to change the society, but to strengthen the one that existed. Roosevelt, in this sense, like a man who when fire breaks out in his apartment immediately builds a stove around it, gave a flexibility to the American ruling class that it could not have survived without. (Baraka, *Home*, 136)

Rather than lionize Olson's beloved FDR as the champion of working-class Americans, Baraka instead situates him as a compromised power-broker maneuvering behind the façade of reform. Such social criticism had its roots in Baraka's Cuban experience and the exchanges with fellow poets that followed. Olson, even more so than Dorn, refused to accept this critique.

In a 1964 letter to Baraka—a letter that went unanswered—Olson was critical of his friend's racial politics. Although compassionate and sympathetic, Olson felt that Baraka's engagement with political action was mistaken, a substitution of abstract "signs and symbols" for the concrete reality of personal experience:

> Because of size one is talking in signs and symbols unless one includes only one's own doings—the personal therefore turns about and becomes both the arbitrary and the politics. (*Selected Letters*, 305)

In this way, Olson felt that Baraka was deceiving himself. As he notes, the threat of global capitalism is the rule of a wage slavery that will affect, in his mind, "Soviets and Chinese and Mexicans and Negroes and Whites" equally (306). The fit response to this, for Olson, was not "political action," but a broad, transnational artistic movement that rejected such forms of life outright (306). In this regard, Olson ends the letter in ambivalence, sympathizing with Baraka's anger, but questioning his turn toward politics:

> I don't for a minute think the White Man you describe isn't the same filthy bastard I know who is completely unable to live either, and is easily as dangerous as you describe him; and in fact the Negro you describe is in fact also the retained brother—retention brother—of this other fellow. But that the violence so engendered is not as interesting as the world-wide violence and shit and that why in fact should the Negro be any specialist in redeeming that fact??????? (*Selected Letters*, 306)

While Olson's frustration here is palpable, there are answers to his question in Baraka's book. As Baraka makes plain at the beginning of *Blues People*, American racism, born out of the "peculiar institution" of American slavery, is culturally and historically unique:

> To the Romans, slaves were merely vulgar and conquered peoples who had not the rights of Roman citizenship. The Greeks thought of their slaves as unfortunate people who had failed to cultivate their minds and wills, and were thus reduced to that lowly but necessary state. But

these slaves were still human beings. However, the African who was unfortunate enough to find himself on some fast clipper ship to the New World was not even accorded membership in the human race. (*Blues People,* 2)

This distinctive experience, that Africans in the New World were deprived of all humanity, is elaborated on the following page with an apposite metaphor:

There was no communication between master and slave on any strictly human level, but only the relation one might have to a piece of property—if you twist the knob on your radio you expect it to play. It was this essential condition of nonhumanity that characterized the African slave's lot in this country of his captivity, a country which was later and ironically to become *his land* also. (*Blues People,* 3)

The comparison to a radio here is instructive: for the white reader who refused to hear the legacy of slavery in jazz, Baraka seems to suggest tuning the radio. In a new version of an old relationship—a "changing same"—white listeners often expected African American musicians to perform like walking jukeboxes, from the previous generations' struggle to establish bebop, over and against the dominance of swing, to the then contemporary battles over the status of avant-garde jazz, of the "new thing." The metaphor thus forces readers to consider these cultural battles as never simply about musical style or taste, but, more expansively, about the legacy of slavery embedded in the relationship between white audience and Black performer. For Baraka, this musical struggle certainly had its parallel in poetry, and particularly in the space where one's interior monologue may simply reproduce the advertisements on the radio. As a result, his artistic development crossed with his growing political concerns, where the performance of a vernacular voice, and its attendant desire for liberation, clashed with the abstraction of voice as such, of projectivism's assumption of a homogeneous sense of breath that could transcend the politics of race.

These changes can be seen most readily in Baraka's mid-1960s writing. More than any other piece, he repeatedly referenced his semi-autobiographical fiction from the period, *The System of Dante's Hell,* as a turning point in his career. Published in 1963, excerpts from the novel appeared as early as 1961. Baraka was arrested and faced trial for publishing a version of "The Eighth

Ditch," a dialogue dramatizing a homosexual encounter in the military, in the newsletter he edited with Diane di Prima, *The Floating Bear*. As with *Blues People* and the poems collected in *The Dead Lecturer*, the novel embodies a turn in Baraka's writing through its weaving together of art and politics, taking its cue, after all, from the first poet to champion the vernacular in *De vulgari eloquentia*. *The System of Dante's Hell* reviews Baraka's vulgar, vernacular experiences as a way of reconnecting with a previous self. As he recalls in his *Autobiography*, the desire to meld these two together after his trip to Cuba required a new, and more personal, style:

> At the same time I had begun a long prose work. It was as if I wanted to shake off the stylistic shackles of the gang I'd hung with and styled myself after. . . . I had the theme in my mind. My early life, in Newark, at Howard, in the air force, but the theme was just something against which I wanted to play endless variations. Each section had its own dynamic and pain. Going so deep into myself was like descending into hell. I called it *The System of Dante's Hell*. (*Autobiography*, 246)

Returning to his life before the "white friend blues," as a character in *System* has it, seemed essential for Baraka to free his writing from the influences that had begun to dominate his work (*System of Dante's Hell*, 91). Chief among them were Black Mountain poets: "I was tearing away from the 'ready-mades' that imitating Creeley or Olson provided. I'd found that when you imitate people's form you take on their content as well" (*Autobiography*, 246–47). Similarly, in a 1977 interview with Kimberley Benston, he stressed these poets' importance: "I was trying to get away from the influence of people like Creeley and Olson. I was living in New York then and the whole Creeley-Olson influence was beginning to beat me up" (*Conversations with Amiri Baraka*, 106). As often throughout his career, music would be essential to this turn.

In "Statement," Baraka wrote that *System*'s stylistic development, its movement beyond the forms of Olson and Creeley, can be traced to its soundtrack: Sonny Rollins's "Oleo" and Cecil Taylor's "Of What."[7] This is in keeping with his later reflections in his *Autobiography*, where he recalled himself as writing in a way parallel to that of an improvising musician:

> So I scrambled and roamed, sometimes blindly in my consciousness, to come up with something more essential, more rooted in my deepest

experience. I thought of music, I thought of myself as an improvising soloist. I would go into almost a trancelike state, hacking deeper and deeper, my interior rhythms dancing me on. (247)

In reviews from the period, Baraka praised Taylor's and Rollins's compositions for returning the music to its roots in improvisational art. Their method of achieving this would provide Baraka with a useful model for his own work. In terms that could equally describe *System*, he praised Taylor's "Of What" as among his best work to date, claiming for his music a special place in the new jazz landscape: "as 'traditional' as any really fresh and exciting jazz music can be . . . Taylor has taken from the inordinately vital 'history' of jazz and worked over into something for himself" ("Cecil Taylor (The World of Cecil Taylor)," *Black Music,* 111). This ability to work—and re-work—a tradition, to remake it into one's own image, is an essential aspect of Rollins's "Oleo" as well. As Gary Giddens has written, the composition is built upon rhythm changes, the "four-square patterning" that Creeley ("Notes Apropos Free Verse," 494) prized in Charlie Parker's work, but more radically free: "the melody is never definingly stated—the musicians begin free, setting up a spectacular Rollins improvisation: fast, hard, exhilarating. . . . The melody is skirted, never confronted"(Giddens, *Visions of Jazz,* 417). For Baraka, such pathbreaking freedom was precisely Rollins's achievement: " 'Oleo' becomes not merely a set of chords fixed under a set of changes, but a growing and constantly changing work based on the total musical shape of the piece" ("Sonny Rollins (Our Man in Jazz)," *Black Music,* 53). Together, then, Rollins, Taylor, and others revive for Baraka the improvisational life of bop stylings that had hardened into cliché:

> What Rollins (and Coltrane and Coleman and Cecil Taylor, and some others) have done is to reestablish the absolute hegemony of improvisation in jazz and to propose jazz again as the freest of Western music. What Busoni meant when he said, "Music was born free; and to win its freedom is its destiny." ("Sonny Rollins," 54)

As the passage's changes on "free" should suggest, Baraka's discourse about jazz in this period frequently overlapped with that of Civil Rights–era politics: "[T]o win its freedom is its destiny." For Baraka, this musical analogue was instructional, leading him to discover alternative paths to a collective freedom through a distinctively Black art.

Though space precludes an examination of the entire text here, a look at a couple of representative examples should bear this out. Among "The Avaricious and Prodigal," the protagonist's flight is arrested by a memory: "The old houses were slums except mine . . . Wallpaper, and bebop orchestras at the first sex. 'Do anything you want to me . . . but don't hurt me'" (*System of Dante's Hell*, 30). Here, "bebop" and "first sex" merge with "[w]allpaper," furnishing the first-person narrator's bleak memory of his adolescent home. Both offer a seeming freedom, mixed with a fear of pain: "'Do anything you want to me . . . but don't hurt me.'" These conflicted memories were later described by Baraka as "'association complexes,'" Jungian nodes or clusters of ideas centered on a particular memory that seemed to play an essential role in shaping his adult personality (*Autobiography*, 246). One of the ways to read this particular complex, then, is as the desire for freedom, for a freedom represented as the achievement of adulthood. Such, for the young Baraka, was the promise of jazz and sex.

Ultimately, though, this freedom appears elusive. As the subsequent complex has it, it is linked to an inescapable conflict over race: "We skipped together . . . in school . . . But she pressed close to me and stood that way for hours. My fingers loosened and I wished I had curly hair" (*System of Dante's Hell*, 30–31). As the young couple separate, the narrator is beset by frustration over his appearance. What has seemed like a series of associations on the subject of young love, however, transitions into a passage on Baraka's poet mentors:

> More than this is some other doing. Some other word. The man turned away cranes towards his beginning. Olson broke, Allen losing his hair. The faces seep together. (31)

The narrator pivots here, rereading the previous passage as clustering around something other than adolescent love: "Some other word." In fact, it is not Baraka's boyhood that interests the narrator here, but the adult world of the "man" turning backward to make sense of his present: "[Charles] Olson broke, Allen [Ginsberg] losing his hair." The former's poverty and professional frustration were certainly well-known to Baraka. As Olson noted in a letter to Creeley, he had been "saved" by Baraka's efforts in more ways than one (quoted in T. Clark, *Charles Olson*, 278). Ginsberg, meanwhile, entering middle-age and balding, would have been losing the "curly hair" the narrator wished for. Notably, Baraka figures as the "man turned away," away from his past, but also away from Olson and Ginsberg, their white faces oozing like zombies. The narrator, in fact, implicates himself in the following passage: "The prodigal lives in darkness" (*System of Dante's Hell*, 31). Following the love implied by the "other word" of Olson and Ginsberg has thus left him lost in a shadowy world of appearances, dispossessed and isolated.

The full passage's play on light and dark emphasizes this. Shadows and corpses—the narrator's own included—haunt the scene, juxtaposed by white characters, "light-skinned women," and even Baraka and Hettie Cohen's daughter (*System of Dante's Hell*, 31–32). For Baraka, then, these "'association complexes,'" through their mingling of jazz, racial politics, and poetics, reveal a need to go home, to flee the ghostly white company he had joined and embrace the African American community of his youth. In this way, the configuration of lightness and darkness in the passage recalls Baraka's memory of a Halloween party from the period. Among an apartment full of white writers and artists dressed as ghouls and goblins, Baraka appeared as a defeated stereotype: "I came . . . as a 'shade,' with an old window shade around my neck and hanging down my back like a cape . . . a comic manqué of Halloween identity" (*Autobiography*, 238). Such despondency apparently went unremarked by those gathered, shrugged off in what must have been the awkward humor of the costume. For Baraka, however, turning away from such haunts seemed his only path to finding a lasting and meaningful freedom.

His later reflections confirm this. Looking back on this period and taking stock of the personal achievement of *System of Dante's Hell*, Baraka felt it set him moving toward his own mature work:

> I felt, then, [i.e., when *System of Dante's Hell* was done] that I was in motion, that my writing, which I'd been deadly serious about, was now not just a set of "licks" already laid down by Creeley, Olson, etc., but was moving to become genuinely mine. I felt that I could begin to stretch out, to innovate in ways I hadn't thought of before. And in all my poetry which comes out of this period there is the ongoing and underlying contention and struggle between myself and "them" that poetry and politics, art and politics, were not mutually exclusive. (*Autobiography*, 247–48)

This pivot into maturity, once again, is defined by Baraka as a development of Creeley's and Olson's work, as an insistence on its capacity for political engagement. Stretching their poetics in this way would prove to be a hallmark of Baraka's subsequent writing, where the focus on the political concerns conjured by the performative aspect of his work predominates. These aspects appear in his short prose from the period as well.

Several essays from the mid-1960s show Baraka breaking free of Olson and Creeley in a similar way, grounding their poetics in political engagement and uniting both through jazz. As William J. Harris has noted, the essay "Hunting Is Not Those Heads on the Wall" bears several conceptual affinities with Olson's and Creeley's poetics, as well as with concepts native to jazz (*Poetry and Poetics of Amiri Baraka*, 101). Another essay from the period, "This Is LeRoi Jones Talking," however, bends these interests toward a politics that neither Olson nor Creeley embraced in their work. The title itself is reminiscent of Olson's *Partisan Review* piece on the Ezra Pound trial, "This Is Yeats Speaking," itself an echo of Pound's wartime broadcasts, which frequently began and ended with the catchphrase, "This is Ezra Pound speaking" (Olson, 141–44; Pound, "Ezra Pound Radio Speeches"). Olson's piece, at once affectionate and critical of Pound, communicates via the mask of Pound's onetime mentor, William Butler Yeats. The associative line of student and teacher thus traces back a century, with the young Baraka as its present manifestation. In using his own name and persona for the title, Baraka effectively moves before Olson—like Pound—and after, as the former's successor. Similar to Pound, Baraka's concerns here will be political; however, unlike any previous writer in this line, his stance on poetry's relationship to racial politics in the U.S. will be much more radical. The epigraph, taken from a *Village Voice* article on him, frames the essay as a response to these themes: " 'Jones seems to have been taken in, to believe that white society actually reflects the nature of white men' " (quoted in "LeRoi Jones Talking," 179). The irony of the accusation (what else would it reflect?) sets up an argument about race and culture that Baraka had been developing for some time.

Early in the piece, Baraka cites Olson not as a poetic influence, but as a political sympathizer. As he wages war against American capitalism, Olson serves as a useful reference:

> The people who are committed to waging war around the globe to maintain the glories of unnatural advantage are brothers of the people, say, who thought that *How to Succeed in Business* . . . deserved the Pulitzer Prize. . . . People the poet Charles Olson spoke of as "the pimps of

progress." But they are not simply "people," they are, sadly, a nation. ("LeRoi Jones Talking," 181–82)

Though Olson no doubt sympathized with Baraka's situation, he avoided waging the kind of counterinsurgency encouraged by Baraka here. As "The Hustings" demonstrates, Olson understood the poem as the most legitimate and comprehensive political act that a poet could make. Nonetheless, Baraka proceeds creatively, misreading key principles of "Projective Verse" later in the essay. Rather than interpret it as a purely poetic manifesto, he reads it as a test of sincerity, and not merely in the compositional process, but in the field of social action:

> A Negro writer, if he is to get at that place in his be-ing (a verb / participle) where art lives, must do as any other artist, *i.e.*, find out what part of that be-ing is most valuable, and then transfer that energy (again paraphrasing Olson) from where he got it on over to any reader. And by reader I mean simply the openness of infinite "interpretation" as it can be said to reside in an artifact, if that artifact—a play, a solo, a poem, a form of loving—be faithfully made. An artist, any artist, must say where it is in the world that he actually is. And by doing this he will also say who he is. But no matter what a man tries, the products of his thinking, indeed of his life, will identify who and where, and for most Americans this is unfortunate, since they are weakling murderers and liars and the place where they live is named after them, even if the plastic sign on their desks says poet and another on the door says CopOut U. ("LeRoi Jones Talking," 182)

Inserting Olson into the essay at this point pays homage, while also subtly shifting the terms. By transferring energy, as "Projective Verse" insists the poet must, the writer locates him- or herself in a field of force. Shifting those forces involves the body in subtle and important ways. Yet, while Olson's essay seeks to recover the body's role in mediating the poetic act—"the HEAD, by way of the EAR, to the SYLLABLE / the HEART, by way of the BREATH, to the LINE"—his responses to Baraka's political engagement clearly show that he hadn't fathomed the import this would have for any body other than that of a white man (Olson, "Projective Verse," 242). By insisting, first, on the racial significance of these concepts in the opening phrase, "[a] Negro writer," and then shifting into the generalizing, "[a]n artist, any artist," Baraka deftly weaves Olson's poetics into a larger consideration of race and culture, one in which poems like "The Hustings" would be taught at "CopOut U."

In the subsequent section of the essay, Baraka plainly encourages the kind of poetic revolution he had been pondering for some time. Notably, it is not just poetry, but a politicized, innovative poetry, a "screaming in verse" in union with avant-garde art and music, that takes center stage:

> the denial of reality has been institutionalized in America . . . one way Negroes could force this institutionalized dishonesty to crumble and its apologizers to break and run even faster than they are now would be to turn crazy, to bring out a little American dada, Ornette Coleman style, and chase these perverts into the ocean, where they belong. Say, if Negroes just stopped behaving, stopped being what Charles desires, and just flip, go raving into the streets, screaming in verse an honest history of America, walk off their jobs . . . and watch the country grind to a halt. . . . It is a good, and practical, idea. Why don't you try it, Negroes? ("This Is LeRoi Jones Talking," 183)

The revolutionary "screaming in verse" imagined here may seem distant from Olson's intentions for a "Projective Verse," but its emphasis on the "force" of "breath," its ability to sound identity across a field of opposing energies, marks a cognate development, a prodigal extension of open field poetics. Read as a mock broadcast, in line with Pound's often informal rants and antisemitic attacks, the very personal, pugilistic style of address is fitting. In this way, Olson's presence in the essay sheds light on Baraka's increasingly complex development of his mentor's poetics. In "This Is LeRoi Jones Talking," Baraka manages an Olsonian response to his *Village Voice* critic that doubles as a challenge to Olson and his Black Mountain and Beat friends. Many of the poems collected in *The Dead Lecturer* embody a similarly conflicted resonance.

While examples of this abound, one instance worth considering in greater detail is "A Poem for Speculative Hipsters." Though it may not be apparent at a first view, the poem responds to Olson in several ways, principally through its distinctive use of projective verse, especially with its focus on the breath line and use of shifting margins. Though in this regard it may seem merely imitative, Baraka draws close to the example of Olson and Creeley as part of a larger intervention into the practice of projective verse. As he emphasized in reflecting on *System of Dante's Hell*, the novel's prose had led him beyond producing the "'ready-mades' that imitating Creeley or Olson provided" and into "something more essential" (*Autobiography*, 246). Read in conjunction with *The System of Dante's Hell*, then, "A Poem for Speculative Hipsters" opens on a similarly Dantean situation, with the poet lost in the dark wood of imitation:

> He had got, finally,
> to the forest
> of motives. ("Poem for Speculative Hipsters," 76)

Much of *System of Dante's Hell*, certainly, could be described as "the forest / of motives," especially the passage cited, where Olson's ghostly face appears, haunting the prodigal narrator (*System of Dante's Hell*, 31). Like Dante, his ambitions have forced a kind of imaginative exile, even from self. Retrospectively, too, Baraka would also describe his life in the Village as a kind of hellish exile from the African American community of his childhood (*Autobiography*, 290–91). In regard to projective verse, however, "motives" takes on a special importance. Olson begins "Projective Verse" by hinting that his poetics involves not simply writing, but a new "stance toward reality," an ethic by which, as he declares at the essay's end, "each of us must save himself" ("Projective Verse," 239, 248). Such "motives" are thus interwoven into the call to craft a poetry that gets at the root of the word in motion, "MOVE, INSTANTER" (240). These interrelated concerns for the ethics or morality of form are unpacked in more detail elsewhere. In the *Letters for Origin*, for instance, Olson instructs Cid Corman to understand the two as interwoven:

> THE MORAL IS FORM, &
> nothing else
> and the MORAL ACT is the honest—"sincere" motion
> in the direction of FORM (82)

In many ways, this is the heart of Olson's poem "The Hustings": rather than locate the moral in some action outside of the poem, as he sees Baraka attempting to do, he encourages him to reconsider this maxim concerning the ethics of form itself. For Baraka, however, such maxims, divorced from any further political engagement, rang hollow—they led, in fact, to a dark wood. Coming to terms with this situation was, in many ways, the work of *The System of Dante's Hell*. Realizing this, "A Poem for Speculative Hipsters," seeks to unmask this perspective as just another speculation, another theory from "CopOut U."

The allusion to D. H. Lawrence in the subsequent lines turns toward this:

There were no
. . . Connie Chatterley's
resting beautifully
on their backs, having casually
brought socialism
to England. ("Poem for Speculative Hipsters," 76)

The first sentence, read along with the opening, echoes ideas from "Hunting Is Not Those Heads on the Wall," which, as Harris has shown, incorporates Olson's poetics while swerving in a radically different direction, reading them as leading to Baraka's own growing Black nationalist and Marxist sympathies (W. J. Harris, 101–2). The reference to *Lady Chatterley's Lover*, however, strikes an even richer vein. One of the first enthusiasms Olson and Creeley shared in their correspondence was for Lawrence. At Black Mountain, they would team-teach a course on Lawrence in 1954, with Creeley leading discussions of his prose, and Olson leading sessions on his verse (Olson, Literature Program Catalogue Description, 8). At the time the poem was composed, between 1961 and 1964, Grove Press, both Baraka's and Olson's publisher, had gone to court over publishing an unexpurgated edition of Lawrence's novel in 1959. The censorship ban on *Lady Chatterley's Lover* was lifted because of the successful case won by Barney Rosset, who owned Grove, and his lawyer, Charles Rembar, in the New York Court of Appeals.[8] In defending the novel from obscenity charges, they relied on the famous case involving James Joyce's *Ulysses* as precedent and so lifted a ban that had stood in America since the initial publication of *Lady Chatterley's Lover* in 1929. This history would have been well-known to Baraka. Not only was he a Grove author, but, as noted, along with Diane di Prima, he was arrested in October of 1961 on a similar charge of obscenity for a homosexual passage from *The System of Dante's Hell* that authorities had discovered printed in *The Floating Bear*. As he recalled in his *Autobiography*, at the trial the *Ulysses* precedent was essential to his defense: "I defended myself before the grand jury, however. I read all the good parts of Joyce's *Ulysses* . . . and then read Judge Woolsey's decision on *Ulysses*" (251). While Baraka certainly agreed with di Prima's recollection that they had been arrested for "a good cause," for what they "both conceive to be the line of duty," his conscience went further (di Prima, *Recollections of My Life as a Woman*, 271). As his disagreement with Dorn over Cuba during the same period shows, freedom of speech was part, but only a small part, of a larger battle that Baraka felt he and his friends should be waging. By 1964, his frustration with their lack of engagement led him to believe that neither poetry nor fiction had "brought socialism," or the kinship of humanity it promises, any closer to reality, either at home or abroad.

In Baraka's poem, then, these insights are countered through the shorthand of allusion. Rather than elevate Lawrence's example, Baraka finds it wanting, ironically, in its failure to inspire any significant revolution in society. Lacking this, he presents the novel's frank sexuality as no more interesting than mere "casual" sex. Though Lawrence's portrayal, and the novel's subsequent obscenity trial, could be read as evidence of the author's political seriousness, Baraka's phrasing questions this. It is as though he had second thoughts about the significance of his own novel's subsequent obscenity charge. In his *Autobiography*, for instance, Baraka notes that by the mid-1960s he had come to see the sexual license of his Village friends as using the "cover story of Art to provide arrogance and a sense of superiority for some finally low shit" (*Autobiography*, 238). The critique of Lawrence in the poem runs parallel. Rather than sexual liberation, or an assault on gendered hierarchies, Baraka reads such activity at this stage of his career as an escape from politics, its once threatening transgressions subsumed into the commonplace, if mildly frowned upon, narrative of the bourgeois affair.

The poem's closing, too, offers a critique of Baraka's Village friends. In this regard, the projectivist line-breaks, with their approximation of hipster speech, conjure Creeley and other Black Mountain associates:

Like,
he was *really*
nowhere. ("Poem for Speculative Hipsters," 76)

Baraka's employment of the emphatic use of the adjective "Like" here, accentuated by the heavy pause caused by the coupling of line-break and comma, enacts a hipster or beatnik vernacular that he knew intimately, one that is also woven throughout the Olson-Creeley correspondence. Much of that exchange was already in print at the time in the form of selections made for the 1954 Diver's Press edition of the *Mayan Letters*. The line also echoes—and inverts—the sarcasm of Dorn's noncommittal response to the Cuban situation: "*Sides*, are a bigassed drag. The biggest small-talk of all, like which one are you on?" (Dorn, 53). Such responses are critiqued in the poem as escaping to the "nowhere" of noncommitment, an evasion of politics, rather than the aesthetic redress Dorn and others intended. In all these ways, then, "Poem for Speculative Hipsters" functions as a critique of the downtown scene in general, and of Olson, Creeley, and projectivist poetics in particular, as a riposte to what Baraka saw as the narrowing of their white voices.

As his autobiographical writings detail, Baraka sought throughout this period to inspire a political engagement commensurate with the aesthetic approach of his Village friends. In terms of his own poetry, this can be seen most clearly in his attempts to uncover the roots of projectivist poetics, to reveal the latent politics challenging its social and musical affinities. As Baraka later explained, at this time he consciously fought to develop his writing beyond mere imitations of Olson and Creeley:

> I was really writing defensively. I was trying to get away from the influence of people like Creeley and Olson. I was living in New York then and the whole Creeley-Olson influence was beginning to beat me up. I was in a very closed, little circle—that was about the time I went to Cuba—and I felt the need to break out of the type of form that I was using then. I guess this was not only because of the form itself but because of the content which that form enclosed, which was my politics. (Benston, *Conversations with Amiri Baraka*, 106)

The poems collected in *The Dead Lecturer* witness this "break out" through their questioning of projective verse's potential for political engagement. While Olson and Creeley pioneered a materialist poetics that sought to locate politics in the writerly act, for Baraka, such acts rang hollow. As his correspondence with Olson and Dorn shows, he became increasingly frustrated by his friends' unwillingness to join in the revolutionary discussion surrounding the situation in Cuba, by their failure to offer any material support for the battle for civil rights at home, and by their reluctance to even consider his attempts to adapt projectivist poetics by broadening their conception of voice to accommodate political commitment. While the general outline of this story may be well known, what has been overlooked is that at the root of this frustration lay the thwarted attempt to persuade Olson and Creeley of the political commitment inherent in the poetics of breath and voice.

Decades later, Baraka still labored to demonstrate this. In a 2008 lecture on his friend Ed Dorn, for instance, Baraka scorned the critique that his own career lacked consistency: "People are always asking me that ignorant bit of small talk turned question. Why have your views changed . . . ? It's a silly question whose only merit is seeking after real information" ("Ed Dorn and the Western World," xvi). Such reality, of course, was more complex. As Baraka recalls, through continued conversation in later decades, he came to understand the New American poetics of breath and voice under two guises:

> I was fed the myth and reality of Black Mountain up close from some
> of its most loyal students: Joel Oppenheimer, Fielding Dawson, Basil
> King, who I saw almost nightly. What Dorn thought about Black
> Mountain and its primary teachers Olson and Creeley, I got, actually, in
> antidote to the aforementioned whose juiced up recollections frequent-
> ly bordered on the sentimentally surreal. ("Ed Dorn and the Western
> World," xvi)

Dorn, despite his earlier disagreement with Baraka over the situation in Cuba, later offered an antidote to the mythologizing tendency in the form of an insistence on Olson's commitment to a politically engaged poetry, over and above whatever inspiration other disciples of Black Mountain may have taken away. As Baraka recalled, "[i]t was Dorn" who sought to continue the conversation with him in subsequent years on the Civil Rights Movement and the question of "what was in that field in this world to be reported and how was a poem to do that" ("Ed Dorn and the Western World," xvi). The irony, then, was that other poets in the Beat and Black Mountain scenes could interpret his increasingly political verse as a break rather than a change or development necessitated by the terms of their common poetics. As he noted in exasperation, "some of this crowd of poets could say to me poetry and politics don't mix even while paying homage to intensely political poets like Ginsberg or Olson" ("Ed Dorn and the Western World," xvi). Even at the end of his career, Baraka framed his work as a continuing intervention, a broadening of the poetics of breath and voice.

Chapter Five

SPITTING FIRE

THE BLACK ARTS MOVEMENT AND

THE NEW AMERICAN POETRY

Stephen Henderson, in *Understanding the New Black Poetry*, introduced what was then the New Black Poetry of the 1960s and early 1970s, by questioning the very adjective that continues to define it. In terms of the poetics of "form," he admits that "often there is little (sometimes nothing) on the page to tell a reader at first sight that a 'Black' poem was not indeed composed by e. e. cummings, Jack Spicer, or Paul Blackburn" (28). The quotation marks around "'Black'" threaten any attempt to describe such poetry as essentially different from the work of whites. As Henderson continues, however, he highlights the source of the discrepancy in the interracial poetics of the New American Poetry:

One must admit that typographically, at least, contemporary Black poets have been greatly influenced by white poets and frequently admit it, as least the older ones do. Imamu Amiri Baraka (LeRoi Jones) has said on several occasions that he owes a great technical debt to William Carlos Williams, and his early poetry embodies many of the attitudes and utilizes many of the techniques of the Beats. . . . Much the same can be said of Bob Kaufman. . . . But more fundamental than all of this is the fact that along with their immersion in Zen, the Beats themselves were enamored of jazz in particular and the Black life-style in general, and at times sought to communicate what has to be called a "Black feeling" in their work. Often their formal model was alleged to be jazz, so that accurately or not, Allen Ginsberg described Jack Kerouac's writing as a kind of "bop prosody." The words give us an important clue. They let us know that the Beats in their writing were striving to capture the rhythms and phrasings of Black music, to notate somehow those sounds on the printed page. (*Understanding the New Black Poetry,* 29–30)

Once again, the question of poetics returns to considerations of musical performance, of transcribing the breath. As shown in earlier chapters, the development of this poetics involved an interracial, if not always equally integrated, poetic community, one solidified by an enthusiasm for jazz music and an engagement—sometimes practical, sometimes merely theoretical—with the politics of race. Here, however, Henderson emphasizes the belatedness of that attempt in his recovery of the Blackness of the new poetry: "But the point needs to be made that this was a generation after Langston Hughes had done the same thing—and with greater success" (30). As suggested in the preface to this study, Hughes's role at the heart of postwar American poetry has long been overlooked and misunderstood. In reclaiming his primacy, Henderson, like many poets and theorists of the Black Arts Movement, demonstrates the critical difference such essentialism provides. As he argues, the "technical and thematic" problems broached by the Beats (and other white poets inspired by jazz) "have been approached from the *inside*" by Black poets (S. Henderson, 30).

Henderson, of course, was not alone in stressing this crucial difference. James Smethurst, in his comprehensive study *The Black Arts Movement,* has noted that "Langston Hughes and other Black writers did have a major, though generally unacknowledged, influence on the New American Poetry through their impact on Popular Front poetics. And Black music served as both icon and formal resource for many of the New American poets" (135).

Like Henderson, Smethurst too reverses the question of influence: rather than portray Olson and Ginsberg as influences for a younger generation of Black poets, these poets influence the complicated legacies of Olson and Ginsberg by unearthing the unacknowledged importance of Hughes and Black music in the formation of their shared poetics. Consequently, Black Arts poets, as the example of Henderson's work shows, viewed the New American Poetry as inherently Black—albeit naively—having grounded its poetics in the experience of Black expressivity. As the previous chapters of this study have also demonstrated, this characterization reveals a great deal concerning interracial friendships and the development of such poetics. What remains to be shown, however, is that this process did not end with the advent of the Black Arts Movement; in fact, it continued through it. After all, in this reading Black Arts poets were in a unique position to recover the primacy of Black experience for the postwar avant-garde by revealing the performative inspiration at the heart of the New American Poetry.

Amiri Baraka, of course, focused his attention on similar problems. After decamping from the Lower East Side and relocating to Harlem, he sought to reimagine New American poetics as well. In doing so, however, he remained close to his poetic "bible," "Projective Verse" (Baraka, *Autobiography*, 282). In his rereading of Olson, Baraka came to share Henderson's perspective on typography and his focus on performance. As Henderson argues, Black poets needed to explore a methodology that could break free from the pervasive influence of bop prosody and projective verse on the "structure" and "typography" of their work (28–30). In doing so, he points repeatedly to Larry Neal's conception of "'the destruction of the text,'" in which the text of a poem is merely a "'score,'" a chart, as jazz musicians would say, for performers to improvise over (quoted in S. Henderson, 30). Baraka certainly sympathized with this aim. In a 1970 essay on how the "Black creator" needed to break away from the slavery of European machines, he mocked projectivism as, in the hands of white writers, being unnecessarily tied to the typewriter:

A typewriter?—why shd it only make use of the tips of the fingers as contact points of flowing multi directional creativity. If I invented a word placing machine, an "expression-scriber," *if you will*, then I would have a kind of instrument into which I could step & sit or sprawl or hang & use not only my fingers to make words express feelings but elbows, feet, head, behind, and all the sounds I wanted, screams,

grunts, taps, itches, I'd have magnetically recorded, at the same time, &
translated into word—or perhaps even the final xpressed [*sic*] thought/
feeling wd not be merely word or sheet, but *itself*, the xpression, three
dimensional—able to be touched, or tasted or felt, or entered, or heard
or carried like a speaking singing constantly communicating charm. *A
typewriter is corny!!* (Baraka, "Technology & Ethos," 156)

Humor aside, Baraka's aim here is to argue for a "three dimensional" Black
aesthetic, a charmed performance that could draw on the talking book tradition, on oral storytelling, and on the large and growing field of African
American music, genres that too often were regarded by white writers and
scholars as merely folk or popular media. In his attempt to create a form of
communicative charm, Baraka, like Larry Neal, Stephen Henderson, and
other artists and writers involved in the Black Arts Movement, sought to
align print with speech, high culture with low, through privileging the act
of performance as the epitome of African American poetic achievement.
In reconfiguring "Projective Verse" as a first step toward an improvisatory
performance art, then, Black Arts writers like Baraka acknowledged the
significance of Olson's poetics, while also moving past them in ways that
revise and integrate the New American Poetry.

In tracing the development of Black Arts poetics in this chapter, then, I
want to focus on one such instance of this literary history: the adoption and
adaptation of the New American poetics of breath and voice by prominent
figures in the Black Arts Movement. In particular, I want to draw attention
to the poetry of Lorenzo Thomas, Sonia Sanchez, and Jayne Cortez. As an
important scholar and poet of the Black Arts Movement and of its precur-
sor, Umbra, Thomas holds an important place as a writer who has played
a central part in both transitioning away from downtown poetics and in
shaping the later reception of this work. Sanchez's poetry, meanwhile, moves
beyond transitional gestures to embrace a performance poetry that is now
synonymous with the Black Arts Movement. As much as Baraka or any
other poet associated with the movement, her work marks one of the most
readily identifiable and representative instances of the poetics chronicled
here. Perhaps more than any other, though, the weaving together of these
strands can be observed in the poetry and performance of Jayne Cortez. As
both a Black Arts poet and a vocalist for the band the Firespitters, Cortez's
employment of open field concepts mark the fullest realization of its per-

formative potential. Of course, other examples could be drawn on as well. Calvin Hernton, Tom Dent, Larry Neal, Askia Touré, Haki Madhubuti, Eugene Redmond, Carolyn Rodgers, and more could be cited as instances of the poetics considered here. In focusing on Thomas, Sanchez, and Cortez, however, the aim is to demonstrate the variety of ways in which compositional strategies associated with the New American Poetry were not imitated but returned to their source in Black expressivity. In this way, the work of Black Arts poets reconfigures standard narratives of postwar poetic influence and inspiration, discovering, in the process, the fullest expression yet of the poetics of breath and voice.

REDISCOVERING AMERICA

In his brief memoir, "Alea's Children," Lorenzo Thomas details life on the Lower East Side in the early 1960s. Among the features distinguishing the community of artists, writers, and musicians gathered there, the most salient for him was its interracial character: "The most remarkable thing about the Lower East Side scene was that, while race remained a powerful engine of social upheaval, the artists seemed able to work together almost in spite of it . . . there was a kind of integrated society that did not seem to exist elsewhere" ("Alea's Children," 575). As instances of this, he lists the white poet Art Berger's participation in the predominantly Black Umbra Workshop and Clavin Hernton and Norman H. Pritchard's recording with white poets Jerome Badanes and Paul Blackburn (575). As these instances—only a few among many—indicate, the "relative lack of racial animosity, at least among the artists, was a notable feature of life on the Lower East Side" (577). This view of the early 1960s downtown scene reflects the experience of other Black poets like Amiri Baraka and A. B. Spellman as well. As the piece's title suggests, however, Alea, the goddess of chance, had other plans: "The goddess Alea, in all her un-predictability, for all that the artists themselves shamelessly worshipped her, ordained a change of course" (577). Without naming a specific event, Thomas simply concludes by recalling that the "moment of the African American avant-garde writer on the Lower East Side was superseded in the second half of the 1960s by the Black Arts Movement, and interracial collaborations were replaced with a different mood" (577). As an autobiographical gloss on his own poetic development, the memoir offers little explanation for the impetus behind this "different mood"; still, it does witness to the fact that the Black Arts Movement constituted for Thomas a "change of course" in the development of "the African American avant-garde writer on the Lower East Side" (577).

Elsewhere, he has reiterated the continuity that this reading suggests, as a way of emphasizing the critical development from one period to the next. As noted earlier in this study, in his scholarship Thomas repeatedly asserted that "Black Arts poets maintained and developed the prosody that they had acquired from Black Mountain and the Beats" (*Extraordinary Measures*, 201). Despite other critics' focus on performance, Thomas maintained the continued relevance of downtown strategies, such as Olson's use of typography:

> Henderson spends little time on the typographical strategies that poets devised. . . . Typography, however, was important. In the work of the best poets, typography showed readers the mechanism of "taking the poem off the page." To anyone familiar with Olson's *Projective Verse*, the text of Sonia Sanchez's "Queens of the Universe" functions precisely as a *score*. (*Extraordinary Measures*, 211)

The point, of course, is not to obscure the genuine originality of a poet like Sanchez's work; nor is it to attribute any rigid, traditional sense of poetic influence. Instead, Thomas's argument here connects with his memoir by widening the lens, showing us that the movement from downtown to uptown was not simply a break, but equally a matter of development and transformation. Sanchez's "Queens of the Universe" does not merely employ Olsonian typographical practices; it transforms them, reimagining projective verse as a weapon that "Black/woooomen" might use in their battle against "this crackerized country" (Sanchez, "Queens of the Universe," 115).

Thomas, for his part, employed the downtown poetics of breath and voice to various ends throughout his own career as a poet. The early poem "Political Science," originally published in the fall of 1963 in Ted Berrigan's *C: A Magazine*, exemplifies one such use. James Smethurst has argued that second generation New York School circles like Berrigan's were in fact the heart of interracial collaboration in the downtown scene (*The Black Arts Movement*, 136). Thomas's writing was certainly a crucial component of that effort, mixing collaborators and styles in his work. As Daniel Kane notes, Thomas's poem combines Olsonian typography and New York School "surface lightness" to create a new, hybrid approach, one that develops O'Hara's occasional incorporation of racial politics in his poems (*All Poets Welcome*, 119–20). While the surrealism of the piece, most evident in the concluding line, manages to hold any simple didacticism at bay, the ethnic and racial references—"jew," "christianize," "yellow"—weave a more serious undertone throughout, forcing the reader to search for ways to align surface and depth. Thomas's approach works to exile and estrange the reader much like the situation of the speaker in the Robert Browning reference that opens the poem:

> Now could I read Browning.
>   "Home
> Thoughts from abroad ("Political Science" n.p.)

Browning's "Home-Thoughts from Abroad," after all, captures the imagination in exile. As in similar poems written by American immigrants, like, for instance, Claude McKay's "Subway Wind," Browning's poem offers an elegiac reflection on time and distance. On the other hand, the sense of cultural superiority apparent in Browning's work complicates any easy comparison with others. Browning's closing complaint about the "gaudy" melon-flowers of his adopted home in Italy, compared to the "buttercups" of England, sounds a somewhat patronizing note (Browning, 16). The problems inherent in seeing the world through such an Anglo-American lens, through the perspective of western hegemony in this period, is essential to Thomas's reference, however. "Now could I read Browning" is not the same, after all, as "Now I sympathize with Browning" ("Political Science"). It bears mentioning that Thomas was also something of a transplant, having been brought to the United States from Panama at the age of four. Still, at the time this poem was published, he had spent virtually his entire life in New York City. His sense of exile, therefore, is less a matter of home as nation and more a sense of it as a space mapped by psychological and cultural discourses; it is "home" in the sense of Amiri Baraka's collection of social essays of the same name, itself a meditation on the struggle of African Americans to be at home in the United States.

The poem's closing speaks to the frustrations inherent in this meditation. The 1963 publication closes with a mixing of the racial and ethnic signifiers alluded to earlier: "entire geography history a jumbled a yellow in fireside" (Thomas, "Political Science"). Crossing space and time in a domesticated conflagration, the line eschews traditional syntax and grammar in its purposeful confusion of identity. Such a "yellow" may refer to the products of interracial couplings, to the color of the flame, or both. That such couplings nonetheless end in flames presents well the frustration of any attempt to transcend the Jewish-Christian cultural divide, or, indeed, any other. The science of politics would thus appear to be a disciplining through ascription, the designation of ethnic or religious identity as a way of dividing populations and asserting control, over and above any attempts to cross such boundaries. That he published such a poem in a predominantly white magazine at this time speaks to some of the leading concerns of Thomas's fellow Umbra poets, at once embracing and participating in the interracial ambitions of the downtown scene while also critiquing its hypocrisies. A later version of the piece, the one published in the *Collected Poems of Lorenzo Thomas* (2019), appends several lines to the conclusion and ends with a telling image:

> "There will always be a place for you
> you can be the epee
>   when I paint the heart on my chest ("Political Science," 445)

Though not the only addition ("magnetize" in line eight is changed to "magazine," as though hearkening back to the poem's original place of publication), this image involves the reader in the imagined violence of the poem. For the many white readers of *C*, there would certainly "always be a place" in America where they could feel at home; in fact, such at-homeness becomes in itself a sword, an "epee," carving a bleeding heart on the poet's chest, itself an ironic suggestion of the failures of the era's well-intentioned liberals, both Black and white.

Related struggles are broached in later poems that reflect on this era. One of the most complicated and telling is "Historiography," at once a celebration and a critique of beatnik sensibility. A "Bird Poem" that engages with the politics of Black music, "Historiography" takes the performance and reception of Charlie Parker's work as its main subject, replete with explanatory "Liner Notes" appended to the poem's metaphorical record. In the "Notes," Thomas describes the poem as a "tonal evocation of the spirit of Charles Parker . . . designed for oral recitation" ("Liner Notes," 89). In this way the poem accords well with the New American poetics of breath and voice. Like Ginsberg, Thomas goes on to describe it as "a solo constructed in the bop saxophone style," while, like Creeley, he explains that "the poem is an investigation of the sonic developments pioneered by Parker and his associates" ("Liner Notes," 89). Such glosses position the piece at the center of the New American Poetry's attempts to adapt bop principles gleaned from Parker's music. As Thomas has written elsewhere, quoting Alain Locke, one beneficial aspect of such appropriative inspiration was the creation of an interracial aesthetic: "It was in this atmosphere of jazz as an 'interracial collaboration'—with segregated dressing rooms—that the first notes of bebop were heard" ("Evolution of the Bop Aesthetic," 94). The sarcasm noted here certainly translated to Thomas's view of the politics of the period as well. As he insists later in the same piece, bebop practitioners espoused a union of the aesthetic with the political:

> There are two major considerations that need attention in order to understand bebop as more clearly part of an African American cultural continuum. . . . On the one hand, bebop challenges Eurocentric standards by aggressively interrogating their hegemonic status. . . . On the other hand, bebop does represent a development of African American cultural nationalism that identifies the evolution of a popular performance style toward a more sophisticated or "serious" art form as well as a social and political statement. ("Evolution of the Bop Aesthetic," 97)

Here, Thomas makes plain that any thorough understanding of bebop, of Parker's innovations in jazz, must attend equally to the music as both an aesthetic challenge to white standards and as a statement of political resistance. A related perspective has been observed earlier in the writings of Bob Kaufman. Similarly, Ted Joans, whose work is referenced ironically in the epigraph that opens "Historiography," expressed parallel concerns in his poetry and art, infamously graffitiing "Bird Lives!" all over New York city in the late 1950s as a response to Parker's death that combines both art and politics, an affirmation of the ongoing revolution inaugurated by his music. Regardless, for most whites involved in the integrated poetic communities of the period, aesthetic debates remained curiously apolitical, as earlier looks at Ginsberg, Kerouac, Spicer, Wieners, Creeley, and Olson have, to various degrees, shown. Thomas's poem thus plunges into this divide by reclaiming the flawed, fragile human being at the heart of the Bird legend.

To begin, the first section of the poem ironically conflates Parker's power with his perceived martyrdom. As the opening lines assert, "the junkies . . . the sports / And the high living down looking ones" appreciate Parker's playing ("Historiography," 86). Accordingly, Thomas associates Bird's fans with drug addicts, casual friends, and privileged hipsters, none of whom appear to possess any understanding of his art on a human level. Instead, they appreciate merely a mix of "music and terror and lames," an empowering combination that allows them to revel in the thought that "in Bird's end [they] would someday do better" (86). Such appreciation is less inspiration than fantasy, the cult of personality that attends the death of almost any relatively young artist, musician, or writer, from Parker to Jimi Hendrix to Jean-Michel Basquiat. What gets lost in such transformations is the material basis of their work, the human caught in networks of ideological control. In fact, what is often celebrated is a life captured, edited, and recorded for the whims of future playback. As Thomas's enjambment in stanza two suggests, "some come to prefer" not only the "tv," but Parker's spiraling "down in disaster," ignoring the "keening cry of the Bird / Nailed to the wax they adored" ("Historiography," 86). Like a Christ figure, Parker becomes an object of adoration, his records a kind of crucifix-like talisman to be worshipped, all the while the suffering he endured in Jim Crow America is conveniently elided, unheard. The poem's larger suggestion attends to the racial politics at the heart of Parker's reception in the lines that follow, "Every cat caught with // A white girl wailed Bird Lives" (86)! Referencing Joans's graffiti and the many interracial couples who populated New York's downtown scene, the lines portray a biting irony: Parker's pain is their pleasure. In fact, legend-making slogans like "Bird Lives!" serve in some ways to keep the human at the heart of his music "chilly and gone" ("Historiography," 86).

Sections two and three develop this irony further, musing on the "Pretty music. For all that // Pain" ("Historiography," 87). In particular, section two questions how "the young ones remember the pain / And almost forget the dances," wondering who could "[s]teal the prints and the master and burn down / The hope of his rage when he raged" (87)? At issue here is the separation of aesthetics and politics that occurs in the transformation from flawed performer to immortal martyr. In an attempt to wrest Parker back to earth, each of the first two sections of the poem ends with the refrain, "Bird // Was a junkie" (86–87). The jarring reminder of the phrase resounds a criticism not merely of Parker but of the political situation that played such a prominent part in his suffering and of the ignorant elision of this on the part of many downtown hipsters. As has been demonstrated throughout this study, the New American Poetry certainly took part in disseminating the myth of Bird that is here critiqued, while ignoring the appropriation such mythmaking entails. Section three of "Historiography" faces this fact squarely, turning to the first-person to address Parker's revolutionary playing:

> According to my records, there was something
> More. There was space. Seeking. And mind
> Bringing African control on the corny times
> Of the tunes he would play. There was Space. (88)

The "Space" that appears at the beginning and ending of the passage hearkens back to Olson's conjuring of the same term in "Projective Verse," only here the sound of it is perceived in Parker as something primary, as the poetic inspiration his music truly was. As Olson would admit, "there was no poetics. It was Charlie Parker. Literally, it was Charlie Parker" (*Muthologos*, 281). Thomas's lines witness as much here, while also anticipating the "corny" typewriters of Baraka's critique ("Technology & Ethos," 156). Displacing the white, "corny times" of Tin-Pan-Alley "tunes," Parker effectively exercises "African control" over American cultural discourse, thereby opening a revolutionary "space" for listeners to enter. In this way, when Thomas plays Parker's "records," he hears the possibility of freedom from the "dull system // Of our own enslavements" ("Historiography," 88). Such liberation, however, becomes audible only through his blues-inflected playing, through the distinctively African American sufferings that drove his drug addiction and so, in turn, informed his work. As Thomas concludes the poem, with a variation on the previous refrain that echoes in a manner similar to a blues triplet, "[b]ut Bird *was* a junkie!" (88).

While "Historiography" embodies one of Thomas's fullest engagements with the poetics of breath and voice in this period, his long career witnesses many others. In *Sound Science*, for instance, the many love poems that comprise the collection take part in a play of voices, a dance that moves between the most intimate closeness and the most distant beyond. In fact, the collection's title is taken from Sun Ra who, in his poem "The Outer Bridge," writes of "the half-between world" where "the sound scientists" dwell ("The Outer Bridge," *Immeasurable Equation*, 293). For Thomas, too, "the half-between world" of avant-garde jazz composition translated into moving poetry. In fact, in discussing free jazz's relationship to the Black Arts Movement, he was keen to echo Henderson's characterization of Black poets in this period as modern griots, emphasizing the degree to which both poetry and music at this time rooted themselves in African American performance traditions (Thomas, "Ascension," 128–30). Poems like "My Calling," "The Offering," and "Low Speech," from *Sound Science*, represent this intention well. In fact, the latter imagines the beloved's lips as kissed by a "bright polished bell of brass" and her talk as the "[e]xtravagant sounds" of "song" ("Low Speech," 188–89, 191). In "My Calling," the encounter between the two lovers figures as an improvised saxophone solo, a passion that thrives at a moment's notice:

> When I call you . . .
> I want a saxophone player to play
> Because as I say I love you
> That "you" makes me blaze. ("My Calling," 188)

In the communion between the two people here, timing is everything. Much like a soloist embarking upon an improvisation, rhythm typically determines what will or will not resound. As the unusual punctuation of the opening fragment has it, "[w]hen" governs the poet's "calling." Analogous to a saxophone's cry, the "I love you" of the poem avoids sentimentality in the manifold reference of its ambiguity. A writer's calling, traditionally, is to engage a reader. The poet's relationship with the reader therefore parallels the musician's with the listener and the lover's with the beloved. As opposed to the catharsis that attends upon the communion of two people in a more traditional love lyric, the fiery "blaze" that ends this piece incinerates all of the aforementioned, leaving nothing but ashen embers. For Thomas, then, despite the piece's seemingly placid, quiet surface, music calls the Black Arts poet to burn down traditional, Eurocentric forms in a performance of revolutionary passion.

As all of these attest, Thomas's work in this period uncovers new potential in the spoken, in the adaptation of the New American Poetry's poetics of breath and voice to fit the needs of an emerging Black Arts Movement. As he writes in "Discovering America Again," a poem commemorating the life of Umbra founder and friend Tom Dent, their shared poetics at this time centered on speech:

> Discovering America again,
> We found
> The simplest of all mysteries

Called speech
Retains the register
Of fear
Encountering
What we do not know we know
Disguised as other people. (298)

Focusing on their close collaboration, the stanza encourages one to read their shared accomplishments by focusing on the "simplest" of New American insights: that poetry is performed speech. While this may appear obvious and even banal in retrospect, the privileging of American speech, and particularly African American vernacular, continues to cause controversy even today. "Discovering" this freedom becomes, in Thomas's words, an aesthetic awareness that "speech / Is breath made lovely / Shaped and shaping"; it is thus the "secret" that Dent knew and that many of the poets associated with both Umbra and the later Black Arts Movement would reveal for an African American audience ("Discovering America Again," 299). Consequently, Dent appears as a kind of mentor to the younger Thomas, as one who initiated him into the life of poetry. As the poem concludes, Thomas remembers him as a "man who spoke with people / Who asked you questions / So that you could breathe" (299). In this way, Thomas's commemoration of Dent bears a clear resemblance to Olson's writing in "Projective Verse," from the emphasis on breath and speech to the larger insistence that attending to these things necessarily affects the poet's "stance toward reality" ("Projective Verse," 239). Of course, Thomas was no doubt aware of this. Writing of Olson's influence on poetry readings, he recalled that "gatherings of poets in the 1960s were sometimes life-changing events" ("New and Old Gospel," 152). Such, certainly, was the case in his encounter with Dent and the Umbra circle. For fellow poets involved in the Black Arts Movement later in the decade, a parallel conjunction of speech-based poetics, Black power politics, and avant-garde jazz would produce similarly life-changing results.

SCRREEEEEEECHHHING LOVE

As noted, Thomas has credited Sonia Sanchez with adapting Olson's poetics of breath to suit the needs of African American female poets (Thomas, *Extraordinary Measures*, 211–12). Such adaptations, it must be emphasized, complicate any traditional sense of linear influence. As Sanchez herself has insisted, conceptions of orality that often accompany the poetics of breath and voice carry an especial burden for African American poets:

> On many levels, it is so much easier to relegate our art to what we call primitive art. Or it's so much easier to relegate our form to being always oral form. . . . But that doesn't make me an "oral" poet. They want to relegate you. When Allen Ginsberg reads his poetry aloud, and he has learned how to read it well from listening to Baraka and other people who have read their poetry well, when he chants, whatever, in his poetry no one says, "Well, he's an oral poet." (*Conversations with Sonia Sanchez*, 108)

The problems broached here are manifold. First of all, there is the presumption that Black Arts poetry is primarily oral, and that, as such, it should be understood as a merely primitive art. In addition to this, there is the double-standard apparent in the judgment of white poets like Ginsberg, who work in a related style, but whose oral performances are often viewed as a complementary wildness enlivening and enriching his sophisticated texts. As Sanchez suggests, the difference in treatment is clearly racialized. In fact, I would argue that it is one of the primary reasons why connections between the Black Arts Movement and the New American Poetry have been misunderstood for so long. Though many white poets in the period perceived such double standards and struggled to overcome them, both in the surrounding world and in their own personal lives, most did not succeed. Scholarship, by and large, has struggled to account for these discrepancies as well.

Rather than dismissing Sanchez's work as merely oral poetry, I want to consider it here as a development of the poetics of breath and voice. In this way, the noticeable orality of her work appears not as primitive, but as practical: a reworking of the New American Poetry. As Jean-Philippe Marcoux has written, Sanchez follows Amiri Baraka's adaptations of the poetics of breath and voice to create "assassin poems" aimed at hegemonic whiteness (*Jazz Griots*, 110). Her poetry also engages equally in the period's typographic debates. By adapting what Olson called "the fruits of the experiments of Cummings" ("Projective Verse," 245), Sanchez noticeably drops conventional rules for capitalization and adopts an arch tone. In fact, she often does so in the service of enfranchising a vernacular speech that is unique to African American communities. Like other writers whose work experiments with the use of AAVE, Sanchez borrows key compositional principles from jazz and the blues, from Black music. Again, as Olson insists in "Projective Verse," the musical, performative use of lyric always returns to the speaking voice (245). In fact, in quoting the famous opening of *Twelfth Night*, Olson argued that the gap between Shakespeare's music and the academic poetry dominant at midcentury resulted largely from the privileging of print: "What we have suffered from, is manuscript, press, the removal of verse from its producer and its reproducer, the voice, a removal by one, by two removes from its place of origin *and* its destination" ("Projective Verse," 245). Though Olson could not have foreseen it, such a responsive, communal poetics clearly resonated with Black Arts strategies of reading, where audience engagement is clearly audible on archived recordings and where many inspired younger writers were certainly in attendance. In a prose style that attempts to chart the emphasis inherent in his own speech rhythms—consider the otherwise unnecessary comma after "from"—Olson here encourages the print practices that Thomas has since credited Sanchez with reimagining and extending through her attempts to create a score for performance (*Extraordinary Measures*, 211).

One of the first attempts by Sanchez to achieve such a poetry is apparent in the early piece "homecoming." The title poem of her first collection, it embodies elements of projectivism in its intentional, Cummings-like misuse of capitalization, in the Olsonian employment of shifting margins, and in Sanchez's own distinctive engagement with vernacular speech. Commenting on the titles of her works, she has reflected on the process of composing the collection as a whole:

> I did one called *Home Coming*, a lot of writers, from Ngugi on, had written a book called "homecoming." We were all coming home, at a certain time, people were coming home to themselves, to their identities, their sense of selves, and that's what happened with me. And then I started playing with words, "We a baad people"—and they didn't understand the terminology, and we had to say, "No, no, no, we be bad, as in good. We the good people, the really hip people." The spelling of all those kinds of things, also for the first times, in the early seventies, I started to notate musically, the sense of a word, how a poem should be read. (*Conversations with Sonia Sanchez*, 150)

Here, Sanchez frames the collection as a discovery of self, of identity as woven into a sense of home. Congruent with the home that Thomas longs for in "Political Science," Sanchez's perspective also aligns well with his in "Discovering America Again." As she says, coming home to oneself meant for her "playing with words" and "spellings," employing the home speech of vernacular. Realizing the musicality of the spoken language, rather than, say, avoiding it as incorrect or nonstandard, forms the core of her efforts to come home. As Thomas knew, recovering the power of one's vernacular speech uncovers a version of self that allows you to "breathe" ("Discovering America Again," 299).

The titular poem "homecoming" engages with these perspectives in precisely this way. To open the piece, Sanchez begins with a bracing use of vernacular:

> i have been a
> way so long
> once after college
> i returned tourist
> style to watch all
> the niggers killing
> themselves with
> 3 for oners
> with
> needles
> that
> cd
> not support
> their
> stutters. (*Collected Poems of Sonia Sanchez*, 3)

The use of "niggers," the most egregiously racist epithet in American English, regardless of intent, continues to draw criticism even today. Sanchez's familiar use of it here, however, attests to its common deployment among speakers of AAVE for both positive and negative attributions. Faithful to the spoken word, over and above the rules and conventions of print decorum, the poem proceeds to involve the audience in the lingo of drug dealers, one that would remain unintelligible to the typical middle-class, white reader of the time. The phrase "3 for oners" refers to selling drugs, heroin, in this case, at a discount, typically to new users as a way of gaining new customers. These vernacular references to the business of street life mark Sanchez's home in the poem as distinctly impoverished, and identifiably Black. Clearly, this is the point. As one of the few fortunate enough to go away to "college," the poem's diminutive "i" has experienced a very different community, one where the "I" is capitalized, with the added suggestion that the socialization in this kind of community provides the cultural and financial independence that allows for self-determination. The lowercase usage, therefore, could be read as marking a lessening of such independence, a cutting-it-down-to-size, so as to return it to its home community. Nevertheless, the poem knows that the business of addiction cannot remove the source of "their / stutters," a phrase that is itself emblematic of the syncopation inherent in the vernacular usage that stumbles in the face of white convention.

Capable of staying or leaving, of adopting or resisting such conventions by virtue of her education, the speaker of the poem faces a clear choice. To represent the crucial turning points in the poem, Sanchez adopts a typical Olsonian tool, the indented margin:

>   now woman
> i have returned
> leaving behind me
> all those hide and
> seek faces peeling
> with freudian dreams.
> . . .
>   black
>   niggers
>   my beauty. ("homecoming," 3)

Having "returned" home, her classmates and professors at college appear childlike, with "hide and / seek faces," wrapped up in the desire of their own superficially "freudian dreams." The use of the lowercase form again suggests a resistance to convention, in this instance, in fact, a resistance to academic, Freudian explanations. As opposed to these "dreams," she chooses home as a representation of reality, phrased as "black / niggers / my beauty." The indentation creates space to linger over and emphasize each word.

Consequently, it draws out at least two responses. For many Black readers, it encourages a celebratory evocation of the spoken, "real" life of the street. By contrast, for many white readers, it conjures a jarring response, one that requires them to recognize, on one hand, the racism inherent in the epithet, while, on the other, perceive, at a distance, the beauty of an essential Blackness, of a racialized identity founded in opposition to white hegemony. As the conclusion of the poem notes—taunts—life in this home "ain't like they say / in the newspapers" ("homecoming," 3). As opposed, then, to the predominantly white world of newsprint, the spoken, "real" experience of Black community is outside the bounds of that world, a tacit recognition, in other words, of a beauty that is only fully accessible to Black readers.

Such beauty is celebrated throughout Sanchez's work, presented most frequently through a version of projectivist poetics rooted in jazz compositional paradigms. In an interview with Sascha Feinstein, Sanchez has elaborated her conception of writing as jazz: "In other words, the composition of the poem is jazz, the delivery of the poem is jazz, and the juice, infusing it, is jazz" (*Conversations with Sonia Sanchez,* 164). Among the pieces she lists during the interview as being composed especially in this manner is the bluesy "I Have Walked a Long Time" (*Collected Poems of Sonia Sanchez,* 165). The opening lines confound any conventional sense of past or present with their lament that "I have walked a long time / much longer than death that splinters" (84). In this way, the "i" of the poem no longer resembles the poet, as in "homecoming," and instead takes on a kind of ancestral persona. As Sanchez has said, her work, like that of Spicer, Wieners, and Jonas, gives voice to the ancestral alongside the contemporary, understanding its jazz influence as a cognate form of *cante jondo:*

> The *cante jondo*—the deep song—is in each one of our cultures. One of the *cante jondo* is the blues. The *cante jondo* that became urban—more modern—is jazz, in my head. At some point, when you hear that wail, that song, that fusion, that movement off the ground into the sky— then you know this is ancient and modern at the same time. (*Conversations with Sonia Sanchez,* 162)

This conjunction of the ancient and the modern can be felt in "I Have Walked a Long Time," particularly in the shifting registers, the counterpointing of more conventional lines, such as "my life, ah my alien life" and "ah, I have not loved," with those in vernacular, "bringen blue screens to bury clouds / rinsen wite stones stretched among the sea" ("I Have Walked a Long Time," 84). Such delicate shifting of voices also reveals a development and complication of the poetic inaugurated by the earlier "homecoming." The use of indentation, of the shifting margins of projectivism, is elaborated further as well here, with whole stanzas, as opposed to short lines, responding to others anchored by the left-hand margin. In their questioning refrain—"you, man, will you remember me when I die?"—they trouble any linear reading, involving the audience in a kind of call-and-response, in an act of comprehension that is once again rooted in jazz compositional practices, just as much as it is an adaptation of New American poetic strategies ("I Have Walked a Long Time," 84–85). In all of these ways, the approach here heightens the attempt found throughout Sanchez's work to sound a distinctively Black femininity. As Marcoux has noted, the poet's ability to score speech makes audible the "black female voice" as an "example of what Sanchez means when she sloganizes that the 'personal is political'" (121).

A similar approach can be seen in a poem like "Sequences," another piece Sanchez describes as a jazz poem resonant with Coltrane's influence (*Conversations with Sonia Sanchez*, 165). There, surrealist imagery combines with a more formal, conventionally literary voice to displace the authorial persona and locate the poem in a kind of ancestral *now*. Once again, shifting margins shape a counterpointed chorus, a sort of call-and-response dialogue between the capital "I" who speaks at the opening and the lowercase "i" of the indented stanzas ("Sequences," *Collected Poems of Sonia Sanchez*, 71–72). Again, the focus is on movement—or lack thereof—on countering a "breath" dried "in paint" with "movements that run / green then blue again" (71–72). Though the clown imagery repeated in the poem echoes Smokey Robinson and The Miracles' famous hit "The Tears of a Clown," the chant-like rhythms employed for commemorating the dead gives the piece a ritualistic property that resembles prayer, much like Coltrane's music. As Sanchez recalls, "Coltrane was holy to us all. When people asked did you pray, you'd say yes, I play Coltrane. And they weren't being facetious either—because of just how mystical his music was, and how his music kept a lot of people alive at a time they wanted to be kept alive" (*Conversations with Sonia Sanchez*, 36).

Coltrane's influence can be seen more clearly, however, in Sanchez's perhaps best-known piece, "a / coltrane / poem." The poem exhibits all of the projectivist elements of her other work, but to an even greater degree. The use of typographical techniques common to projectivist poets are especially evident, such enfranchisement of forward slashes, backslashes, abbreviations, the use of all-caps to mimic shouting, the incorporation of vernacular speech, and the deployment of constantly shifting margins to create an active, noisy page where writer and reader are forced to "MOVE, INSTANTER" throughout the poem (Olson, "Projective Verse," 240). Of course, as has been shown, Olson's projectivist formulations themselves owe a debt to the playing of Charlie Parker. Sanchez thus has little need of referencing New American poetics, opting instead to go straight to the musical source of their shared aesthetic. Rather than Parker, though, Sanchez's particular source here is John Coltrane. As Meta DuEwa Jones has written, Sanchez's poem adapts the saxophonist's use of "multiphonics" to the printed page via what Jones terms *"multiphonemics,"* a form of verbal play that "captures orthographically a sense of the intensity and layered texture of sound on the page" (102). Similarly, Feinstein has argued that the poem presents a "phonetic equivalent to the explosive sound of Coltrane's saxophone" (*Jazz Poetry, from the 1920s to the Present,* 124). "a/coltrane/poem" achieves these ends masterfully, reworking what might be called the projectivist influence on Sanchez's writing so that such strategies appear, instead, as what they are: poetic techniques inspired by Black music. Though I have followed Thomas in citing Olson throughout this chapter to demonstrate the degree to which his work is confluent with Black Arts poets, it is important to emphasize that his presence here in no way connotes a subservient, mentor-student relation of influence. Such influence itself is strenuously resisted by poets like Sanchez and Baraka through their attempts to reach back before the advent of the New American Poetry to a jazz aesthetic that predated and, in fact, exerted a considerable influence on it. Still, Black Arts writing differs significantly from the jazz poetry of Hughes, despite his considerable importance, and, as Thomas has argued, from the larger Black Mountain and Beat poetics of breath and voice in the intervening period. As Kimberly Benston has shown, the Coltrane Poem typically champions the "subversive instinct" apparent in the saxophonist's music (*Performing Blackness,* 119). Perhaps, then, the best model for understanding the persistence of the poetics of breath and voice among poets of the Black Arts Movement is Ludwig Wittgenstein's notion of "family resemblances," where "gait, temperament, and so on and so forth—overlap and criss-cross" in constantly new and unexpected ways

(*Philosophical Investigations*, 36). For Black Arts poets who spent their formative years as part of the interracial downtown scene, such crisscrossing was no doubt inevitable, as the deep indebtedness of their white peers to Black cultural expressivity shows.

In using such crossed and interwoven techniques to celebrate the artistry and achievement of avant-garde jazz's patron saint, "a/coltrane/poem" resounds with the period's aesthetic. After all, line one references Coltrane's biggest commercial hit, "My Favorite Things," itself a reworking of a show tune written by Rodgers and Hammerstein for their popular 1959 musical *The Sound of Music*. Coltrane's fourteen-minute performance essentially deconstructs a pop standard, and so engages with white art in a manner parallel to Sanchez's and other Black Arts poets' adoptions of New American poetic techniques. In a similar way, the forward slashes used to fragment and, in so doing, fork and branch the sense of a phrase in previous poetry like Olson's are here employed to augment the poem through the addition of a form of vernacular speech that complicates the more conventional phrasing and diction of counterpointed passages. Shifting margins add to this countering instinct, creating a dynamic rhythm of stops and starts as passages weave together multiple registers. Consider, for instance, the opening passage:

> my favorite things
> > > is u/blowen
> > > > > > yo/favorite/things
> > stretchen the mind
> > > > till it bursts past the con/fines of
> > solo/en melodies.
> > > > to the many solos
> of the
> > mind/spirit. ("a/coltrane/poem," 361)

Here, projectivist techniques align fully with their jazz inspiration. From forward slashes to margins to the breath of the spoken voice, all moves in syncopated fashion, troubling any linear reading with a polyrhythmic, polyvocal performance. This latter element is drawn out even more so in the following reference to "Frère Jacques," where "Brother John" becomes Coltrane himself, as Sanchez has noted:

Of course it's my response to Coltrane and "My Favorite Things," but it's also counterpoint; I do something and then all of a sudden I stop it, and do that little chant: "Are you sleeping, are you sleeping, brother John, morning bells are ringing, morning bells are ringing." It's paying respect to Brother John—everyone called John Brother John—but it's also to emphasize that he's not really dead, so I say sleeping instead, to bring back the whole idea of life and death at the same time. (*Conversations with Sonia Sanchez*, 36)

As "counterpoint," then, the allusion again complicates the voice; doubly so, since the lyrics are altered to fit the speech patterns of AAVE, "brotha john," and to emphasize the frustrated, dampened hopes attendant upon Coltrane's absence, "no mornin bells / are ringen here. only the quiet / aftermath of assassinations" ("a/coltrane/poem," 361). The mention of "assassinations" in the passage, conjuring the ghosts of Patrice Lumumba, Malcom X, Martin Luther King, Jr., Fred Hampton, and John and Robert Kennedy, brings to the surface the political undertone of Coltrane's significance. As a pioneer of "freedom music," his work was heard as a goad and accompaniment to the Civil Rights and Black Power movements. Such polyphony thus creates once again the effect of a call-and-response, one which inspires the protest that Sanchez hears in Coltrane's music and then responds to it in kind throughout the remainder of the poem.

There, the future is inaugurated by Coltrane's overblown horn. As James Smethurst has written, Black Arts poets, in enfranchising both vernacular speech and jazz poetics, often made prominent use of nonverbal sounds (*Black Arts Movement*, 99). Sanchez does so in the poem through mimicking, and then extrapolating, the abrasive resistance to cultural convention and white hegemony implicit in Coltrane's forays into the art of noise:

> A LOVE SUPREME
> scrEEEccCHHHHH screeeeEEECHHHHHHH
>   sCReeeEEECHHHHHH SCREEEECCCCHHHH
>   SCREEEEEEEECCCHHHHHHHHHHH
>
> . . .
>
> a lovesupremealovesupremealovesupreme for our blk
> people.
>   BRING IN THE WITE/MOTHA/fuckas
>   ALL THE MILLIONAIRES/BANKERS/ol

. . .

      GITem.

            PUSHem/PUNCHem/STOMPem. THEN

      LIGHT A FIRE TO

               THEY pilgrim asses.

. . .

screeeeeeeeeeeeeeeeeeCHHHHHHHHHHH

SCREEEEEEEEEEEEEECHHHHHHHHHH

screeEEEEEEEEEEEEEEEEEEEEEEEE

EECCCCHHHHHHH ("a/coltrane/poem," 361–62)

The righteous anger animating the passage appears here as a form of love. As such, it gives meaning to an artistry that many white listeners heard as merely noise in Coltrane's later work. A call to revolutionary resistance, to oppose the racist capitalism of America's ruling class, Coltrane's screeching horn becomes also, for Sanchez, a love song "for our blk / people," a tender and rebellious voicing that sounds the breath of a paradigmatic artistry. Beginning with a reference to the saxophonist's most famous composition, "A Love Supreme," a song with its own chanting, prayer-like sequence, the poem takes projectivist strategies to new heights in its embrace of the nonverbal as both aesthetically beautiful and politically responsive. As Sanchez has explained in retrospect, being asked to perform the poem for the first time at Brown University in the late 1960s instilled in her a freedom to compose musically for the rest of her career:

> I said, "I've never read that poem out loud. . . . Give me a minute to look it over." . . . [T]hank goodness for an appreciative audience. When I got to it, I *did* the music. I did Coltrane. The voice did everything. [Sings a brief, rising tone.] It just came to me. And from that point on, I was literally released to do whatever I wanted to do with a poem, with music, with sound. . . . I began to notate. . . . I began the whole process of [thinking about] the poem and the music as one. (*Conversations with Sonia Sanchez,* 159)

While the unity of poetry and music was apparent in earlier writers covered in this study, Sanchez's achievement in "a/coltrane/poem" certainly surpasses their attempts to write poetry as jazz by augmenting their strategies in a dramatic presentation centered on the performance of the body. As a female African American poet, the challenges implicit in this approach are manifold. By embracing avant-garde jazz's convention shattering noise, however, Sanchez finds a complementary mode to weave new perspectives into the era's experimental poetics. In this way, she shows that the jazz poetics of the New American Poetry could be turned back to the roots of their inspiration, reinvigorating Black writing in the process. As the conclusion of the poem has it, Coltrane's playing provides the inspiration for new life:

> yeh. john coltrane.
> my favorite things is u.
>> showen us life /
>>> liven.
> a love supreme.
>> for each
> other
> if we just
> lisssssssSSSTEN. ("a / coltrane / poem" 364)

The poem thus closes with a hiss of dissonance. In this way, Coltrane's music reveals a deep love for Black experience and a counter to white hegemony through its resistance to musical convention. Following his lead, Sanchez adopts an avant-garde poetics and, similarly, pushes it beyond the horizons of the moment to sound the body of a dissonant, loving community. Other female poets in the Black Arts Movement were certainly listening.

VERY FINE ENCUENTROS[1]

Among the Black Arts poets whose writing exemplifies the critiques of Henderson, Baraka, and Thomas, Jayne Cortez's work holds a special significance. Having been married early in her career to avant-garde saxophonist Ornette Coleman, Cortez would become a performer in her own right with her band the Firespitters, which featured their son, Denardo Coleman, on drums. Her poetry witnesses the fulfillment of a performance tradition inaugurated by Black music, extended by Olson, and reimaged by Baraka, Thomas, Sanchez, and other writers involved in the Black Arts Movement. As she recalled, her initiation into the world of performance poetry came via Paul

Blackburn's reading series at Dr. Generosity's, a bar on New York's Upper East Side, in 1969 (Melhem, *"A MELUS Profile and Interview: Jayne Cortez"* 72). That her earliest forays into this field should involve Blackburn is perhaps no coincidence. After all, he collaborated with Umbra poets and worked as both a writer and impresario in organizing important downtown reading series earlier in the decade, including the St. Mark's Poetry Project, and he helped to distribute the *Black Mountain Review* in the mid-1950s. Blackburn's connection to Cortez stands as another instance of the networks connecting Black Arts poets to the downtown scene in ways that have been chronicled throughout this book. In many ways, Cortez's career brings the poetry and poetic history explored here full circle.

In doing so, her writing, even more so than that of her predecessors and peers, dwells at the intersection between poetry and music. As Renee Kingan has noted, Cortez's work dwells in a "space neither poetry nor music can inhabit in isolation" (" 'Taking it Out!,' " 153). Partly, this aspect of her work can be traced to her personal involvement with avant-garde jazz, through her first husband and their son, and experimental jazz poetics, through Blackburn, Sanchez, and others. Naturally, it would seem, a writer intimately involved in these circles would find new ways to bring them together. The effect of such frequent encounters on her own aesthetic is telling. As she explained, there was for her no clear division between print and aural composition: "Music is another dimension with which to compose. I have no preference" (Melhem, *"A MELUS Profile and Interview,"* 78). This blurring of the line between the two can be seen in her publication history. For instance, her 1991 poetry collection, *Poetic Magnetic*, consists almost wholly of lyrics from her musical albums *Maintain Control* and *Everywhere Drums*. As a result of this approach, the references to jazz compositional practices used metaphorically by earlier poets in developing their unique approaches appear more concretely in Cortez's work. In many cases, these concerns in her writing converge on the figure of the female body. In fact, Cortez's imagination, even more so than other poets considered in this study, grounds itself time and again in such figurations. This inherent physicality is at the heart of her compositional process:

I use dreams, the subconscious, and the real objects, and I open up the body and use organs, and I sink them into words, and I ritualize them and fuse them into events. I guess the poetry is like a festival. Everything can be transformed. (*Melhem,* 74)

This sense of poetry as ludic ritual, as transformative performance, whether on the page or the stage, resounds throughout her career. Her work represents a "fusion" of avant-garde poetry and jazz in the flesh of the performer, one that fulfills, in many ways, the poetic imaginations of Olson, Ginsberg, and even Hughes, while transcending their most ambitious expectations.

An early poem that brings together the musical and the poetic, locating their convergence in the body, is "Tapping." The poem blends tap-dancing lingo—"locomotive," "scissor," "heel slide"—with a host of famous saxophonists, composers, and singers to conjure a projectivist jazz poetry focused on the body of the performer. The piece is dedicated to the famous "Baby Laurence, and other tap dancers," an indication of the larger celebration of the art form that Cortez's poem intends. Structured, like much of her poetry, around two anaphoric refrains, "when" and "I'm gonna," "Tapping" builds up a catalogue of preparatory movements before pivoting into a declaration of artistic arrival, one accompanied by the recognition of a bemused audience ("Tapping," *Coagulations*, 17–18). The opening, for instance, uses projectivist spacing and margin shifts to embody a poetry whose rhythmic alternations are as dynamic as dance:

> When I pat this floor
>   with my tap
>
> when I slide on air
>   and fill this horn intimate with
> the rhythm of my two drums
>
>   when i cross   kick
> scissor   locomotive
>
>   take four for nothing
> four we're gone (17)

The projective space apparent on the page creates the interplay of taps and rests needed to realize the dancer's rhythm. To follow the beats and observe the pauses, in fact, is to witness a dance of the intellect more subtle, and certainly different, than anything Pound could have anticipated and offers a broadening of Olson's interest in dance. In this way, the page of Cortez's poetry performs as remarkably as her well-known recitations. In fact, the imagination here crosses over into the physical in striking ways, with the dancer's feet figured as "two drums" filling the bell of a "horn" with their percussive, "intimate" power. It is as though the call-and-response relationship between instruments in a jazz combo, or voices in a projectivist poem, becomes here a model for the connection between music and the dancer's body. This physicality is, as I have been emphasizing, a hallmark of Cortez's adaptation of New American poetics.

Of particular note in this regard is the movement from lowercase "I," immersed, like Sanchez's, into the world of the poem, into the musical dialogue of the piece, and the uppercase "I" that signals the turn from the opening section to its answering part. There, the speaker emerges momentarily as the assertive, individualized "I" who is "gonna spotlite my boogie / in a Coltrane yelp / echo my push in a Coleman Hawkins whine" ("Tapping," 18). This spotlighted self steps out from the group to take a turn before returning to the lowercase accompaniment of "Ellington," "Ayler," "Satchmo," and "Rainey" (18). Rather than dance steps, this more assertive self gives body to a voice that "yelps," "whines," "cries," and adjusts its "pitch" to a larger jazz and blues performance tradition as part of an attempt to "pay my dues" and so prepare for a career of her own (18). Like Sanchez, whose paradigmatic use of nonverbal sounds in "a/coltrane/poem" gives voice to a counter tradition, a noisy otherness, Cortez sounds the emergent artist in a note of onomatopoetic dissonance:

i'm gonna steal no steps

i'm gonna pay my dues

i'm gonna 1 2 3

and let the people in the apple
go hmmmp hmmmmp hmmmmmp (18)

Thus her New York audience, the "people in the apple," are put on notice. Like the young Cortez preparing her first reading at Dr. Generosity's, the tap dancer in this poem envisages a coming-of-age moment. Stealing no previous artist's steps, yet having paid her dues, she follows the rhythm—"1 2 3"—to discover her own unique sound in the dissonant "hmmmp" of a nonverbal stomp. In this way, the piece literally sounds the body as a founding poetic act. In doing so, it builds off the projectivist strategies of Olson, the expressive sounding of the early Baraka, and the resistant, feminist art of Sanchez and others. "Tapping" thus demonstrates many of the key elements of Cortez's poetics in a work that introduces a strikingly new performance paradigm.

Similar takes on these strategies can be seen in "Strike Up the Band." There, the audience is addressed as a woman preparing for a night of dancing. In the opening, a projectivist attention to space and rhythm is paired with the surrealist personification evident in "Tapping":

> At midnight
> in your rusty industrial cockpit
> of oxtail stew
> in your hiccuping buttocks made
> radioactively ready to prance
> khaki uterus &
> AK-47 tongue
> blow through your ghost words
> your coyote microphone
> your wildebeest virtuoso crying pipe
> let chickens get tired of chicken shit
> your throat is like a two-headed drum. ("Strike Up the Band," 77)

Encouraging the "you" of the poem to break out of her "rusty industrial cockpit," to take off, Cortez again uses the silences of blank space on the page to time rhythmic interventions. The hesitating, wavering introduction, set amidst the gloom of a radioactive, postwar industrialism, replete with working-class food, "oxtail stew," and the flatulence that accompanies it, frames a self trapped and at odds with a distinctively late-twentieth century form of anomie. In this context, the "AK-47 tongue" that murders "ghost words" becomes a sign of life, a willingness to fight back, to pilot the self in a struggle for a more authentic existence. It is one grounded in a body "ready to prance," with a voice breaking out into song. The anaphoric "your" of the left-hand margin, as with the similar use of this form of repetition in "Tapping," compiles the liberatory aspects of the voice in a celebratory riff on the poetics of breath. As opposed to "ghost words," the voice here appears violent, wild, and animal, opposing "chicken shit" fears with the assertion of a "two-headed drum," a rhythm that beats a percussive catalogue of personified attributes.

The body once again becomes the site of a struggle for authenticity. Consequently, the poem develops toward a sense of self-possession that is witnessed in its penultimate section:

> let the dawn babble through a mouth of mildew blankets
> there is nothing better than wearing
> your own shoes
> your own panty liner
> your own jock strap
> your own sweat
> inside your own navel of archaeological digs
> heat up the site. ("Strike Up the Band," 77)

As the catalogue has it, ownership of the night becomes a pathway to owning the self. Tomorrow morning may "babble" on in the aftermath of a night out, but such concerns are shrugged off as secondary to the primal need for self-possession. This taking oneself back from the alienating world of radio-active industrialism is possible through music, through a rhythmic, physical response to the band. Significantly, it is the body, in all of its intimacy, that is celebrated here, from panty liners to jock straps to belly buttons. Cortez's unflinching ownership of these details signals a homely confidence in one's flesh as the site of a hidden power, a stolen life. Rediscovering this, giving it back to both writer and reader, becomes therefore a central aim of her poetry. As D. H. Melhem has written, Cortez's work witnesses "the relent-less searchlight of her perceptions," an intense commitment that "exposes what is wrong with the world" as part of a larger struggle to show us that "we can make things right, or somewhat better, or at least that we can hold annihilation at bay" ("A MELUS Profile and Interview," 79). In the poem, the simple act of dancing after midnight achieves this by reminding the reader that the social can be reclaimed through the intimately personal:

> whoever possesses the land will possess your bones &
> make love to your night life   uh hunh
> strike up the band. ("Strike Up the Band" 77)

The dance therefore becomes an act of love, with the vernacular "uh hunh" signing its authenticity. An embodied poetics of breath and voice, whether in the sense of a lyric performed with the accompaniment of instruments, or in the form of the rhythms and intonations charted on the page, clearly marks her primary mode of achieving such agency.

"I See Chano Pozo," one of Cortez's best-known pieces, combines all of these elements in a passionate performance with her band, the Firespitters. Like her other work, the poem applies Black Arts and implicitly feminist perspectives through a cross-cultural genealogy, drawing inspiration, ostensibly, from both projectivist poetics and the music of the famous Afro-Cuban conga drummer Chano Pozo. Having appeared simultaneously in her 1982 collection *Firespitter* and in her band's album of the same year, *There It Is*, the piece oscillates between print and audio performance, combining elements of both in her reading. In doing so, however, the text borrows many of the typographical innovations associated with Olson's projective verse, from the unusual spacing and shifting margins, to its use of the performer's breath to determine line breaks. All of these combine in an encounter with the liberatory power of jazz music, of its engagement with the body in an act of celebratory freedom.

The poem's subject, it should be noted, lived a short but eventful life. Growing up in Havana, Chano Pozo learned to play congas while plying several trades, ranging from newspaper boy to Mafia hit man.[2] At the same time, he became a devotee of Santería, the polytheistic, African diasporic religion that syncretized elements of Yoruban religious traditions and Christianity. Pozo, in fact, pledged his allegiance to Shango, the Yoruban God of thunder, syncretized as the Roman Catholic Saint Barbara, and patron of the drums (Cortez, "Glossary," 111). Taking these experiences with him, Pozo emigrated to the United States in the late 1940s, where he was introduced to trumpeter Dizzy Gillespie. Their collaborations on songs such as "Manteca" and "Tin Tin Deo" brought his music to prominence, spawning the Latin Jazz genre and leading to a host of imitators throughout the 1950s, including, most famously, Desi Arnaz. Unfortunately for Pozo, however, he did not live to see these developments, as he was shot and killed in a Harlem bar in 1948. The influence of his music, however, would persist, its cross-cultural mix of African drumming, Latin American rhythms, and Caribbean sensibility enriching Gillespie's and a younger generation's approach to jazz through its diasporic aesthetic.

Cortez's poem celebrates Pozo as an embodiment of the diasporic imagination, as a new world conjurer of various Yoruban, Ashanti, and other African "talking" drums—Atamo, Atumpan, Ntenga, Bata—drums used in various West African religious rites (Cortez and Firespitters, "I See Chano Pozo," 65, 67). In this way, his drumming gives voice to the forgotten histories of slavery, colonialism, and the struggle for freedom. The conga here works as both protest—brought over by enslaved Africans, the dance was outlawed in Cuba by Gerardo Machado and only occasionally permitted by Fulgencio Batista—and play. Consequently, Pozo's "very fine conga of sweat" registers this history through the ambiguous "groans," "growls," and "yells" of "revolutionary spirits" in the opening rites ("I See Chano Pozo," 65). This is transferred to Africa later, where late-1960s civil wars in Angola and Nigeria (Calabar in the colonial era), which also served as proxy battles between the U.S. and the Soviet Union, bring to bear the complicated histories of colonialism and Cold War politics ("I See Chano Pozo," 66). As both a Lucumi, a devotee of Santería, as well a member of an Abakwa, an Afro-Cuban secret society, Pozo appears as a "healer" to these divisions, as a "very fine encuentro" ("I See Chano Pozo," 66–67). To have "heard," "oye," Chano Pozo, then, is for Cortez also to locate him in the cross-cultural here of the poem, to chart such encounters through the performance of this history.

The Firespitters' music reinforces this dynamic sense of encounter in various ways. The recording similarly casts Pozo as a heroic figure for music's celebration of African diasporic rhythms and religion. In doing so, it also reconfigures the field of projective verse, opening it up to a Black Arts understanding of performance that blends the innovations of Black Mountain poetics with the musical experimentation of Pozo, Gillespie, and others. The musical piece opens with Coleman's conga drumming, followed by the entire band chanting "I see . . . Chano Pozo" over a driving bass line (Firespitters, 00:00:01–00:00:33).[3] Sonically, the effect echoes and updates Pozo's own music; meanwhile, Cortez's unadorned spoken word renders the poem largely as it appears on the page. Perhaps the greatest difference in this regard is the subtle additions to the audio recording. Aside from the band's refrain, chanted following Cortez's own repetition of the phrase at the break of each verse, she also embellishes the text at various points with a seemingly improvised "yeah," "oye," or "Chano" to soften the line breaks and respond to the music's pulsing rhythm (Firespitters, 00:00:34–00:07:32). For similar reasons, it would seem, the line "Lucumi   Abakwa   Lucumi   Abakwa," with its lengthy pauses and heavy accents, was omitted from the recording ("I See Chano Pozo," 67). Nevertheless, the sense of an extended, imagined community emerges through the intergenerational encounter that Cortez and her son Denardo make with Pozo's diasporic spirit. In this way, Coleman's drum solos recall Pozo's own playing, giving the effect of hearing both Coleman and Pozo at the same time (Firespitters, 00:03:03–00:03:45; 00:04:53–00:05:20). So, too, Cortez's shouts of "oye" and "olé I say," which can be heard at times on Pozo's recordings as well, sound a ghostly double-voice, conjuring the spirit of the drummer via a syncopated delivery that is represented by the shifting margins on the page ("I See Chano Pozo," 66; Firespitters, 00:00:34–00:07:32). In fact, using the page as a score, or chart, for vocal delivery effectively adapts Olson's typographic innovations, thereby reimagining projective verse as an essential component of a larger performance aesthetic. For instance, when reading the poem while listening to the recording, the text's indentations move throughout to enact the dramatic pauses necessary to syncopate the reader's rhythm, much like Pozo's and Coleman's drumming. Similarly, the heavily weighted line-breaks complicate sentence grammar, much like those of Robert Creeley's poetry, disrupting prepositional phrases and stringing together independent clauses into long, complex chains of anaphoric drumming.[4] Beating interrogatives and imperatives into a rhythmic chant, the poem commands the reader to move in tune to Pozo's "mediation," to engage with the performance as a dramatic encounter. Cortez's delivery enacts much the same, particularly in the changes of tempo necessitated by her son's drumming and the consequent omission and addition of phrases and pauses to the text of the original, which, in a larger sense, open the poem to the kind of improvisatory encounter that Larry Neal sought in advocating " 'the destruction of the text' " and the advent of a dissonant performance art that would, in Baraka's words, move beyond the constraints of the writing to embrace a world of distinctively Black physicality (Neal, as quoted in Stephen Henderson, 30; Baraka, "Technology & Ethos," 156). In all these ways, then, the result is, much like Chano Pozo's drumming, an embodied, hybrid poetic that integrates both African and European aesthetics in a fine encounter.

This braiding of body, text, and music recurs throughout the work of Black Arts poets. Even the titles of Cortez's early collections, for instance, resound with these concerns. From the gritty physicality of *Pissstained Stairs and the Monkey Man's Wares* to *Scarifications*, *Mouth on Paper*, and *Firespitter*, these titles all witness an attempt to score the text, both in the sense of a chart for performance, as earlier poets had also done, but also as a scarring, a tattooing of the page. As Tony Bolden has written, Cortez's poetry exemplifies a blues-based performance poetic that consistently opposes the hegemony of white print culture (" 'All the Birds Sing Bass,' "62). This intention clearly goes hand in hand with a perception shared by Sanchez, Thomas, and other Black Arts poets who understood the poem as embodied voice, spitting a liberatory fire into the minds and ears of readers and listeners. As Adriana Cavarero has argued, such an embrace of voice's stubborn physicality witnesses a thorough resistance not only to the racist ideologies that have historically governed the assumed privilege of the printed over the performed word, but to long-held patriarchal assumptions as well:

> Symptomatically, the symbolic patriarchal order that identifies the mas-culine with reason and the feminine with the body is precisely an order that privileges the semantic with respect to the vocal. In other words, even the androcentric tradition knows that the voice comes from "the vibration of a throat of flesh" and, precisely because it knows this, it catalogs the voice with the body. This voice becomes secondary, ephemeral, and inessential—reserved for women. Feminized from the start, the vocal aspect of speech and, furthermore, of song appear together as antagonistic elements in a rational, masculine sphere that centers itself, instead, on the semantic. To put it formulaically: woman sings, man thinks. (6)

As any reader of either Cortez's or Sanchez's work can tell, the hierarchy implied by the formula overlooks the life-affirming potentiality to be found in the obstinacy of flesh. Sounding such flesh through the voice's stubborn resistance to the dichotomy "woman sings, man thinks" thus poses a dissonant reading of such perspectives, one that adapts the New American poetics of breath and voice to the discursive aims of a thoroughly feminist approach to Black Arts aesthetics that would have widespread implications for male practitioners as well.

Taken together, then, Thomas, Sanchez, and Cortez witness a reimagin-ing of midcentury avant-garde poetics. Combining a projectivist attention to charting breath with a Beat enthusiasm for vocalized performance and converting these to the liberatory ambitions of Free Jazz and the physicality of Black Power politics, they devised a poetry that could consciously sound dissonant voices. By taking the revolution implicit in the New American poetics of breath and voice off the page, their work as poets engaged in the Black Arts Movement completes a crucial period in postwar American poetry, one that scholars, poets, activists, politicians, and, last but not least, listeners and readers, continue to grapple with today.

Conclusion

OUT AND GONE

In the early 1970s, as the Black Arts Movement dispersed outward from New York, San Francisco, and other metropolitan centers and formed a truly national network of writers, poets, musicians, artists, and activists, it became intertwined with local leftist institutions. As James Smethurst has written, though the Movement developed "differently from place to place," its participants found new homes by interweaving their work into "what remained of the formal and informal networks . . . of the Old Left," as well as those of "the old nationalism of Garveyites, Pan-Africanists, and so on" (*Black Arts Movement*, 368). In his return to Newark and embrace of Marxism, a similar pattern can be seen in the development of Amiri Baraka's career. As he recounts it in his 1984 *Autobiography*, the moment he and a small of group of fellow travelers emerged from the subway in Harlem in 1965 to found the Black Arts Repertory Theater, "we felt like pioneers of the new order. Back in the homeland to help raise the race" (295). Though such enthusiasm can be attributed in part to the optimism of youth, it was also, as this study has shown, clearly inspired in Baraka's case by his conflicted experiences on the Lower East Side. In retrospect, he now imagines himself as appearing to fellow Harlemites like the typical "middle class native intellectual," as a character who, "having outintegrated the most integrated, now plunges headlong back into what he perceives as blackest, native-est" (295). Of course, this revisionist portrait of the "fanatical patriot" he felt that he had become during his nationalist period was written almost two decades after he had decamped from the Village (295). By that stage in Baraka's career, the essentialism of the Black Arts Movement seemed to be at odds with his later attempts to reconstruct an integrated Popular Front, one led by a vanguard of "Blacks, Browns, Reds, Yellows + Whites" (*Hard Facts*, 5).

In terms of poetics, much had changed as well. While poets like Baraka, Thomas, Sanchez, and Cortez would continue to develop their work along the paths they had embarked upon in the 1960s, new movements—and a new avant-garde—had emerged in place of both the New American Poetry and the Black Arts Movement. While some had found a home in academia, many poets from the early 1970s through the turn-of-the-century remained on the margins as a largely a-political, self-expressive confessionalism maintained dominance despite the emergence of language poetry, conceptualism, and even flarf at one end of the spectrum, and a resurgent neo-formalism at the other. For a younger generation of African American writers inspired by the innovative poetics of the Black Arts Movement, none of these avenues offered easy admittance. Of course, in sketching such a broad outline, it should be recalled that the reasons for this situation could be as idiosyncratic as the individual poets involved. Space precludes an investigation into the range of difficulties facing even the major writers in these late-twentieth-century groupings. Still, within this general framework, I want to focus briefly here on one particular tension in the transition from the New American poetics of breath and voice to the poetics of the language poets as a way pointing beyond the horizon of this study and toward important critical work yet to be done. In framing the transition in this way, I should note that I follow Alan Golding's assessment that language poetry, like any other group or movement, is not a homogeneous field (*From Outlaw to Classic,* 151). Still, the poetics associated with language have posed special problems for African American writers. The piece considered by many practitioners to be among the very founding gestures of language poetry complicates core principles of the Black Arts' adaptation of New American poetics and so has affected subsequent discussions of the poetry studied here.

Often referenced as effecting a break between the New American poetics of breath and voice and a subsequent generation of avant-garde poets and writers, Robert Grenier's short essay "On Speech" has been read as inaugurating what has subsequently come to be termed language poetry. As Ron Silliman wrote in the introduction to his pioneering anthology of like-minded poets, *In the American Tree*, Grenier's essay marked "a new moment in American writing" (xv). Certainly, his piece attempted to break new ground. In it, Grenier writes, "why not exaggerate . . . to rid us, as creators of the world, from reiteration of the past dragged on in formal habit. I HATE SPEECH" ("On Speech," n.p.). Here, the desire to move beyond the strictures of the New American poetics of breath and voice is apparent. Creating a new world certainly necessitates breaking with old habits. "I HATE SPEECH," in fact, has subsequently formed a rallying cry for opposing the constraints imposed by the New American Poetry's emphasis on orality. As he adds in his next paragraph, "[w]e don't know the restrictions imposed by speech pattern/conventions . . . won't until a writing clears the air." Operating as such a clearing, Grenier's piece risks exaggeration in order to open up a space for new work—for an approach to writing that, aligned with a poststructuralist critique of voice, would invert the primacy of speech. Of course, it should go without saying at this point that such a position threatened also to invert the very core of both New American and Black Arts poetics, and, in doing so, further complicated the already fraught racial politics surveyed here. When speech-based poetics, and with them the jazz-inspired performance tradition cultivated by the midcentury avant-garde, lost their currency, so too did a great deal of the impetus behind earlier efforts to forge integrated poetic communities. This is not to say that interracial collaboration did not continue in some way—or that emergent avant-gardes resisted such opportunities. In many ways, Baraka's embrace of Marxism shared much in common with the social critiques of language poets like Silliman and Barrett Watten. However, as Baraka and Watten's infamous encounter at the Opening of the Field poetry conference in 2000 shows, such common ground was rarely shared.[1] For these reasons, then, a brief look at language's pivot away from the poetics of breath and voice will reveal much about the dissolution and evolution of the poetic communities studied here.

For some time, the New American poetics and, often tacitly, the Black Arts Movement's performance-based poetry, have been judged from the perspective of a somewhat narrow and uncritical interpretation of language poetry's origins in Grenier's short essay, as though shifting the attention away from speech necessitated a hostility to sound and embodiment altogether. Admittedly, the central poetic documents of the New American Poetry, from "Projective Verse" to "Notes for 'Howl'" and "How You Sound??," do privilege speech and the body via the "conventions" Grenier associates with it. Building upon William Carlos Williams's celebration of American English, which, clearly, can only be distinguished via an appeal to vernacular differences with British English, spoken language certainly became a primary concern, as has been documented throughout this study. For African American poets in the period, such attention to spoken forms became a necessary foundation in establishing a poetics that is identifiably black through its privileging of vernacular. As with the many female and homosexual poets engaged with the midcentury avant-garde, such attention to the conventions of speech, coupled with the many vibrant reading series of the time, foregrounded the unique physicality of each writer, making visible, and audible, a dissonant resistance to the dominant culture's attempts to enforce racial segregation and gender conformity. Of course, resistance to hegemony is equally—if not more so—embedded in language poetry. Language's "ludic" resistance to linguistic conventions such as "grammatical constraint," as Steve McCaffery has shown, involves an essential opposition to both traditional poetics and state control ("Language Writing," 149–50). Its manner of doing so, however—as a form of play—complicates that resistance in a way that has sometimes been seen as ignoring the full-throated activism of many New American and most Black Arts writers. As Charles Bernstein playfully puts it, in his parody of Olson's projectivist manifesto, "Introjective Verse," there are in language poetry "no realities outside the poem: no stances only dances" ("Introjective Verse," 111). At first glance, the statement can appear to waive away any concern for ideological stances or, indeed, activism in general. Taken seriously, of course, the phrase can be understood as nicely sloganizing the playfully trenchant politics at the heart of, say, Georges Bataille's general economy, or even of Asgar Jorn's pataphysical take on situationism, to name only two notable examples.

In their very serious concern for sound and intonation, language poets have not totally opposed key features of the poetics of breath and voice. Consequently, it is important here to stress what is apparent in such writing, though often missed in subsequent readings of speech-based poetics: i.e., that the materiality of speech witnesses a differential polyvocality that is every bit the vehicle for poetry that a Derridean focus on writing as *écriture* would yield, as even Grenier himself suggests ("On Speech"). As is evident in the work of African American poets from the period, the spoken can have a political valence without imposing a metaphysics of presence, without privileging speech as originary. Voices—even the vocalization of an individual at different moments and ages—necessarily engage in a play of differences, just as writing does. By coupling Adriana Cavarero's and Fred Moten's insights into voice's stubborn physicality, I have been arguing throughout for a reconsideration of voice's embodied dissonance in the work of 1950s and 1960s poets. For instance, I have attempted to demonstrate that the performance of AAVE, whether in print or at the microphone, should be read as an instance of what Stuart Hall has termed the "strategic essentialism" necessary for resistance to white hegemony ("What Is This 'Black' in Black Popular Culture?," 110). In doing so, I should emphasize that such resistance can also be conceived as play, i.e., without being imbued with a metaphysical understanding of Blackness. Something similar could be said about the deployment of American vernacular in Williams and his disciples. I would add that the popularity of public readings in the period studied here suggests that the poetics of breath and voice may be understood as strategic in another way as well: as a means of facilitating larger discussions concerning the status of alternative poetry communities at a time when access to mainstream print outlets was scant or nonexistent. Further, even when major readings were sponsored by academic institutions, such as the now legendary Berkeley poetry conference, the readings that transpired didn't often align with any clear sense of disclosing a traditional, one-dimensional performance of self-presence such as, say, that of a more popular figure like Robert Lowell would have done. From the hindsight of criticism, we might now come to view the New American Poetry's appeals to breath and voice simply as oppositional tactics suited to a particular moment in a larger culture war, despite whatever naïve assumptions writers at the time may have had · (and, to a certain degree, there was in fact a great deal confusion over the subject) concerning speech's supposed primacy. After all, for most, it was the charting of the spoken on the page that constituted a poetics of breath and voice, not so much the performance of such charts at a reading or the Heideggerian revelation of self-presence. Again, the Berkeley conference offers a prime example of this. In what has become, in retrospect, the gathering's keynote event, Charles Olson did not so much read his poetic charts as perform a freewheeling train of associational thinking. While this may belie a larger faith in the speaking moment as primary, it also complicates any easy identification of the poem's originary status with its vocal performance.

A related complication should also be brought to bear on language poetry's early attempt to differentiate itself from the New American Poetry through its opposition to speech. Though the establishment of the narrative certainly helps to differentiate language from the poetics of breath and voice, and so to situate it as the succeeding avant-garde, the boundaries in fact are not that firm. First of all, the work of many poets associated with language relies heavily on sound and performance. Consider, at one end of the spectrum, the performance poetry of Steve McCaffery, David Antin, or Jerome Rothenberg. Meanwhile, at the other end, it could be shown that even the printed poetry of language's most ardent practitioners, Ron Silliman, Charles Bernstein, Bob Perelman, Susan Howe, etc., depends on the spoken, on the reader's or listener's apprehension of subtle intonations of voice and changes of delivery for the dynamic shifts in register, disjunctive syntax, and satirical deployment of references to affect an audience. As Scott Pound has written, an irony of Grenier's famous "I HATE SPEECH" is that the passage itself attempts to score a shout through its use of all-caps ("Language Writing and the Burden of Critique," 10). Of course, none of this is meant to refute the originality, humor, or overall critique proffered by language poets, only to point out that, although the New American Poetry became at times the focus of their critical ire, such critiques could equally and, in many ways, more persuasively be made against the dominant confessional mode practiced in the United States at this time, with its heavy emphasis on personal expression.

In fact, privileging writing over speech runs the risk of recreating the very binary oppositions that these writers intend to explode. As Scott Pound has argued, many language practitioners align themselves with a Derridean critique of speech that is itself flawed in significant ways: "to name the hybrid object from this analysis *writing* (*écriture*) and by choosing to validate it in opposition to *speech*, Derrida reproduces the binary logic he had so adeptly displaced" ("Language Writing and the Burden of Critique," 17). A similar argument is made by Cavarero. As she recalls, in his reading of the *Phaedrus* Derrida deconstructs speech as the guarantor of presence and stabilizer of meaning in favor of writing as an ambiguous *pharmakon*, as both remedy and poison (*For More Than One Voice*, 228).[2] In doing so, however, she notes that his conception of speech is rooted in his earlier readings of Heidegger and Husserl, where the voice of one's interior monologue, of the Cartesian *cogito*, is revealed as the "matrix" of western metaphysics (Cavarero, 213). The autoaffection of this interior voice, the immediacy of its seeming presence, covers over, as Derrida has shown, its relationship to writing, to the play of *differánce* that troubles the phenomenological understanding of consciousness itself (Cavarero, 225). Language poets have adopted elements of this critique in their readings of projectivist and Beat poetics. However, while crediting Derrida with revealing such crucial insights, Cavarero also shows that his reading of Plato is not immune to critique. Most importantly, she argues that Derrida's understanding of voice there and elsewhere fails to take account of the shiftiness of speech itself, of the degree to which it, as opposed to interior monologue, is not, in fact, a guarantor of stable meaning precisely because it is grounded in the wayward and fragile flesh of the speaker, and the equally fallible ear of the listener: "When the silent *dia-logos* of the soul with itself is vocalized, it is transmitted into an extraneous, corporeal, unstable, untrustworthy element" (Cavarero, 232). In fact, Derrida's account misses this dialogic element in both Plato's dramatic fiction and in the everyday exchanges that feature in Cavarero's readings of voice. In doing so, it also conflates the Platonic metaphysics of the idea with the Husserlian, autoaffective conception of the interior voice of thought. Such an approach therefore misses what Cavarero calls the "polyphony" of voice's "relational horizon" by ignoring its manifold materiality (Cavarero, 234). To put it in Grenier's terms, the Derridean reading of voice risks sharing with the metaphysical tradition it seeks to deconstruct a deafness to the "[v]arious vehicle that American speech is in the different mouths of any of us" ("On Speech," n.p.).

Working within this situation, innovative African American poets writing within the Black Arts tradition have reimagined the uses of music, breath, and vernacular as a polyphonic materiality in similar ways. Doing so, however, involves bridging often unrecognized and overlooked divides in contemporary poetics. As Nathaniel Mackey has framed it, "[t]he distinction between a formally innovative willingness to incur difficulty, on the white hand, and a simple disclosure of innovative content, on the Black, is a simple or simplistic one, but nonetheless telling" ("Expanding the Repertoire," 241). As he insists, the inherent segregation at the heart of such distinctions continues to perpetuate itself, perhaps in more sophisticated ways, in critical discussions of contemporary poetics:

Racialized dichotomies between content and form, accessibility and difficulty, conventionality and innovation, and the like rest on a division of cultural labor black experimental writing has to contest and overcome. The grid of expectations enforced by such dichotomies has had a great deal of influence on the critical legitimation of African American writing and experimental writing as well, categories that are generally treated as entirely separate, nonoverlapping. ("Expanding the Repertoire," 241)

Certainly, a primary ambition of this study has been to overcome these divisions by exploring earlier attempts to do the same, whatever our estimates may be of their successes and failures. In that vein, Mackey's own writing draws together aspects of what critics often consider distinctively African American with other aspects deemed experimental, particularly in the mode of language poetry and its avant-garde successors. Drawing on perspectives aligned with performance and sound studies, his poetry and fiction have brought a musicality to procedures otherwise associated with language poetry and experimental writing. By weaving jazz perspectives into a poetics that is responsive to both the theoretical influences and technical innovations of language poetry, Mackey's work has helped to integrate the late-twentieth-century American avant-garde.

Perhaps the best place to observe these aspects of Mackey's work is in the conjunction of jazz concepts like improvisation with innovative poetic techniques, like serial composition, which itself descends from Jack Spicer and has since been incorporated in various ways by language practitioners and others. In a 2011 interview with Charles Bernstein, Mackey describes himself as a "slow improviser," explaining that he treats the process of serial composition as a form of improvisation (Mackey, "Close Listening," 00:25:50–1). Such a perspective entails seeing published writing as the amalgamation of several spontaneous performances. As Mackey notes, "I think of writing as performance. . . . I think of the words as performers too" ("Close Listening," 00:24:59–00:25:07). The implications of this are elaborated later in the interview, where he makes plain that his writing process is intended to capture the dynamic energy of an improvised performance, rather than the static clarification of a predetermined theme:

It's not, "I was trying to say something in this patch of writing that I just didn't get to," and I revise to make more clear what I was trying to say. It's usually not at that level. . . . It's feeling that there's something more there, that you don't know quite how to say what it is, but you work towards getting that more out. And that more's not necessarily a more precise statement, you know, of what was already there. It's often, and most interestingly, something else. ("Close Listening," 00:27:09–00:27:50)

In this regard, Mackey's expansive aim in revising differs significantly from the standard proofreading and clarification, as well as from earlier attempts by poets studied here to chart the voice. As he says later, it involves, instead, looking for "clues within the writing itself," for openings, for "[s]omething you hadn't noticed before" ("Close Listening," 00:27:58–00:28:03). This approach certainly resonates with aspects of jazz improvisation, where often scales and melodies are deconstructed and reconstructed, altered, pushed further out, and then revisited in new and unforeseen ways. It also elaborates, in unique ways, the "introjective" ambitions of Bernstein and others through its recurrent focus on playing and re-playing the text. As Adalaide Morris observes, such work demonstrates "Operatic Tilt," an "improvisatory, self-reflexive, over-the-top poetics" Mackey shares with peers and predecessors like H.D. (Morris, "Angles of Incidence / Angels of Dust," 235). A similar process is at work in Mackey's understanding of serial improvisation:

New stuff comes out of revision, you re-see, you revisit, certainly, and that's part of it, but that re-visitation, you know, can take where you were before into an unpredictable place. So, part of what I mean by saying I'm a slow improviser is to say that it is *all* improvisation. It's not as though at one point I have a score and then I go off from that. ("Close Listening," 00:28:33–00:29:02)

Here, Mackey attests to a larger poetics of improvisation, to an understanding of the very process of composition as an improvised performance. By insisting that "it is *all* improvisation," Mackey directs the reader to understand his writing as performance, with the concomitant requirement that it be experienced, interacted with, rather than passively read, in a manner akin to the readerly expectations that many language poets, including Bernstein, describe in their critical work ("Close Listening," 00:28:53–00:28:57).

Connections between poetry and improvised performance can be traced through Mackey's other comments on the subject as well. As early as 1991, in an interview with Edward Foster, Mackey described his own writing as modeled on the example of Cecil Taylor, whose music he calls "improvisational" (Mackey, *Paracritical Hinge*, 278).[3] Responding to a question about the apparently Jamesian nature of his writing, Mackey redirects the conversation toward Taylor and the practice of improvisation:

> When you talk about this particular mix of formal writing—formal in a kind of Jamesian way—that is extolling and explicating music whose key ethic is improvisational, constant redefinition of the formal, I think of Cecil Taylor, who, in his way of accommodating that conservatory, academic background of his with the improvisational tradition that his music is performed in the context of, would be one of the models that I have had in mind. I'm post-bebop. (*Paracritical Hinge*, 278–79)

Treating Taylor, rather than Henry James, as a model requires thinking of improvisation in an analogical way. What I want to focus on here, however, is the phrase "post-bebop." Distinguishing the jazz influence on his work from that of New American poets like Creeley and Ginsberg, Mackey's free jazz inspiration is in line with many writers in the Black Arts tradition. Yet, as opposed to their frequent references to historical jazz figures like Duke Ellington and Billie Holiday, or celebration of pivotal ones like Charlie Parker in the many poems dedicated to him, Mackey's references typically draw on the work of the most avant-garde of the 1960s' "new thing," on Taylor, Anthony Braxton, and Don Cherry. In this way, he situates his writing as post-bop, as post-New American Poetry, in ways that complicate the relationship between later experimental writing and Black music.

Similarly, Mackey's understanding of improvisation can be applied to several aspects of his poetry, through what he has referred to as the "itineracy endemic to the medium" (Mackey, *Splay Anthem*, x). Such elements require the reader to participate in the performance of reading, to improvise, in fact, a meaning, in a manner akin to the endless deferment theorized by Derrida and incorporated, playfully, in language's "Introjective Verse." Like the band of nomads who travel throughout Mackey's serial poetry, overarching interpretations must be abandoned in favor of the partial and provisional. The result is a poetry that explores postmodern poetics through heeding

Coltrane's directive, heard in the Sun Ship sessions, that his fellow performers "keep, keep, you know, keep a *thing* happening all thru it" (Coltrane, as quoted in *Atet A.D.,* volume 3 of Mackey's *From a Broken Bottle*, 526). This sense of constant movement, of Derridean *différance*, is most clearly evident in the fact that the travelers seek, but never arrive, at their destination. In this way, a new leg of the journey must always be improvised in place of their sought-after arrival.

Mackey's first full-length collection, *Eroding Witness*, in fact, features his initial work on the two serial poems that have preoccupied his career: *Song of the Andoumboulou* and *"Mu."* Even the epistolary fiction that comprises his multivolume work *From a Broken Bottle Traces of Perfume Still Emanate* finds its beginnings here in the sixth and seventh sections of *Song of the Andoumboulou*. In pursuing a postmodern poetic, both pieces take their cue from recordings: *Song of the Andoumboulou* from *Les Dogon*, a 1956 recording of West African Dogon music made by François Di Dio, as noted by Mackey in *Eroding Witness* (31), and *"Mu,"* from a two-part recording of the same name by trumpeter Don Cherry (Mackey, *Eroding Witness,* 60). As such, the poems broach concerns regarding the African diaspora and situate their content in a transnational, and transhistorical, context. The epigraph to the first *Song of the Andoumboulou* conveys this situation well:

> The song of the Andoumboulou is addressed to the spirits. For this reason the initiates, crouching in a circle, sing it in a whisper in the deserted village, and only the howling of dogs and the wind disturb the silence of the night. (François Di Dio, quoted in *Eroding Witness*, 31)

In an instance of what the poet Will Alexander has termed Mackey's "archetypal Nubia," a kind of imagined community emerges, one perpetually calling, yet perpetually out of reach, as a microcosm of the larger ambitions, and problems, embodied by Mackey's serial poems (Alexander, "An ashen finesse," 702). The desire to sing for the dead, to give them a voice, is fraught with difficulties that can never be fully resolved, just as the travelers of the poems never fully arrive. As section one has it, the dead may "get / our throats," but, as section seven admits, the whole endeavor may also prove to be nothing more than "courting a lack" (Mackey, *Eroding Witness,* 33, 54). The proliferation of voices, and of perspectives, gives the self-reflexive passages of the series a kind of call-and-response effect. Like the call-and-response of a Ring Shout, or the metaphorical form of it that takes place when multiple instruments respond to each other's improvisations in jazz, these passages reopen and reimagine themes hinted at or touched on earlier—as though the living were singing to the dead who, in turn, respond through the throats of the living, in a swirl of experience that troubles any attempt to claim a precise beginning or ending.

Such elements are evident even earlier, in *Song of the Andoumboulou: 6*. The section itself will be reworked later, as Mackey revisits the epistolary form for his first novel, *Bedouin Hornbook*. Now, however, it plays backward, revisiting the unsung, or only partially sounded, source of *Song of the Andoumboulou: 3*:

> Dear Angel of Dust,
>
> In one of your earlier letters, the one you wrote in response to *Song of the Andoumboulou: 3*, you spoke of sorting out "what speaks of speaking of something, and what (more valuably) speaks *from* something, i.e., where the source is available, becomes a re-source rather than something evasive, elusive, sought after." Well, what I wanted to say then was this: We not only can but should speak of "loss" or, to avoid quotation marks notwithstanding, any such inkling of self-pity, speak of *absence* as unavoidably an inherence in the texture of things (dream-seed, habitual cloth). (Mackey, *Eroding Witness*, 50)

The passage is remarkable for its ability to reimagine the earlier piece while also engaging the reader in a habit of reading unique to serial poetry. As a stand-in for the imagined addressee, the reader can either acquiesce in the "Angel of Dust" moniker, the one who really does "seem to believe in, to hold out for some first or final gist underlying it all," or, following "N.," a kind of authorial cipher, embrace "that very absence," who appears as "an unlikely Other whose inconceivable occupancy glimpses of ocean beg access to" (*Eroding Witness*, 50). Whereas the Angel of Dust looks for a clear "source" to be made present and so provide an origin from which to understand the series, N. insists that the absence or inaccessibility of such a source is precisely what needs to be told. Unmoored, the poems then journey endlessly toward a goal that, though it can never be abandoned, can never be fully attained. Certainly, a form of Derridean *différance* is evident in the nomadic drift of the writer's improvised response. As N. playfully concludes the letter, "Not 're-source' so much for me as re: Source," re-turning upon the Angel of Dust's words from the opening in a phrase that gestures toward, rather than seeks to make present, an absent source (*Eroding Witness*, 50). In all of these ways, then, Mackey's work complicates the approaches to voice found in earlier Black Arts and New American poets. His writing functions as a bridge between a performance tradition and musical inspiration common to Black Arts and New American poetics, as well as to a Derridean aesthetic apparent in the work of language and other innovative poets who succeeded them.

In this, however, Mackey is not alone. Though space precludes a deeper investigation into the host of poets whose writing also works this ground, Harryette Mullen's poetry adds an important instance. Especially helpful in this regard is her deployment of vernacular speech in *Muse & Drudge*. While her early work, even more so than Mackey's, witnesses a Black Arts inheritance, her writing post-*Trimmings* evidences the growing influence of language and innovative poetics in general on her compositional approach. *Muse & Drudge*, as she has indicated, attempts an integration between the two inspirations by way of response to a critical quandary:

> The assumption remains, however unexamined, that "avant-garde" poetry is not "black" and that "black" poetry, however singular its "voice," is not "formally innovative." It is my hope that *Muse & Drudge* . . . might alter or challenge that assumption, bridging what apparently has been imagined as a gap (or chasm?) between my work as a "black" poet and my work as a "formally innovative" poet. ("Poetry and Identity," 12)

Seeking, therefore, to overcome the "[r]acialized dichotomies" and the "grid of expectations" identified by Mackey, Mullen situates *Muse & Drudge* as a "bridge" between the supposedly separate, (mis)perceived poles of African American writing and innovative poetics (Mackey, "Expanding the Repertoire," 241). Like Mackey, Mullen too draws on the vast resources of Black music to form this bridge. In *Muse & Drudge*, as she notes, "I have been influenced by instrumental and vocal improvisations of blues and jazz musicians" ("Kinky Quatrains," 16). The question of voice thus returns to the fore. Rather than imagine her poetics as jazz performance in the sense of Sonia Sanchez or Jayne Cortez, however, Mullen instead employs an inherited form, the quatrain, in order to open up possibilities for multiple registers and vocal textures:

I was attracted to the form primarily because I saw that . . . I could make these four-line stanzas quirky, irregular, and sensuously kinky in terms of polyrhythm (as opposed to regular meter) and polyvocality (as opposed to the persistence of a single lyric voice or narrative viewpoint). ("Kinky Quatrains," 16)

Mullen's description grounds *Muse & Drudge* in a poetics of voice that nonetheless eschews any naïve assumptions concerning authorial intention or a metaphysics of presence. Voice here is spliced through "a wide range of lexical choice," "the various possibilities of rhyming or not rhyming," "'found poetry,'" and "semantic and syntactic tensions within and between lines" ("Kinky Quatrains," 16). All of these strategies are marshalled in opposition to "the persistence of a single lyric voice," thereby differentiating her approach from that of earlier poets working in the same traditions. Her larger discussion of *Muse & Drudge*'s cross-cultural influences makes plain her intention for the poem to function as a bridge:

Some of the lines I write aspire to certain moments in jazz when scat becomes a kind of inspired speaking in tongues, or glossolalia, moments when utterance is pure music. Improvisatory methods I have used in poetry also follow from my interest in the literary techniques and experiments of Oulipo, as well as Saussure's investigation of anagrammatic, tabular readings of poetic texts. ("Kinky Quatrains," 16–17)

Such "pure music" thus combines jazz performance techniques with avant-garde experiments, effectively bridging the "gap (or chasm?)" between African American and innovative writing (Mullen, "Poetry and Identity," 12). Even the poets she mentions exhibit this tendency, from Steve McCaffery and Bernadette Mayer, on one hand, to Paul Laurence Dunbar, Langston Hughes, Margaret Walker, and Gwendolyn Brooks, to list only a few, on the other ("Kinky Quatrains," 17). The result is a poem that, by intention and ambition, attempts to overcome the persistent segregation of Black and innovative writing traditions through a thoroughly integrated poetics of voice. In a nod toward previous attempts to do the same, Mullen credits Lorenzo Thomas's example as "most influential," praising him for his "attention to the communal drum," adding that his "commitment to his own offbeat solo music demonstrates the flexibility of traditions, forms, and genres in the hands of an adept aesthetic innovator" ("Kinky Quatrains," 17). Certainly, the same attention and commitment is apparent in *Muse & Drudge*.

Several stanzas and passages from it could be drawn as examples. From the very beginning, in fact, the reader's attention is drawn to the musicality of shifting speech registers:

> Sapphire's lyre styles
> plucked eyebrows
> bow lips and legs
> whose lives are lonely too
>
> my last nerve's lucid music
> sure chewed up the juicy fruit
> you must don't like my peaches
> there's some left on the tree. (*Muse & Drudge*, 1)

While introducing the poem's main subject, Sapphire, a contemporary character whose identity is doubled, mixed with the ancient Greek poet Sappho, the opening stanzas move through layers of consonance and alliteration, reproducing a music akin to hip-hop and replete with a vernacular resistance to grammatical conventions ("you must don't like"). In this way, the poem plays with conventions of voice and musicality established in popular song, in African American poetry, and in postmodern conceptions of innovative poetics. This updating, then, of the aesthetic traced throughout this study is encapsulated well in a metapoetic moment that occurs later in *Muse & Drudge*, one where Sapphire is described as an innovative, post-language poet of sound:

> hooked on phonemes imbued with exuberance
> our spokeswoman listened for lines
> heard tokens of quotidian
> corralled in ludic routines. (*Muse & Drudge*, 49)

Like Bernstein's "introjective" poet, Sapphire is "hooked" on language games, on "phonemes" and "ludic routines." And yet, at the same time, like a projectivist or Black Arts poet, she "corralled" her poetry from the "heard . . . quotidian," from the sounds of everyday life. Whereas this passage seems to emphasize the experimental side of the poem without any clear reference to race, others highlight the distinctly African American take on experiment attempted by Mullen and presented throughout as a bridge.

In fact, the muse of the poem appears as a cross between Sappho, blues matriarchs like Ma Rainey, and hip-hop idols like LL Cool J's "Around the Way Girl." The latter—the "extensions" wearing, "street slang" talking, "real independent" woman celebrated in his 1990 hit—appears to be referenced early in Mullen's piece:

> fixing her lips to sing
> hip strutters ditty bop
> hand-me-down dance of ample
> style stance and substance
>
> black-eyed pearl
> around the world girl
> somebody's anybody's
> yo-yo fulani
>
> occult iconic crow
> solo mysterioso
> flying way out
> on the other side of far. (*Muse & Drudge*, 40)

Here, the allusion to LL Cool J expands a frame of reference beyond the muse whom "poets salute . . . with haiku" to include the contemporary "stance and substance" of an "around the world girl," someone, in other words, whose persona echoes and expands the character of the song, stretching back into world history and beyond to present someone dwelling "on the other side of far" (*Muse & Drudge*, 40). This composite, elusive character shrugs off the burden of her role as cross-cultural and transhistorical muse by remaining at the vanguard of inspiration. As Mullen has written, quoting this very passage, *"Muse & Drudge* . . . locates itself in a space where it is possible to pay dues, respects, and 'props' to tradition while still claiming the freedom to wander to the other side of far" ("Kinky Quatrains," 17). Such combinations thus situate an empowered, resonant form of Black femininity at the horizon, at the far-out edge of avant-garde composition, successfully bridging the gap between the two.

From the outset, the poets surveyed in this study all share a perspective that continues to inspire the work of contemporary writers like Mullen and Mackey, namely, that any distinctively American avant-garde must necessarily draw from the vanguard of African American cultural expression. Early on, white poets like Charles Olson, Robert Creeley, Allen Ginsberg, and Jack Spicer consistently sought to imbue their poetics with compositional strategies drawn from jazz, and particularly the bebop of Charlie Parker, as a way of both distinguishing their work from modernist predecessors and also grounding their writing in postwar American culture. In doing so, they benefitted greatly from African American writers like Bob Kaufman, Amiri Baraka, and Stephen Jonas. Meanwhile, poets like John Wieners, Ed Dorn, and others, continued to develop Black Mountain and Beat poetics along these lines, basing their own careers on the inspiration drawn from interracial friendships and a shared enthusiasm for jazz. At the heart of these encounters was a commitment to poetry as the charting of breath and voice, to the poetic page as a score for performance. This particular aspect was seized upon by Umbra and Black Arts poets like Lorenzo Thomas and Sonia Sanchez in their negotiations of the oppositional materiality of African American voices. Such embodied dissonance can be seen more fully in the work of Jayne Cortez, whose poetry and song lyrics blur the line between the spoken and the written, thereby forging a poetics at once distinctive of a Black Arts Movement performance tradition while at the same time realizing the deeper inspirations of the New American Poetry. As this study has shown, the integrative efforts working this narrative arc shaped an essential strand of innovative poetry in midcentury America.

Poets at the time did not take this for granted. Consider, for instance, Amiri Baraka's appearance in the posthumously published third volume of Charles Olson's *Maximus Poems*. In a haunting moment documented in a section dated February 11, 1966, Olson finds himself identifying his own working-class, immigrant background with the struggles of Baraka (then LeRoi Jones) and others:

. . . my father a Swedish
wave of
migration after
Irish? like Negroes
now like Leroy [*sic*] and Malcolm
X the final wave

of wash upon this
desperate
ugly
cruel
Land this Nation
which never
lets anyone
come to
shore. (*Maximus*, III.118–19)

The frustration evident here aligns Olson at once with Jones and the then recently assassinated Malcolm X. Though admittedly hyperbolic in one sense—neither LeRoi's nor Malcolm's ancestors came to the U.S. as part of a "wave of / migration," at least not in the sense that Olson's father did—the solidarity expressed appears nonetheless genuine. In this way, the passage also looks back at the broken friendship with Baraka, then removed to Harlem, with some sense of revisionist clarity. The passage goes on to angrily question "how many waves . . . of hurt and punished lives" shall be necessary before America can become the egalitarian nation it purports to be (*Maximus*, III.120). At this time, of course, Baraka had embarked upon the pioneering work of helping to "raise the race" as part of the Black Arts Movement (*Autobiography*, 295). Olson, meanwhile, was left to contemplate what he termed their "genetic failure," as though, in their opposition to segregation and embrace of the avant-garde, their poetic successes marked distinctively American forms of failure (*Maximus*, III.120). Though the passages occupy a small portion of a larger meditation upon his father, clearly Olson felt a paternal responsibility for Baraka's poetic path as well, perhaps as some lingering need to set straight the record of their abbreviated friendship.

Near the end of his own life, Baraka would find himself doing much the same. Shortly before his death in January 2014, Baraka gave the Charles Olson lecture at the Cape Ann Museum in Gloucester, titling it "Charles Olson and Sun Ra: A Note on the Out." In it, he celebrated Olson as an anti-imperialist leader of the American counterculture, singling out a passage from "Song 3," in the first volume of *The Maximus Poems*, in particular:

In the land of plenty, have
nothing to do with it

take the way of
the lowest,

including
your legs, go
contrary, go

sing. (*Maximus*, I.15)

Imploring the reader to drop out of middle-class ambition, to "have / nothing to do with it," Olson's writing here realizes a perspective akin to Baraka's Marxism. The anti-capitalist stance of the poem exhibits something like the "genetic failure" that Olson himself would pen later (*Maximus*, III.120). For Baraka, such choices create solidarity among the "out and gone," witnessing an anti-imperialist ethic that is every bit as radical as the poetics in which it is presented ("Olson and Sun Ra," 00:15:19–00:16:01). The freedom that "Projective Verse" granted to "break down the restrictions of literary, closed verse," offering instead the opportunity to compose out of the manifold materiality of "your breath," proved pivotal for Baraka and other poets of his generation ("Olson and Sun Ra," 00:07:43–00:08:05).

Such conceptions, moreover, linked Olson's poetics, in Baraka's mind, with the advances of avant-garde jazz. As he notes, like Sun Ra, who changed his name in the same year that Olson arrived at Black Mountain, Olson too understood "space" as integral to his larger aesthetic; the space of the page, with its open field, parallels in many ways to Sun Ra's otherworldly sounds ("Olson and Sun Ra," 00:13:33–00:14:20). The Arkestra, in fact, as its name suggests, harbored listeners during a turbulent time, availing itself of interstellar metaphors as a way of conjuring other worlds, replete with alternative systems of value. In this way, Ra's space jazz parallels Olson's meditations on the polis's imagined community. For Baraka, both proved to be ways of dropping out of a corrupt, racist society and creating alternative spaces for new forms of living. In this way, as he concludes the lecture by noting, together "Olson and Sun Ra were the perfect mentors" for a young poet at midcentury ("Olson and Sun Ra," 00:22:45–00:22:51). In fact, Baraka insists that if we want to understand the relationship between jazz and the innovative poetry of the 1950s and 1960s, to truly integrate postwar poetics, we have to attune ourselves to the dissonant voices sounded in the very texture of their performance.

Notes

PREFACE. INTEGRATING BLACK MOUNTAIN

1. For an introduction to the abundant scholarship on Ezra Pound's infamous association with Italian Fascism, see, for instance, Tim Redman, *Ezra Pound and Italian Fascism* (Cambridge: Cambridge University Press, 1991), and the more recent discussion in A. David Moody's *Ezra Pound: Poet*, vol. 2, *The Epic Years* (Oxford: Oxford University Press, 2018). For further information on the Bauhaus's complex political alignments, see Elaine S. Hochman's *Architects of Fortune: Mies van der Rohe and the Third Reich* (New York: Grove Press, 1989) and Elizabeth Otto's *Haunted Bauhaus: Occult Spirituality, Gender Fluidity, Queer Identities, and Radical Politics* (Cambridge, MA: MIT Press, 2019).

INTRODUCTION. DISSONANT VOICES

1. See also Garrett Stewart, *Reading Voices: Literature and the Phonotext* (Oakland: University of California Press, 1990).

2. See, for example, Stanley Cavell, *Philosophy the Day after Tomorrow* (Cambridge, MA: Harvard University Press, 2005); Shoshana Felman, *The Scandal of the Speaking Body: Don Juan with J. L. Austin, or Seduction in Two Languages* (Stanford, CA: Stanford University Press, 2002); and Judith Butler, *Giving an Account of Oneself* (New York: Fordham University Press, 2005).

3. See both Baraka's *Blues People: The Negro Experience in White America and the Music That Developed from It* (New York: William Morrow, 1963), written under the name LeRoi Jones, and "The Changing Same (R&B and New Black Music)," in *Black Music* (New York: William Morrow, 1967), 180–211.

4. See David R. Roediger, *The Wages of Whiteness: Race and the Making of the American Working Class*, new ed. (New York and London: Verso, 2007).

5. See Andrew Epstein, *Beautiful Enemies: Friendship and Postwar American Poetry* (Oxford: Oxford University Press, 2009), and Michael Magee, *Emancipating*

Pragmatism: Emerson, Jazz, and Experimental Writing (Tuscaloosa: University of Alabama Press, 2004).

CHAPTER ONE. FORM IS NEVER MORE
THAN AN EXTENSION OF BIRD

1. I have used the abbreviation *O & C Cor*, with accompanying volume and page number, for excerpts from Charles Olson and Robert Creeley, *Charles Olson & Robert Creeley: The Complete Correspondence*, ed. George F. Butterick and Richard Belvins, 10 vols. (Boston, MA: Black Sparrow Press, 1980–1996).

2. Charles Olson, "Projective Verse," *Poetry New York*, no. 3 (1950).

3. See Joseph Pizza, "All That Is Lovely in Jazz: The Creeley-Rice Collaboration for Jargon 10," *Journal of Black Mountain College Studies* 9 (2019).

4. For example, consider the standard histories by Gary Giddens, *Visions of Jazz: The First Century* (Oxford: Oxford University Press, 1998), and Ted Gioia, *The History of Jazz*, 2nd ed., (Oxford: Oxford University Press, 2011), as well as the perspectives gathered in Nat Shapiro and Nat Hentoff, *Hear Me Talkin' to Ya: The Story of Jazz as Told by the Men Who Made It* (New York: Dover, 1966), and the essay collection *The Jazz Cadence of American Culture*, edited by Robert G. O'Meally (New York: Columbia University Press, 1998).

5. See Amiri Baraka [LeRoi Jones], *Black Music* (New York: William Morrow, 1967).

6. Use of the common abbreviation *sic* for "thus" to indicate that material has been reproduced as originally written, regardless of any seeming stylistic, typographical, or grammatical error, has proven especially difficult in this study. Given the regular use of irregular spellings, spacings, indentations, and punctuation marks among innovative poets in this period, I have attempted to keep employment of the abbreviation to a minimum. As such, my policy has been to use it only where such deviations from current conventions seem likely to confuse readers.

7. For further details on bebop's cultural and musical revolution, see Scott DeVeaux, *The Birth of Bebop: A Social and Musical History* (Oakland: University of California Press, 1997), and Ingrid Monson, *Freedom Sounds: Civil Rights Call Out to Jazz and Africa* (Oxford: Oxford University Press, 2010).

8. See Eric Lott, *Love and Theft: Blackface Minstrelsy and the American Working Class* (Oxford: Oxford University Press, 1993).

9. Norman Mailer, "The White Negro: Superficial Reflections on the Hipster," *Dissent* 4 (1957): 276–93.

10. See Norman Mailer, *Advertisements for Myself* (New York: G. P. Putnam's Sons, 1959).

11. For discussions of Parker's technique of extending and reworking standards, see his own comments in *Hear Me Talkin' to Ya: The Story of Jazz as Told by the Men Who Made It*, ed. Nat Shapiro and Nat Hentoff (New York: Dover, 1966), 354–55; and, for the evolution of "Scrapple from the Apple," see Ted Gioia, *The Jazz Standards: A Guide to the Repertoire* (Oxford: Oxford University Press, 2012), 360–61.

12. For discussion of Olson's reception in Britain, see my recent article, "Continental Drift: Charles Olson and *The English Intelligencer*," *Contemporary Literature* 59, no. 3 (2018): 277–307.

13. For the Wilde reference implicit in the phrase "especially wish i had sd," see Oscar Wilde's famous exchange with J. M. Whistler, " 'I wish I had said that.' 'You will, Oscar, you will,' " recounted in Leonard Cresswell Ingleby, *Oscar Wilde, Some Reminiscences* (London: T. W. Laurie, 1907), 67.

14. Charles Olson, *The Mayan Letters*, ed. Robert Creeley (Littleton, NH: Divers Press, 1954).

15. See Heriberto Yépez, *The Empire of Neomemory*, trans. Jen Hofer, Christian Nagler, and Brian Whitener (N.p.: Chainlink, 2013).

16. On Holiday's use of syncopation, see, for example, Scott DeVeaux and Gary Giddens, *Jazz: Essential Listening* (New York: W. W. Norton, 2011), 179–80, or Ted Gioia, *The History of Jazz*, 2nd ed. (Oxford: Oxford University Press, 2011), 165–66.

17. Passages from this section have appeared previously in Joseph Pizza, "All That Is Lovely in Jazz: The Creeley-Rice Collaboration for Jargon 10," *Journal of Black Mountain College Studies* 9 (2019).

18. For further background information, see chapters seventeen and twenty-one of Ekbert Faas and Maria Trombacco, *Robert Creeley: A Biography* (Lebanon: University Press of New England, 2001), 151–62, 188–96.

19. On Creeley's creative mishearing of William Carlos Williams, see his letter to the editors of *Sagetrieb* 9, nos. 1–2 (1990): 270–71. For the "Rock Drill #3" performance, see the Robert Creeley page at *Pennsound*, Center for Programs in Contemporary Writing, University of Pennsylvania, accessed September 9, 2019, http://writing.upenn.edu/pennsound/x/Creeley.php.

20. Listen, for instance, to Miles Davis, trumpeter, "Moon Dreams," recorded March 9, 1950, track 3 on *Birth of the Cool*, released in 1956 on Capitol Records.

21. See, for instance, the use of traditional terms for feet and meter in the Charles Olson essay "Projective Verse," in *Collected Prose*, ed. Donald Allen and Benjamin Friedlander, introd. Robert Creeley (Oakland: University of California Press, 1997), 239–49.

22. For a useful discussion of the reader's perception of absent beats in poetic rhythm, see Derek Attridge, *The Rhythms of English Poetry* (London and New York: Routledge, 1982).

1. See Joseph Torra's introduction to *Arcana: A Stephen Jonas Reader*, ed. Garrett Caples, et al. (San Francisco: City Lights Books, 2019), 17–27, and Aldon Lynn Nielsen's essay "No Saints in Three Acts: Stephen Jonas" in his volume *Integral Music: Languages of African American Innovation* (Tuscaloosa: University of Alabama Press, 2004), 59–97.

2. See, additionally, Nathaniel Mackey's discussion of *duende* in "Limbo, Dislocation, and Phantom Limb: Wilson Harris and the Caribbean Occasion," in *Discrepant Engagement* (Tuscaloosa: University of Alabama Press, 1993), 162–79.

3. See Frank O'Hara, "The Day That Lady Died," *Lunch Poems* (San Francisco: City Lights Books, 1964), 25–26.

4. Take for example Wieners's poem "Like a Rolling Stone," from the 1965 journal titled "Blaauwildebeestefontein," where he laments that "these people [his family] have / crushed me" in *Stars Seen in Person: Selected Journals*, edited by Michael Seth Stewart (San Francisco: City Lights Books, 2015), 102–3.

5. See Lori Chamberlain, "Ghostwriting the Text: Translation and the Poetics of Jack Spicer," *Contemporary Literature* 26, no. 4 (1985): 426–42; and Daniel Katz, "Jack Spicer's *After Lorca*: Translation as Decomposition," *Textual Practice* 18, no. 1 (2004): 83–103.

6. See the transcript of this discussion, collected as "Duende, Muse, and Angel," in Charles Olson, *Muthologos*, ed. Ralph Maud (Vancouver, BC: Talon Books, 2010), 63–75.

7. Here, I'd like to thank the anonymous second reader of this manuscript for the encouragement to consider whether or not a "Bird Poem" had developed prior to, or in parallel with, the better-known Coltrane poem of the Black Arts Movement.

8. See Clayton Eshleman, "The Lorca Working," *Boundary 2: An International Journal of Literature and Culture* 6, no. 1 (1977): 31–50.

9. For quotations in Lorca's Spanish, I have used the bilingual edition of *The Selected Poems of Federico García Lorca*, ed. Francisco García Lorca and Donald M. Allen (New York: New Directions, 1955). As Lorca's brother makes plain in the preface, the texts presented here were reproductions from manuscripts and the earliest published editions.

CHAPTER THREE. HOWLING PARKER

1. See Nancy McCampbell Grace, "A White Man in Love: A Study of Race, Gender, Class, and Ethnnicity in Jack Kerouac's *Maggie Cassady, The Subterraneans,* and *Tristessa*," in *The Beat Generation: Critical Essays*, ed. Kostas Myrsiades (New York: Peter Lang, 2002), 95–120.

2. For the details of Dylan's gift to Ginsberg, I am indebted to Lytle Shaw's discussion of *The Fall of America* in his *Narrowcast: Poetry and Audio Research* (Stanford, CA: Stanford University Press, 2018), 35–36.

3. See James Smethurst, " 'Remembering When Indians Were Red': Bob Kaufman, the Popular Front, and the Black Arts Movement," *Callaloo: A Journal of African Diaspora Arts and Letters* 25, no. 1 (2002): 146–64; and Amor Kohli, "Saxophones and Smothered Rage: Bob Kaufman, Jazz, and the Quest for Redemption," *Callaloo: A Journal of African Diaspora Arts and Letters* 25, no. 1 (2002): 165–82.

CHAPTER FOUR. BROADENING THE VOICE

1. See, for instance, his discussion of the "aesthetic analogies" jazz had provided to midcentury visual art and literature, in LeRoi Jones [Amiri Baraka], *Blues People: The Negro Experience in White America and the Music That Developed from It* (New York: William Morrow, 1963), 233–34.

2. See, for example, two early studies of Baraka: Kimberly Benston, *Amiri Baraka: The Renegade Mask* (New Haven, CT: Yale University Press, 1976), and Werner Sollors, *Amiri Baraka/LeRoi Jones: The Quest for a Populist Modernism* (New York: Columbia University Press, 1978).

3. See Nathaniel Mackey, "The Changing Same: Black Music in the Poetry of Amiri Baraka," in his *Discrepant Engagement: Dissonance, Cross-Culturality, and Experimental Writing* (Tuscaloosa: University of Alabama Press, 1993), 22–48. For Baraka's essay, see LeRoi Jones [Amiri Baraka], "The Changing Same (R&B and New Black Music)," in *Black Music* (New York: William Morrow, 1968), 180–211.

4. See Fred Moten, *In the Break: The Aesthetics of the Black Radical Tradition* (Minneapolis: University of Minnesota Press, 2003).

5. I have explored Dan Rice's jazz-inspired work in greater detail in the following: Joseph Pizza, "All That Is Lovely in Jazz: The Creeley-Rice Collaboration for Jargon 10," *Journal of Black Mountain College Studies* 9 (2019).

6. See Tom Clark, *Charles Olson: The Allegory of a Poet's Life* (Berkeley, CA: North Atlantic Books, 2000), 46.

7. For this fact I am indebted to Nathaniel Mackey's "Breath and Precarity: The Inaugural Robert Creeley Lecture in Poetry and Poetics," where he notes the source: LeRoi Jones [Amiri Baraka], "Statement," *New American Story*, ed. Donald M. Allen and Robert Creeley (New York: Grove Press, 1965), 267–68.

8. For a first-hand account of the trial, see Charles Rembar, *The End of Obscenity: The Trials of Lady Chatterley, Tropic of Cancer, and Fanny Hill* (New York: Random House, 1968).

CHAPTER FIVE. SPITTING FIRE

1. Passages from this section have appeared previously in "Spitting Fire: Black Mountain and the Black Arts Movement in the Poetry of Jayne Cortez," *Journal of Black Mountain College Studies* 12 (2021).

2. For the biographical details used in this section, I have drawn from the account of Pozo's life in Ted Gioia, *The History of Jazz*, 2nd ed. (Oxford: Oxford University Press, 2011), 205–7, unless otherwise cited.

3. The Firespitters, "I See Chano Pozo," recorded July 1982, track 3 on *There It Is*, Bola Press, vinyl LP.

4. Consider Cortez's "I See Chano Pozo," *Coagulations: New and Selected Poems* (New York: Thunder's Mouth Press, 1984), 65–67, alongside the Firespitters, "I See Chano Pozo," *There It Is*, Bola Press, 1982, vinyl LP.

CONCLUSION. OUT AND GONE

1. See, for instance, Mark Nowak's brief account of the exchange in his recently published *Social Poetics* (Minneapolis, MN: Coffee House Press, 2020), 109.

2. See Jacques Derrida, *Dissemination*, trans. Barbara Johnson (Chicago: University of Chicago Press, 1981).

3. Since they are not given titles, I have cited all excerpts from interviews published in the prose collection *Paracritical Hinge* by book title and page number.

Works Cited

Adorno, Theodor. "The Curves of the Needle." In *Essays on Music*, 271–76. Translated by Thomas Y. Levin. Selected by Richard Leppert. Oakland: University of California Press, 2002.

Alexander, Will. "An ashen finesse." *Callaloo* 23, no. 2 (2000): 700–2.

Alighieri, Dante. *La Commedia secondo l'antica vulgata*. 3 vols. Edited by Giorgio Petrocchi. Segrate (Milano), Italy: Mondadori, 1966–1967.

Allison, Raphael. *Bodies on the Line: Performance and the Sixties Poetry Reading*. Iowa City: University of Iowa Press, 2014.

Arendt, Hannah. *The Human Condition*. Chicago: University of Chicago Press, 1958.

Attali, Jacques. *Noise: The Political Economy of Music*. Translated by Brian Massumi. Minneapolis: University of Minnesota Press, 1985.

Attridge, Derek. *The Rhythms of English Poetry*. London and New York: Routledge, 1982.

Baldwin, James. "The Black Boy Looks at the White Boy." In *Collected Essays*, 269–85. New York: Library of America, 1998.

Baraka, Amiri. *The Autobiography of LeRoi Jones*. Brooklyn: Lawrence Hill Books, 1997.

Baraka, Amiri. *Black Music*. New York: William Morrow, 1968.

Baraka, Amiri. "Cecil Taylor (*The World of Cecil Taylor*)." In Baraka, *Black Music*, 110–12.

Baraka, Amiri. "Charles Olson and Sun Ra." *YouTube*, uploaded by Ferrini Productions, October 28, 2013. https://www.youtube.com /watch?v=WWx6Sp6YSm4.

Baraka, Amiri. *The Dead Lecturer*. New York: Grove Press, 1964.

Baraka, Amiri. "Ed Dorn and the Western World." In *Amiri Baraka and Edward Dorn: The Collected Letters*, edited by Claudia Moreno Pisano, xiii–xxiv. Albuquerque: University of New Mexico Press, 2013.

Baraka, Amiri. *Hard Facts*. Newark, NJ: Revolutionary Communist League, 1975.

Baraka, Amiri. "'Howl' and Hail." *American Poetry Review* 35, no. 2 (2006): 8–9.

Baraka, Amiri. "Sonny Rollins (*Our Man in Jazz*)." In Baraka, *Black Music*, 52–55.

Baraka, Amiri. "Technology & Ethos." In *Raise Race Rays Raze: Essays Since 1965*, 155–57. New York: Random House, 1969.

Baraka, Amiri [LeRoi Jones]. "*An Agony. As Now*." In Baraka, *The Dead Lecturer*, 15–16.

Baraka, Amiri [LeRoi Jones]. *Blues People: Negro Music in White America*. New York: William Morrow, 1963.

Baraka, Amiri [LeRoi Jones]. "The Bridge." In *Preface to a Twenty Volume Suicide Note*, 25–26. New York: Totem Press/Corinth Books, 1961.

Baraka, Amiri [LeRoi Jones]. "Cuba Libre." In Baraka, *Home*, 11–62.

Baraka, Amiri [LeRoi Jones]. *Home: Social Essays*. New York: William Morrow, 1966.

Baraka, Amiri [LeRoi Jones]. "How You Sound??" In *The New American Poetry*, edited by Donald Allen, 424–25. New York: Grove Press, 1960.

Baraka, Amiri [LeRoi Jones]. "Hunting Is Not Those Heads on the Wall." In Baraka, *Home*, 173–78.

Baraka, Amiri [LeRoi Jones]. "A Poem for Speculative Hipsters." In Baraka, *The Dead Lecturer*, 76.

Baraka, Amiri [LeRoi Jones]. "Statement." In *New American Story*, edited by Donald M. Allen and Robert Creeley, 267–68. New York: Grove Press, 1965.

Baraka, Amiri [LeRoi Jones]. *The System of Dante's Hell*. New York: Grove Press, 1963.

Baraka, Amiri [LeRoi Jones]. "This Is LeRoi Jones Talking." In Baraka, *Home*, 179–88.

Baraka, Amiri [LeRoi Jones]. "What Does Nonviolence Mean?" In Baraka, *Home*, 133–54.

Barthes, Roland. *The Pleasure of the Text*. Translated by Richard Miller. New York: Hill and Wang, 1975.

Benston, Kimberly. *Amiri Baraka: The Renegade Mask*. New Haven, CT: Yale University Press, 1976.

Benston, Kimberly. *Conversations with Amiri Baraka*. Edited by Charlie Reilly. Jackson: University Press of Mississippi, 1994.

Benston, Kimberly. *Performing Blackness: Enactments of African-American Modernism*. London and New York: Routledge, 2000.

Berliner, Paul F. *Thinking in Jazz: The Infinite Art of Improvisation*. Chicago: University of Chicago Press, 1994.

Bernstein, Charles. Introduction to *Close Listening: Poetry and the Performed Word*. Edited by Charles Bernstein, 3–28. Oxford: Oxford University Press, 1998.

Bernstein, Charles. "Introjective Verse." In *My Way: Speeches and Poems*, 110–12. Chicago: University of Chicago Press, 1999.

Black Mountain College. Faculty Minutes. November 21, 1951. Box 9. Black Mountain College Collection. Western Regional Archives, Asheville, NC. October 19, 2020.

Blake, William. "London." In *The Complete Poetry and Prose of William Blake*, rev. ed., edited by David V. Erdman, commentary by Harold Bloom, 26–27. New York: Doubleday/Anchor Books, 1988.

Bolden, Tony. "'All the Birds Sing Bass': The Revolutionary Blues of Jayne Cortez." *African American Review* 35, no. 1 (2001): 61–71.

Brathwaite, Edward Kamau. *History of the Voice: The Development of Nation Language in Anglophone Caribbean Poetry*. London: New Beacon Books, 1984.

Browning, Robert. "Home-Thoughts from Abroad." In *Robert Browning: Selected Poems*, edited by John Woolford, Daniel Karlin, and Joseph Phelan, 16. London and New York: Routledge, 2015.

Butler, Brian E. *Dan Rice at Black Mountain College: Painter among Poets*. Asheville, NC: Black Mountain College Museum and Arts Center, 2014.

Butler, Judith. *Giving an Account of Oneself*. New York: Fordham University Press, 2005.

Butterick, George F. *A Guide to* The Maximus Poems *of Charles Olson*. Oakland: University of California Press, 1980.

Butterick, George F. Introduction to *Charles Olson & Robert Creeley: The Complete Correspondence*, vol. 1, edited by George F. Butterick, ix–xv. Boston: Black Sparrow Press, 1980.

Carter, Jon Horne. "A Community Far Afield: Black Mountain College and the Southern Estrangement of the Avant-Garde." In *The Bohemian South: Creating Countercultures, from Poe to Punk*, edited by Shawn Chandler Bingham and Lindsey A. Freeman, 54–72. Chapel Hill: University of North Carolina Press, 2017.

Cavarero, Adriana. *For More Than One Voice: Toward a Philosophy of Vocal Expression*. Translated by Paul A. Kottman. Stanford, CA: Stanford University Press, 2005.

Cavell, Stanley. *Philosophy the Day after Tomorrow*. Cambridge, MA: Harvard University Press, 2005.

Chamberlain, Lori. "Ghostwriting the Text: Translation and the Poetics of Jack Spicer." *Contemporary Literature* 26, no. 4 (1985): 426–42.

Cherkovsky, Neeli. "Remembering Bob." In Kaufman, *The Collected Poems of Bob Kaufman*, 211–15.

Cixous, Hélène. *Entre l'écriture des femmes*. Paris: Gallimard, 1986.

Clark, Camille. "Black Mountain College: A Pioneer in Southern Racial Inclusion." *Journal of Blacks in Higher Education* 54 (2006): 46–48.

Clark, Tom. *Charles Olson: The Allegory of a Poet's Life*. Berkeley, CA: North Atlantic Books, 2000.

Clark, Tom. *Robert Creeley and the Genius of the American Commonplace*. New York: New Directions, 1993.

Clay, Mel. *Jazz, Jail, and God: An Impressionistic Biography of Bob Kaufman*. San Francisco: Androgyne Books, 2001.

Cornell, Julien. *The Trial of Ezra Pound: A Documented Account of the Treason Case by the Defendant's Lawyer*. New York: John Day Company, 1966.

Cortez, Jayne. *Coagulations: New and Selected Poems*. New York: Thunder's Mouth Press, 1984.

Cortez, Jayne. "Glossary." In Cortez, *Coagulations*, 111–12.

Cortez, Jayne. "I See Chano Pozo." In Cortez, *Coagulations*, 65–67.

Cortez, Jayne. "Strike Up the Band." In *Jazz Fan Looks Back*, 77. Brooklyn: Hanging Loose Press, 2002.

Cortez, Jayne. "Tapping." In Cortez, *Coagulations*, 17–18.

Cortez, Jayne, and the Firespitters. "I See Chano Pozo." *There It Is*. Bola Press, 1982, vinyl LP.

Creeley, Robert. "Autobiography." In *Robert Creeley and the Genius of the American Commonplace*, edited by Tom Clark, 122–44. New York: New Directions, 1993.

Creeley, Robert. *The Collected Essays of Robert Creeley*. Oakland: University of California Press, 1989.

Creeley, Robert. "[Creeley] Interviewed by Linda Wagner." In Creeley, *Tales Out of School*, 24–70.

Creeley, Robert. "Form." In Creeley, *Collected Essays*, 590–92.

Creeley, Robert. "Interview with John Sinclair and Robin Eichele." In Creeley, *Tales Out of School*, 1–23.

Creeley, Robert. Introduction. In Creeley and Rice, *All That Is Lovely in Men*, n.p.

Creeley, Robert. "Notes Apropos 'Free Verse.'" In *Collected Essays*, 492–95.

Creeley, Robert. *The Selected Letters of Robert Creeley*. Edited by Rod Smith, Peter Baker, and Kaplan Harris. Oakland: University of California Press, 2014.

Creeley, Robert. *Tales Out of School: Selected Interviews*. Ann Arbor: University of Michigan Press, 1993.

Creeley, Robert. "Walking the Dog: On Jazz Music and Prosody in Relation to a Cluster of Beat and Black Mountain Poets." *Pennsound*, Center for Programs in Contemporary Writing, University of Pennsylvania, accessed September 9, 2017. http://writing.upenn.edu/pennsound/x/Creeley.php.

Creeley, Robert. "The Whip." In Creeley and Rice, *All That Is Lovely in Men*, n.p.

Creeley, Robert. "The Whip." "Rock Drill #3." *Pennsound*, Center for Programs in Contemporary Writing, University of Pennsylvania, accessed September 9, 2017. http://writing.upenn.edu/pennsound/x/Creeley.php.

Creeley, Robert, and Dan Rice. *All That Is Lovely in Men*. Asheville, NC: The Jargon
   Society/Biltmore Press, 1955.

Damon, Maria. *Dark End of the Street: Margins in American Vanguard Poetry*.
   Minneapolis: University of Minnesota Press, 1993.

Damon, Maria. "John Wieners in the Matrix of Massachusetts Institutions: A
   Psychogeography." *Journal of Beat Studies* 3 (2014): 69–92.

Damon, Maria. *Postliterary America: From Bagel Shop Jazz to Micropoetries*. Iowa
   City: University of Iowa Press, 2011.

Davidson, Michael. *Guys Like Us: Citing Masculinity in Cold War Poetics*. Chicago:
   University of Chicago Press, 2004.

Davis, Miles. "Moon Dreams." *Birth of the Cool*. Capitol Records, 1956, vinyl LP.

Dawson, Fielding. *The Black Mountain Book*. New ed. Rocky Mount: North
   Carolina Wesleyan College Press, 1991.

Derrida, Jacques. *Dissemination*. Translated by Barbara Johnson. Chicago:
   University of Chicago Press, 1981.

Derrida, Jacques. *Specters of Marx: The State of the Debt, the Work of Mourning,
   and the New International*. Translated by Peggy Kamuf. Introduction by Bernd
   Magnus and Stephen Cullenberg. London and New York: Routledge, 1994.

DeVeaux, Scott. *The Birth of Bebop: A Social and Musical History*. Oakland:
   University of California Press, 1997.

DeVeaux, Scott, and Gary Giddens. *Jazz: Essential Listening*. New York: W. W.
   Norton, 2011.

Dewey, John. *The Later Works, 1925–1953*. Vol. 10. Edited by Jo Ann Boydston.
   Carbondale: Southern Illinois University Press, 1984.

di Prima, Diane. *Recollections of My Life as a Woman: The New York Years*. New York:
   Penguin, 2002.

Duberman, Martin. *Black Mountain: An Experiment in Community*. Evanston, IL:
   Northwestern University Press, 1972.

DuBois, W. E. B. *The Souls of Black Folk*. Edited by Henry Louis Gates, Jr.
   Introduction by Arthur Rampersad. Oxford: Oxford University Press, 2007.

Duncan, Robert. "After *For Love*." In *Robert Creeley's Life and Work: A Sense of
   Increment*, edited by John Wilson, 99–100. Ann Arbor: University of Michigan
   Press, 1987.

DuPlessis, Rachel Blau. *Purple Passages: Pound, Eliot, Zukofsky, Olson, Creeley, and
   the Ends of Patriarchal Poetry*. Iowa City: University of Iowa Press, 2012.

Edwards, Brent Hayes. *Epistrophies: Jazz and the Literary Imagination*. Cambridge,
   MA: Harvard University Press, 2017.

Ellingham, Lewis, and Kevin Killian. *Poet Be Like God: Jack Spicer and the San
   Francisco Renaissance*. Middletown, CT: Wesleyan University Press, 1998.

Ellison, Ralph, and Albert Murray. *Trading Twelves: The Selected Letters of Ralph*

Ellison and Albert Murray. Edited by Albert Murray and John F. Callahan. New York: Vintage Books, 2001.

Epstein, Andrew. *Beautiful Enemies: Friendship and Postwar American Poetry.* Oxford: Oxford University Press, 2009.

Eshleman, Clayton. "The Lorca Working." *Boundary 2: An International Journal of Literature and Culture* 6, no. 1 (1977): 31–50.

Faas, Ekbert, and Maria Trombacco. *Robert Creeley: A Biography.* Lebanon, NH: University Press of New England, 2001.

Fazzino, Jimmy. *World Beats: Beat Generation Writing and the Worlding of U. S. Literature.* Lebanon, NH: Dartmouth College Press, 2016.

Feinstein, Sascha. *Jazz Poetry, from the 1920s to the Present.* Westport, CT: Praeger, 1997.

Felman, Shoshana. *The Scandal of the Speaking Body: Don Juan with J. L. Austin, or Seduction in Two Languages.* Stanford, CA: Stanford University Press, 2002.

Ferlinghetti, Lawrence, and Allen Ginsberg. *I Greet You at the Beginning of a Great Career: The Selected Correspondence of Lawrence Ferlinghetti and Allen Ginsberg: 1955–1997.* Edited by Bill Morgan. San Francisco: City Lights Books, 2015.

Foye, Raymond. Editorial Note. In Kaufman, *Collected Poems,* vii–viii.

Foye, Raymond. "Rain Unraveled Tales: Editing Bob Kaufman." In Kaufman, *Collected Poems,* 216–24. San Francisco: City Lights Books, 2019.

Gates, Henry Louis, Jr. *The Signifying Monkey: A Theory of African American Literary Criticism.* Oxford and New York: Oxford University Press, 1988.

Giddens, Gary. *Visions of Jazz: The First Century.* Oxford: Oxford University Press, 2000.

Gillespie, Dizzy, and Al Fraser. *To Be, or Not . . . to Bop: Memoirs.* New York: Doubleday, 1979.

Ginsberg, Allen. "Angkor Wat." In Ginsberg, *Collected Poems,* 306–23.

Ginsberg, Allen. "Beginning of a Poem of These States." In Ginsberg, *Collected Poems,* 369–72.

Ginsberg, Allen. *The Best Minds of My Generation: A Literary History of the Beats.* Edited by Bill Morgan, foreword Anne Waldman. New York: Grove Press, 2017.

Ginsberg, Allen. "Chicago to Salt Lake by Air." In Ginsberg, *Collected Poems,* 490–92.

Ginsberg, Allen. *Collected Poems, 1947–1980.* New York: Harper & Row, 1984.

Ginsberg, Allen. "Continuation of a Long Poem of These States." In Ginsberg, *Collected Poems,* 375.

Ginsberg, Allen. "Crossing Nation." In Ginsberg, *Collected Poems,* 499–500.

Ginsberg, Allen. *Deliberate Prose: Selected Essays of Allen Ginsberg, 1952–1995.* Edited by Bill Morgan and foreword by Edward Sanders. New York: Harper Perennial, 2000.

Ginsberg, Allen. *The Fall of America: Journals 1965–1971*. Edited by Michael Schumacher. Minneapolis: University of Minnesota Press, 2020.

Ginsberg, Allen. "Howl." In Ginsberg, *Collected Poems*, 126–33.

Ginsberg, Allen. "In the Baggage Room at Greyhound." In Ginsberg, *Collected Poems*, 153–54.

Ginsberg, Allen. "Kaddish." In Ginsberg, *Collected Poems*, 209–27.

Ginsberg, Allen. "Kansas City to St. Louis." In Ginsberg, *Collected Poems*, 413–18.

Ginsberg, Allen. *The Letters of Allen Ginsberg*. Edited by Bill Morgan. New York: Da Capo Press, 2008.

Ginsberg, Allen. "The Lion for Real." In Ginsberg, *Collected Poems*, 174–75.

Ginsberg, Allen. "Meditation and Poetics." In Ginsberg, *Deliberate Prose*, 152–53.

Ginsberg, Allen. "Notes for *Howl* and Other Poems." In *The New American Poetry*, edited by Donald M. Allen, 414–18. New York: Grove Press, 1960.

Ginsberg, Allen. "Outline of Un-American Activities." In Ginsberg, *Deliberate Prose*, 32–44.

Ginsberg, Allen. "Poet's 'Voice.'" In Ginsberg, *Deliberate Prose*, 257–58.

Ginsberg, Allen. "Seabattle of Salamis Took Place off Perama." In Ginsberg, *Collected Poems*, 288.

Ginsberg, Allen. "These States: into L.A." In Ginsberg, *Collected Poems*, 376–89.

Ginsberg, Allen. "Wichita Vortex Sutra." In Ginsberg, *Collected Poems*, 394–411.

Ginsberg, Allen, and Gary Snyder. *The Selected Letters of Allen Ginsberg and Gary Snyder*. Edited by Bill Morgan. Berkeley: Counterpoint, 2009.

Gioia, Ted. *The History of Jazz*. 2nd ed. Oxford: Oxford University Press, 2011.

Gioia, Ted. *The Jazz Standards: A Guide to the Repertoire*. Oxford: Oxford University Press, 2012.

Gizzi, Peter. "Jack Spicer and the Practice of Reading." In *The House That Jack Built*, edited by Peter Gizzi, 173–226. Middletown, CT: Wesleyan University Press, 1998.

Golding, Alan. *From Outlaw to Classic: Canons in American Poetry*. Madison: University of Wisconsin Press, 1995.

Grace, Nancy McCampbell. "A White Man in Love: A Study of Race, Gender, Class, and Ethnicity in Jack Kerouac's *Maggie Cassady*, *The Subterraneans*, and *Tristessa*." In *The Beat Generation: Critical Essays*, edited by Kostas Myrsiades, 93–120. New York: Peter Lang, 2002.

Grenier, Robert. "On Speech." *This* 1 (1971): n.p.

Hall, Stuart. "What Is This 'Black' in Black Popular Culture?" *Social Justice* 20, nos. 1–2 (1992): 104–14.

Harris, Mary Emma. *The Arts at Black Mountain College*. Cambridge, MA: MIT Press, 2002.

Harris, William J. *The Poetry and Poetics of Amiri Baraka: The Jazz Aesthetic.* Columbia: University of Missouri Press, 1985.

Henderson, David. Introduction to *Cranial Guitar: Selected Poems by Bob Kaufman,* edited by Gerald Nicosia. Minneapolis, MN: Coffee House Press, 1996.

Henderson, Stephen. *Understanding the New Black Poetry: Black Speech and Black Music as Poetic References.* New York: William Morrow, 1973.

Hickman, Ben. *Crisis and the U.S. Avant-Garde: Poetry and Real Politics.* Edinburgh: Edinburgh University Press, 2015.

Hochman, Elaine S. *Architects of Fortune: Mies van der Rohe and the Third Reich.* New York: Grove Press, 1989.

Hoffman, Tyler. *American Poetry in Performance: From Walt Whitman to Hip Hop.* Ann Arbor: University of Michigan Press, 2013.

Hughes, Langston. "Democracy Is Not a Theory at Black Mountain College." *Chicago Defender* (national edition), March 5, 1949.

Hughes, Langston. Postcard to Carl Van Vechten, February 1949. Box 19, Folder 391. JWJ MSS 1050. Carl Van Vechten Papers Relating to African American Arts and Letters. James Weldon Johnson Collection in the Yale Collection of American Literature. Beinecke Rare Book and Manuscript Library, Yale University.

Hurston, Zora Neale. Letter to Robert Wunsch, February 21, 1944. Box 150, Folder 2. Black Mountain College Collection. Western Regional Archives, Asheville, NC.

Ingleby, Leonard Cresswell. *Oscar Wilde, Some Reminiscences.* London: T. W. Laurie, 1907.

Jacobson, Matthew Frye. *Whiteness of a Different Color: European Immigrants and the Alchemy of Race.* Cambridge, MA: Harvard University Press, 1999.

Jonas, Stephen. *Arcana: A Stephen Jonas Reader.* Edited by Garrett Caples, Derek Fenner, David Rich, and Joseph Torra. San Francisco: City Lights Books, 2019.

Jonas, Stephen. "Cante Jondo for Soul Brother Jack Spicer, His Beloved California & Andalusia of Lorca." In Jonas, *Arcana,* 70–74.

Jonas, Stephen. ". . . . . An Ear Injured by Hearing Things (after a statement of Jack Spicer's)." In Jonas, *Arcana,* 32–33.

Jonas, Stephen. *Exercises for Ear.* In Jonas, *Arcana,* 123–70.

Jonas, Stephen. "Gloucester (Impressions for J.W., III)." In Jonas, *Arcana,* 75–76.

Jonas, Stephen. "Morphogenesis (being a conventionalization 'Morphemes' of Jack Spicer)." In Jonas, *Arcana,* 80–83.

Jonas, Stephen. "Word on Measure." In Jonas, *Arcana,* 89–91.

Jones, Meta DuEwa. *The Muse Is the Music: Jazz Poetry from the Harlem Renaissance to Spoken Word.* Champaign: University of Illinois Press, 2011.

Kane, Daniel. *All Poets Welcome: The Lower East Side Poetry Scene in the 1960s.* Oakland: University of California Press, 2003.

Katz, Daniel. "Jack Spicer's *After Lorca*: Translation as Decomposition." *Textual Practice* 18, no. 1 (2004): 83–103.

Katz, Daniel. *The Poetry of Jack Spicer*. Edinburgh: Edinburgh University Press, 2013.

Kaufman, Bob. "Abomunist Manifesto." In Kaufman, *Collected Poems*, 57–58.

Kaufman, Bob. "ABOMUNIST RATIONAL ANTHEM." In Kaufman, *Collected Poems*, 64–65.

Kaufman, Bob. *The Collected Poems of Bob Kaufman*. Edited by Neeli Cherkovski, Raymond Foye, and Tate Swindell. Foreword by devorah major. San Francisco: City Lights Books, 2019.

Kaufman, Bob. "Crootey Songo." In Kaufman, *Collected Poems*, 105.

Kaufman, Bob. "Excerpts for the LEXICON ABOMUNON." In Kaufman, *Collected Poems*, 60–61.

Kaufman, Bob. "Ginsberg (for Allen)." In Kaufman, *Collected Poems*, 17.

Kaufman, Bob. "Jail Poems." In Kaufman, *Collected Poems*, 42–47.

Kaufman, Bob. "October 5th, 1963." In Kaufman, *Collected Poems*, 119.

Kaufman, Bob. "O-Jazz-O War Memoir: Jazz, Don't Listen to It at Your Own Risk." In Kaufman, *Collected Poems*, 118–19.

Kaufman, Bob. "Walking Parker Home." In Kaufman, *Collected Poems*, 4–5.

Kaufman, Bob. "War Memoir." In Kaufman, *Collected Poems*, 39.

Kaufman, Bob. "War Memoir: Jazz, Don't Listen to It at Your Own Risk." In Kaufman, *Collected Poems*, 140–41.

Kaufman, Bob. "West Coast Sounds—1956." In Kaufman, *Collected Poems*, 8–9.

Kaufman, Bob. "Would You Wear My Eyes?" In Kaufman, *Collected Poems*, 29–30.

Keller, Lynn. *Re-Making It New: Contemporary American Poetry and the Modernist Tradition*. Cambridge: Cambridge University Press, 1987.

Kerouac, Jack. "Essentials of Spontaneous Prose." *Black Mountain Review* 7 (1957): 226–28.

Kerouac, Jack. *On the Road*. New York: Penguin, 1957.

Kerouac, Jack. *The Subterraneans*. New York: Grove Press, 1958.

Kingan, Renee M. "'Taking it Out!': Jayne Cortez's Collaborations with the Firespitters." In *Black Music, Black Poetry: Blues and Jazz's Impact on African American Versification*, edited by Gordon E. Thompson, 149–61. London and New York: Routledge, 2014.

Kohli, Amor. "Saxophones and Smothered Rage: Bob Kaufman, Jazz, and the Quest for Redemption." *Callaloo: A Journal of African Diaspora Arts and Letters* 25, no. 1 (2002): 165–82.

Lee, A. Robert. *The Beats: Authorships, Legacies*. Edinburgh: Edinburgh University Press, 2019.

Lee, Benjamin. *Poetics of Emergence: Affect and History in Postwar Experimental Poetry*. Iowa City: University of Iowa Press, 2020.

Lhamon, Jr., W. T. *Raising Cain: Blackface Performance from Jim Crow to Hip Hop*. Cambridge, MA: Harvard University Press, 1998.

LL Cool J. "Around the Way Girl." *Mama Said Knock You Out*. Def Jam Recordings, 1990, compact disc.

Lorca, Federico García. "Oda a Walt Whitman." In *The Selected Poems of Federico García Lorca*, edited by Francisco García Lorca and Donald M. Allen, 124–34. New York: New Directions, 1955.

Lott, Eric. *Love and Theft: Blackface Minstrelsy and the American Working Class*. Oxford: Oxford University Press, 1993.

Lowney, John. *Jazz Internationalism: Literary Afro-Modernism and the Cultural Politics of Black Music*. Champaign: University of Illinois Press, 2017.

Mackey, Nathaniel. "Breath and Precarity: The Inaugural Robert Creeley Lecture in Poetics." In *Poetics and Precarity*, edited by Myung Mi Kim and Christanne Miller, 1–30. Albany: State University of New York Press, 2018.

Mackey, Nathaniel. "Cante Moro." In *Sound States: Innovative Poetics and Acoustical Technologies*, edited by Adalaide Morris, 194–212. Chapel Hill: University of North Carolina Press, 1998.

Mackey, Nathaniel. "The Changing Same: Black Music in the Poetry of Amiri Baraka." In Mackey, *Discrepant Engagement*, 22–48.

Mackey, Nathaniel. *Discrepant Engagement: Dissonance, Cross-Culturality, and Experimental Writing*. Tuscaloosa: University of Alabama Press, 1993.

Mackey, Nathaniel. *Eroding Witness*. Champaign: University of Illinois Press, 1984.

Mackey, Nathaniel. "Expanding the Repertoire." In Mackey, *Paracritical Hinge*, 240–43.

Mackey, Nathaniel. *From a Broken Bottle Traces of Perfume Still Emanate*. 3 vols. New York: New Directions, 2010.

Mackey, Nathaniel. *Paracritical Hinge: Essays, Talks, Notes, Interviews*. Madison: University of Wisconsin Press, 2005.

Mackey, Nathaniel. *Splay Anthem*. New York: New Directions, 2002.

Mackey, Nathaniel, and Charles Bernstein. Pennsound: "Close Listening." University of Pennsylvania and the Center for Programs in Contemporary Writing, February 1, 2011, http://writing.upenn.edu/pennsound/x/Close-Listening.php.

Magee, Michael. *Emancipating Pragmatism: Emerson, Jazz, and Experimental Writing*. Tuscaloosa: University of Alabama Press, 2004.

Mailer, Norman. "The White Negro: Superficial Reflections on the Hipster." In *Advertisements for Myself*, 299–320. New York: G.P. Putnam's Sons, 1959.

major, devorah. Foreword to *The Collected Poems of Bob Kaufman*, edited by Neeli

Cherkovski, Raymond Foye, and Tate Swindell, ix–xv. San Francisco: City Lights Books, 2019.

Marcoux, Jean-Philippe. *Jazz Griots: Music as History in the 1960s African American Poem*. Lanham, MD: Lexington Books, 2012.

Marshall, Edward. "Leave the Word Alone." In *The New American Poetry*, edited by Donald M. Allen, 323–33. New York: Grove Press, 1960.

McCaffery, Steve. "Language Writing: From Productive to Libidinal Economy." In *North of Intention: Critical Writings, 1973–1986*, 143–58. New York: Roof Books, 2000.

McGann, Jerome. *Black Riders: The Visible Language of Modernism*. Princeton University Press, 1993.

Melhem, D. H. "A MELUS Profile and Interview: Jayne Cortez." *MELUS: Multi-Ethnic Literature of the United States* 21, no. 1 (1996): 71–79.

Monson, Ingrid. *Freedom Sounds: Civil Rights Call Out to Jazz and Africa*. Oxford: Oxford University Press, 2010.

Moody, A. David. *The Epic Years*. Vol. 2 of *Ezra Pound: Poet*. Oxford: Oxford University Press, 2018.

Morris, Adalaide. "Angles of Incidence / Angels of Dust: Operatic Tilt in the Poetics of H.D. and Nathaniel Mackey." In *No Rule of Procedure: H.D. and Poets After*, edited by Donna Hollenberg, 235–54. Iowa City: University of Iowa Press, 2000.

Moten, Fred. *Black and Blur*. Durham, NC: Duke University Press, 2017.

Moten, Fred. *In the Break: The Aesthetics of the Black Radical Tradition*. Minneapolis: University of Minnesota Press, 1993.

Moten, Fred. *The Universal Machine*. Durham, NC: Duke University Press, 2018.

Mullen, Harryette. *The Cracks Between What We Are and What We Are Supposed to Be*. Introduction by Hank Lazer. Tuscaloosa: University of Alabama Press, 2012.

Mullen, Harryette. "Harryette Mullen on Bob Kaufman." *YouTube*, uploaded by PenCenterUSA, July 28, 2008. https://www.youtube.com /watch?v=EppWseVcn9A.

Mullen, Harryette. "Kinky Quatrains." In Mullen, *The Cracks Between*, 13–17.

Mullen, Harryette. *Muse & Drudge*. San Diego, CA: Singing Horse Press, 1995.

Mullen, Harryette. "Poetry and Identity." In Mullen, *The Cracks Between*, 9–12.

Nielsen, Aldon Lynn. *Black Chant: Languages of African-American Postmodernism*. Cambridge: Cambridge University Press, 1997.

Nielsen, Aldon Lynn. *Integral Music: Languages of African American Innovation*. Tuscaloosa: University of Alabama Press, 2004.

Nielsen, Aldon Lynn. *Reading Race: White American Poets and the Racial Discourse in the Twentieth Century*. Athens: University of Georgia Press, 1988.

Nielsen, Aldon Lynn, and Lauri Ramey. "Introduction: Fear of a Black

Experiment." In *Every Goodbye Ain't Gone: An Anthology of Innovative Poetry by African Americans*, 2nd ed., edited by Aldon Lynn Nielsen and Lauri Ramey, xiii–xxi. Tuscaloosa: University of Alabama Press, 2006.

Nowak, Mark. *Social Poetics*. Minneapolis, MN: Coffee House Press, 2020.

O'Hara, Frank. "The Day That Lady Died." In *Lunch Poems*, 25–26. San Francisco: City Lights Books, 1964.

Olson, Charles. *Collected Prose*. Edited by Donald Allen and Benjamin Friedlander. Introduction by Robert Creeley. Oakland: University of California Press, 1997.

Olson, Charles. "Duende, Muse, and Angel." In Olson, *Muthologos*, 63–75.

Olson, Charles. "GrandPa, Goodbye." In Olson, *Collected Prose*, 145–52.

Olson, Charles. "Human Universe." In Olson, *Collected Prose*, 155–66.

Olson, Charles. "The Hustings." In *The Collected Poems of Charles Olson, Excluding the* Maximus *Poems*, edited by George F. Butterick, 532–35. Oakland: University of California Press, 1987.

Olson, Charles. "Letter to Elaine Feinstein." In Olson, *Collected Prose*, 50–52.

Olson, Charles. *Letters for Origin: 1950–1956*. Edited by Albert Glover. Foreword by John Tytell. St. Paul, MN: Paragon House, 1989.

Olson, Charles. Literature Program Catalogue Description. *Black Mountain College Bulletin* 12, no. 1 (1956): 7.

Olson, Charles. *The Maximus Poems*. Edited by George Butterick. Oakland: University of California Press, 1983.

Olson, Charles. "Memorial Letter." *Origin* 20 (1971): 42.

Olson, Charles. *Muthologos: Lectures and Interviews*. 2nd ed. Edited by Ralph Maud. Vancouver, BC: Talon Books, 2010.

Olson, Charles. "The Present Is Prologue." In Olson, *Collected Prose*, 205–7.

Olson, Charles. "Projective Verse." In Olson, *Collected Prose*, 239–49.

Olson, Charles. *Selected Letters*. Edited by Ralph Maud. Oakland: University of California Press, 2000.

Olson, Charles. *The Special View of History*. Edited by Ann Charters. Berkeley, CA: Oyez, 1970.

Olson, Charles. "This Is Yeats Speaking." In Olson, *Collected Prose*, 141–44.

Olson, Charles, and Robert Creeley. *Charles Olson & Robert Creeley: The Complete Correspondence*. Edited by George Butterick, vols. 1–8, and Robert Blevins, vols. 9–10. Boston: Black Sparrow Press, 1980–1996.

O'Meally, Robert G., ed. *The Jazz Cadence of American Culture*. New York: Columbia University Press, 1998.

Otto, Elizabeth. *Haunted Bauhaus: Occult Spirituality, Gender Fluidity, Queer Identities, and Radical Politics*. Cambridge, MA: MIT Press, 2019.

Panish, John. *The Color of Jazz: Race and Representation in Postwar American Culture*.

Jackson: University Press of Mississippi, 1997.

Pater, Walter. *The Renaissance: Studies in Art and Poetry*. Edited by Donald L. Hill. Oakland: University of California Press, 1980.

Paul, Sherman. *Olson's Push: Origin, Black Mountain, and Recent American Poetry*. Baton Rouge: Louisiana State University Press, 1978.

Perelman, Bob. *The Trouble with Genius: Reading Pound, Joyce, Stein, and Zukofsky*. Oakland: University of California Press, 1994.

Perloff, Marjorie. "After Free Verse: The New Non-Linear Poetries." In Marjorie Perloff, *Poetry On and Off the Page: Essays for Emergent Occasions*, 141–67. Evanston, IL: Northwestern University, 1998.

Pisano, Claudia Moreno, ed. *Amiri Baraka and Edward Dorn: The Collected Letters*. Albuquerque: University of New Mexico Press, 2013.

Pizza, Joseph. "All That Is Lovely in Jazz: The Creeley-Rice Collaboration for Jargon 10." *Journal of Black Mountain College Studies* 9 (2019). https://www .blackmountainstudiesjournal.org/lovely-jazz/.

Pizza, Joseph. "Continental Drift: Charles Olson and *The English Intelligencer*." *Contemporary Literature* 59, no. 3 (2018): 277–307.

Pizza, Joseph. "Spitting Fire: Black Mountain and the Black Arts Movement in the Poetry of Jayne Cortez." *Journal of Black Mountain College Studies* 12 (2021). https://www.blackmountainstudiesjournal.org/pizza-black-arts/.

Pound, Ezra. "Ezra Pound Radio Speeches." Edited by Ben Friedlander Richard Sieburth. *Pennsound*, Center for Programs in Contemporary Writing at the University of Pennsylvania, http://writing.upenn.edu/pennsound/x /Pound-Speeches.php.

Pound, Ezra. "How to Read." In *The Literary Essays of Ezra Pound*, edited by T. S. Eliot, 15–40. London: Faber, 1960.

Pound, Scott. "Language Writing and the Burden of Critique." *Canadian Literature* 210, no. 11 (2011): 9–26.

Rampersad, Arthur. *1941–1967, I Dream a World*. Vol. 2 of *The Life of Langston Hughes*. 2nd ed. Oxford: Oxford University Press, 2002.

Redling, Erik. *Translating Jazz into Poetry: From Mimesis to Metaphor*. Berlin: De Gruyter, 2017.

Redman, Tim. *Ezra Pound and Italian Fascism*. Cambridge: Cambridge University Press, 1991.

Rembar, Charles. *The End of Obscenity: The Trials of* Lady Chatterley, Tropic of Cancer, *and* Fanny Hill. New York: Random House, 1968.

Roediger, David R. *The Wages of Whiteness: Race and the Making of the American Working Class*. New ed. New York and London: Verso, 2007.

Rumaker, Michael. *Black Mountain Days: A Memoir*. Brooklyn: Spuyten Duyvil, 2012.

Sanchez, Sonia. "a/coltrane/poem." In *SOS—Calling All Black People: A Black*

Arts Movement Reader, edited by John H. Bracey Jr., Sonia Sanchez, and James Smethurst, 361–64. Amherst: University of Massachusetts Press, 2014.

Sanchez, Sonia. *The Collected Poems of Sonia Sanchez*. Boston: Beacon Press, 2021.

Sanchez, Sonia. *Conversations with Sonia Sanchez*. Edited by Joyce A. Joyce. Jackson: University Press of Mississippi, 2007.

Sanchez, Sonia. "homecoming." In Sanchez, *Collected Poems*, 3.

Sanchez, Sonia. "I Have Walked a Long Time." In Sanchez, *Collected Poems*, 84–85.

Sanchez, Sonia. "Queens of the Universe." *SOS—Calling All Black People: A Black Arts Movement Reader*, edited by John H. Bracey Jr., Sonia Sanchez, and James Smethurst, 114–20. Amherst: University of Massachusetts Press, 2014.

Sanchez, Sonia. "Sequences." In Sanchez, *Collected Poems*, 71–72.

Serres, Michel. *Genesis*. Translated by Geneviève James and James Nielson. Ann Arbor: University of Michigan Press, 1995.

Shapiro, Nat, and Nat Hentoff. *Hear Me Talkin' to Ya: The Story of Jazz as Told by the Men Who Made It*. New York: Dover, 1966.

Shaw, Lytle. *Narrowcast: Poetry and Audio Research*. Stanford, CA: Stanford University Press, 2018.

Silliman, Ron. Introduction to *In the American Tree: Language, Realism, Poetry*, edited by Ron Silliman, i–xxiii. Orono, ME: National Poetry Foundation, 1986.

Siraganian, Lisa. *Modernism's Other Work: The Art Object's Political Life*. Oxford: Oxford University Press, 2012.

Slive, Zoya Sandomirsky. "Another Kind of Hoe Down." In *Black Mountain College, Sprouted Seeds: An Anthology of Personal Accounts*, edited by Mervin Lane, 97–98. Knoxville: University of Tennessee Press, 1990.

Smethurst, James. *The Black Arts Movement: Literary Nationalism in the 1960s and 1970s*. Chapel Hill: University of North Carolina Press, 2005.

Smethurst, James. "'Remembering When Indians Were Red': Bob Kaufman, the Popular Front, and the Black Arts Movement." *Callaloo: A Journal of African Diaspora Arts and Letters* 25, no. 1 (2002): 146–64.

Smitherman, Geneva. *Talkin' and Testifyin': The Language of Black America*. Detroit: Wayne State University Press, 1977.

Sollors, Werner. *Amiri Baraka/LeRoi Jones: The Quest for a Populist Modernism*. New York: Columbia University Press, 1978.

Spicer, Jack. *After Lorca*. In Spicer, *My Vocabulary Did This to Me*, 105–54.

Spicer, Jack. "Dictation and 'A Textbook of Poetry.'" In Spicer, *The House That Jack Built*, 1–48.

Spicer, Jack. "Forest." In Spicer, *My Vocabulary Did This to Me*, 132.

Spicer, Jack. *The House That Jack Built: The Collected Lectures of Jack Spicer*. Edited by Peter Gizzi. Middletown, CT: Wesleyan University Press, 1998.

Spicer, Jack. "Jack Spicer: Letters to Robin Blaser, 1955–1958." Edited by Lori

Chamberlin and Terry Ludwar. *Line 9* (1987): 26–55.

Spicer, Jack. *My Vocabulary Did This to Me: The Collected Poetry of Jack Spicer.* Edited by Kevin Killian and Peter Gizzi. Middletown, CT: Wesleyan University Press, 2008.

Spicer, Jack. "Ode for Walt Whitman." In Spicer, *My Vocabulary Did This to Me,* 126–30.

Spicer, Jack. "A Poem without a Single Bird in It." In Spicer, *My Vocabulary Did This to Me,* 73.

Spicer, Jack. "The Poems of Emily Dickinson." In Spicer, *The House That Jack Built,* 231–36.

Spicer, Jack. "The Poet and Poetry—A Symposium." In Spicer, *The House That Jack Built,* 229–30.

Spicer, Jack. "Poetry in Process and *Book of Magazine Verse.*" In Spicer, *The House That Jack Built,* 97–148.

Spicer, Jack. "Some Notes on Walt Whitman for Allen Joyce." In Spicer, *My Vocabulary Did This to Me,* 55.

Spicer, Jack. "Song for Bird and Myself." In Spicer, *My Vocabulary Did This to Me,* 69–72.

Stevens, Wallace. "Of Modern Poetry." In *The Collected Poems of Wallace Stevens,* 239–40. New York: Vintage, 1990.

Stevens, Wallace. "The State of American Writing." *Partisan Review* 15 (1948).

Stewart, Garrett. *Reading Voices: Literature and the Phonotext.* Oakland: University of California Press, 1990.

Stewart, Michael Seth. Introduction to Wieners, *Stars Seen in Person: Selected Journals,* edited by Michael Seth Stewart, preface by Ammiel Alcalay, xv–xxiv. San Francisco: City Lights Books, 2015.

Stewart, Michael Seth. Introduction to Wieners, *Yours Presently: The Selected Letters of John Wieners,* edited by Michael Seth Stewart, preface by Eileen Myles, xv–xix. Albuquerque: University of New Mexico Press, 2020.

Sun Ra [Herman Poole Blount]. "The Cosmic Equation." In *Sun Ra: The Immeasurable Equation,* 110.

Sun Ra [Herman Poole Blount]. "The Outer Bridge." In *Sun Ra: The Immeasurable Equation: The Collected Poetry and Prose,* 293.

Sun Ra [Herman Poole Blount]. *Sun Ra: The Immeasurable Equation: The Collected Poetry and Prose.* Edited by James L. Wolf and Harmut Geerken. Norderstedt, Germany: Waitawhile, 2005.

Tedlock, Dennis. *The Olson Codex: Projective Verse and the Problem of Mayan Glyphs.* Albuquerque: University of New Mexico Press, 2017.

Thomas, Lorenzo. "Alea's Children: The Avant-Garde on the Lower East Side, 1960–1970." *African American Review* 27, no. 4 (1993): 573–78.

Thomas, Lorenzo. "Ascension: Avant-Garde Jazz and the Black Arts Movement."

In Thomas, *Don't Deny My Name*, 116–33.

Thomas, Lorenzo. *The Collected Poems of Lorenzo Thomas*. Edited by Aldon Lynn Nielsen and Laura Vrana. Middletown, CT: Wesleyan University Press, 2019.

Thomas, Lorenzo. "'Communicating by Horns': Jazz and Redemption in the Poetry of the Beats and the Black Arts Movement." In Thomas, *Don't Deny My Name*, 105–15.

Thomas, Lorenzo. "Discovering America Again." In Thomas, *Collected Poems*, 298–99.

Thomas, Lorenzo. *Don't Deny My Name: Words & Music & The Black Intellectual Tradition*. Edited by A. L. Nielsen. Ann Arbor: University of Michigan Press, 2008.

Thomas, Lorenzo. "Evolution of the Bop Aesthetic." In Thomas, *Don't Deny My Name*, 87–98.

Thomas, Lorenzo. *Extraordinary Measures: Afrocentric Modernism and Twentieth-Century American Poetry*. Tuscaloosa: University of Alabama Press, 2000.

Thomas, Lorenzo. "Historiography." In Thomas, *Collected Poems*, 86–88.

Thomas, Lorenzo. "Liner Notes." In Thomas, *Collected Poems*, 89.

Thomas, Lorenzo. "Low Speech." In Thomas, *Collected Poems*, 191.

Thomas, Lorenzo. "My Calling." In Thomas, *Collected Poems*, 188.

Thomas, Lorenzo. "New and Old Gospel: The Black Arts Movement and Popular Music." In Thomas, *Don't Deny My Name*, 152–75.

Thomas, Lorenzo. "The Offering." In Thomas, *Collected Poems*, 189.

Thomas, Lorenzo. "Political Science." *C: A Journal of Poetry* 1, no. 5 (1963): n.p.

Thomas, Lorenzo. "Political Science." In Thomas, *Collected Poems*, 445.

Torra, Joseph. Introduction to Stephen Jonas, *Arcana: A Stephen Jonas Reader*, edited by Garrett Caples, Derek Fenner, David Rich, and Joseph Torra, 17–27. San Francisco: City Lights Books, 2019.

Wieners, John. "Act #2." In Wieners, *Supplication*, 52–53.

Wieners, John. "Blaauwildebeestefontein" In Wieners, *Stars Seen in Person*, 102–3.

Wieners, John. "Cocaine." In Wieners, *Supplication*, 60.

Wieners, John. "Hanging On for Dear Life." *Boundary 2: An International Journal of Literature and Culture* 2, no. 1–2 (1973): 22–23.

Wieners, John. "Memories of You." In Wieners, *Supplication*, 72–74.

Wieners, John. "Parking Lot." In Wieners, *Supplication*, 82.

Wieners, John. "A poem for cock suckers." In Wieners, *Supplication*, 18–19.

Wieners, John. "A poem for museum goers." In Wieners, *Supplication*, 23–26.

Wieners, John. "A poem for record players." In Wieners, *Supplication*, 6–7.

Wieners, John. "A poem for the dead I know." In Wieners, *Supplication*, 29–32.

Wieners, John. *Stars Seen in Person: Selected Journals*. Edited by Michael Seth

Stewart. Preface by Ammiel Alcalay. San Francisco: City Lights Books, 2015.

Wieners, John. "Stationary." In Wieners, *Supplication*, 80.

Wieners, John. *Supplication: Selected Poems of John Wieners*. Edited by Joshua Beckman, C. A. Conrad, and Robert Dewhurst. Seattle: Wave Books, 2015.

Wieners, John. "We have a flame within us I told Charles." In Wieners, *Supplication*, 84.

Wieners, John. *Yours Presently: The Selected Letters of John Wieners*. Edited by Michael Seth Stewart. Preface by Eileen Myles. Albuquerque: University of New Mexico Press, 2020.

Wilkins, Micah. "Social Justice at BMC before the Civil Rights Age: Desegregation, Racial Inclusion, and Racial Equality at BMC." *Black Mountain College Studies* 6 (2014). http://www.blackmountainstudiesjournal.org/volume6/6-17-micah-wilkins/.

Williams, Alma Stone. "Opening Black Doors at Black Mountain College." In *Remembering Black Mountain College*, edited by Mary Emma Harris, 41. Asheville, NC: Black Mountain College Museum and Arts Center, 1996.

Williams, William Carlos. "The Red Wheelbarrow." In *The Collected Poems of William Carlos Williams*, vol. 1, edited by A. Walton Litz and Christopher MacGowan, 224. New York: New Directions, 1986.

Wittgenstein, Ludwig. *Philosophical Investigations*. 4th ed. Translated by G. E. M. Anscombe, P. M. S. Hacker, and Joachim Schulte. Hoboken, NJ: Wiley-Blackwell, 2009.

Yépez, Heriberto. *The Empire of Neomemory*. Translated by Jen Hofer, Christian Nagler, and Brian Whitener. N.p., Chainlink, 2013.

Zukofsky, Louis. *A*. New York: New Directions, 2011.

Zukofsky, Louis. "An Objective." In *Prepositions: The Collected Critical Essays of Louis Zukofsky*. Expanded ed. Oakland: University of California Press, 1981.

Index

Adorno, Theodor, 14–15

African American Vernacular English (AAVE), 31, 105, 169–70, 176, 193

Alexander, Will, 199

Alighieri, Dante, 50, 86, 150

Allen, Donald, 19

Allen School (Asheville, NC), 27

Allison, Raphael, 4

Antin, David, 194

Arendt, Hannah, 10–11

Armstrong, Louis "Satchmo," 49–50, 55, 62, 181

Ashbery, John, 19

Attali, Jacques, 7

Attridge, Derek, 211n22

Auden, W. H., 38, 56

Ayler, Albert, 181

Baldwin, James, 34

Baraka, Amiri (LeRoi Jones), 1–2, 13–14, 17, 18, 21, 22, 124–25, 129–54, 155, 157–59, 168, 174, 178, 182, 186, 190, 191, 213n7; affinity for Black Mountain, 131–32; *The Autobiography of LeRoi Jones*, 129, 131; *Black Music*, 46, 144, 209n3, 210n5, 213n3; *Blues People*, 139, 141, 142, 143, 209n3, 213n1; friendship with Allen Ginsberg, 100–02, 104–06, 108–13, 145–46; friendship with Charles Olson, 25, 46, 96, 132–35, 137, 140–42, 145–54, 205–07; friendship with Ed Dorn, 137–39, 151–54; *Hard Facts*, 130, 190; relationship with Diane di Prima, 18–19, 142–43, 151–52; *The System of Dante's Hell*, 142–46, 150–51, 165, 207; "An Agony. As Now.," 101; "The Bridge," 135–36; "Cecil Taylor (*The World of Cecil Taylor*)," 144; "Charles Olson and Sun Ra," 1–2, 206–07; "Cuba Libre," 137, 139; "Ed Dorn and the Western World," 154; "How You Sound?," 134–35, 192; "Howl and Hail," 100–01, 111; "Hunting Is Not Those Heads," 147, 151; "A Poem for Speculative Hipsters," 149–53; "Sonny Rollins (*Our Man in Jazz*)," 144; "Statement," 143; "Technology and Ethos," 158, 165, 186; "This Is LeRoi Jones Talking," 147–49; "What Does Nonviolence Mean?," 139

Barthes, Roland, 10

Basquiat, Jean-Michel, 164

Batista, Fulgencio, 138, 185

Beach Boys, The, 106

Beatitude, 112, 116

Beatles, The, 106

Beats, 5, 12, 20, 21, 38, 56, 95–97, 112–13, 115–16, 118, 120–21, 123, 128, 132, 156, 160

bebop, 5, 17, 24–25, 26, 27, 30–32, 37–39, 42, 49, 50, 54–56, 65–66, 95, 97, 99, 114, 127, 139, 142, 144–45, 156, 157, 162, 163, 198, 204–05, 210n7

Benston, Kimberly, 15, 135, 143, 153, 174, 213n2

Berliner, Paul, 7–8

Bernstein, Charles, 10, 192, 194, 196, 197, 203

Berrigan, Ted, 160

Black Arts Movement, 2, 3, 7, 9, 12, 17, 21, 97, 106, 156–60, 165–67, 178, 188, 189–90, 205–06; and projectivism, 21; and "Coltrane Poem," 82, 174

Black Mountain College, 2, 3–5, 7, 9, 12, 13, 17, 18, 19–21, 23–25, 30, 33, 44, 49, 50, 53, 59, 60, 71, 73, 79, 91, 92, 94, 99, 128–33, 136, 137, 143, 149, 151–52, 154, 159–60, 174, 185, 205, 207; and Black music, 26–29; and racial integration, xi–xvi, 27–28

Black Mountain Review, The, 2, 131–32, 133, 179

Black music, 5, 6, 7, 12, 13, 15, 17, 21, 22, 25, 63, 66, 68, 92, 97, 104, 115, 116, 120, 121, 122, 123, 130, 156, 157, 162, 169, 174, 178, 198, 201

Black Panthers, 109

Blackburn, Paul, 9, 155, 159, 179

Blackness: as displacement of singularity, 14–15; as essentialized difference, 15, 136, 156, 172, 193; as marginalization, 105; performance of, 67, 75, 76, 92, 105, 109

Blake, William, 101

Blaser, Robin, 4, 58, 59, 88

blues, 62, 65–66, 68, 103, 121–22, 124, 139, 143, 165, 169, 172, 181, 201, 204

Boldereff, Frances, 23

Brathwaite, Edward Kamau, 12

Braxton, Anthony, 198

Brooks, Gwendolyn, 202

Browning, Robert, 161

Butler, Judith, 10, 209n2

C: A Magazine, 160, 162

cante jondo, 65, 67, 72, 81, 82, 91, 172

Carmichael, Stokley, 109, 110, 111

Castro, Fidel, 104

Cavalcante, Guido, 50

Cavarero, Adriana, 10–13, 99, 100, 187, 194–95

Cavell, Stanley, 10, 209n2

Cherkovsky, Neeli, 112

Cherry, Don, 198, 199

Chessman, Caryl Whittier, 125

Chicago Defender, xv–xvi

Civil Rights Movement, xiv, 5, 30, 92, 106–07, 119, 125, 144, 153, 154, 176

Cixous, Hélène, 10

Clark, Tom, 25, 133, 213n6

Clarke, Kenny, 30

Cleaver, Eldridge, 109, 112

Coleman, Denardo, 178, 186

Coleman, Ornette, 132, 136, 144, 149, 178

Coltrane, John, 135, 144, 173–78

Congress of Racial Equality (CORE), xii, 140

Cool J, LL, 204

Corman, Cid, 57, 91, 150

Corso, Gregory, 116

Cortez, Jayne, 17, 21, 158, 159, 179–88; friendship with Paul Blackburn, 179; and her band The Firespitters, 22, 158, 178, 184–86, 216n3, 216n4; marriage to Ornette Coleman, 178;

and son Denardo Coleman, 178,
186; "Glossary," 184; "I See Chano
Pozo," 184–86, 216n3, 216n4; "Strike
Up the Band," 182–83; "Tapping,"
180–82

Crane, Hart, 29

Creeley, Robert, 1, 2, 5, 6, 17, 20, 21,
23–56, 57, 63, 64, 70, 75, 79, 80, 91, 92,
128, 131–32, 137, 139, 143–47, 149–54,
162, 163, 198, 205, 210n1, 210n2,
211n14, 211n17, 211n18, 211n19, 211n21,
213n5, 213n7; collaboration with
Dan Rice, 50–56; Interview with
John Sinclair and Robin Eichele, 31;
Interview with Linda Wagner, 51;
Introduction to *All That Is Lovely in
Men*, 50; marriage to Ann Creeley,
50; relationship with Cynthia Homire, 50; "Autobiography," 31–32; "cult
of the hipster," 31–32, 36; "Form,"
51–52; "Notes Apropos Free Verse,"
144; "Walking the Dog," 53–54; "The
Whip," 50–54

Cruz, Pastora Pavón, "La Niña de los
Peines," 58–59, 72, 81

Damon, Maria, 59, 61, 75, 91, 92, 96, 127

Davidson, Michael, 4, 60, 89

Davis, Miles, 8, 24, 28, 29, 37, 38, 50, 51,
52, 132, 211n20

Dawson, Fielding, xiii, xiv, 28, 29, 131,
132, 139, 154

De Gruttola, Raffael, 61

Dent, Tom, 159, 166–67

Derrida, Jacques, 113, 194–95, 198, 214n2

DeVeaux, Scott, 210n7, 211n16

Dewey, John, 131

di Prima, Diane, 4, 18–19, 143, 151–52

Dickinson, Emily, 58, 85–87

dixieland, 49, 82

Dodds, Warren "Baby," 46, 49

Dorn, Ed, 4, 21, 29, 128, 137–38, 141,
152–54, 205

duende, 20, 58–69, 72–74, 77, 78, 80–81,
84–85, 90–91, 212n2

Dunbar, Paul Laurence, 202

Duncan, Robert, 2, 19, 33, 50, 71, 73, 78,
79, 81, 91, 131

Dunn, Joe, 58, 59, 82

DuPlessis, Rachel Blau, 19

Durante, Jimmy, 49

Dylan, Bob, 106, 112, 213n2

Edwards, Brent Hayes, 10

Eigner, Larry, 19

Eisenhower, Dwight D., 26

Eliot, T. S., 30, 31, 46, 56, 59, 62, 90, 114

Ellington, Duke, 181, 198

Ellison, Ralph, 34, 75

Empson, William, 43

Epstein, Andrew, 4, 5, 18, 135, 209n5

Eshleman, Clayton, 87, 88, 212n8

Evers, Medgar, 106–07

Fazzino, Jimmy, 22

Feinstein, Sascha, 50, 172, 174

Felman, Shoshana, 10, 209n2

feminist/feminism, 19, 182, 184, 187

Ferlinghetti, Lawrence, 100, 104, 112,
116, 118

Firespitters, The. *See* Cortez, Jayne

Fletcher, Dusty, 103

Floating Bear, The, 18, 133, 143, 151

Foye, Raymond, 113, 114

free jazz, 13, 17, 142, 198

Gates, Henry Louis Jr., 10

Giddens, Gary, 144, 210n4, 211n16

Gillespie, Dizzy, 40, 45, 97, 184, 185

Ginsberg, Allen, 1, 3, 6, 12, 17, 21, 22,

70, 81, 93, 94–128; and Beat poetics, 41, 97–112; *The Best Minds of My Generation*, 97; correspondence with Gary Snyder, 103–04; correspondence with Lawrence Ferlinghetti, 103–04; *The Fall of America*, 100, 108–11, 213n2; friendship with Amiri Baraka (LeRoi Jones), 96–97, 103–12; friendship with Bob Kaufman, 96–97, 112–28; friendship with Jack Kerouac, 95–98; as guest editor of *Black Mountain Review*, 2; *The Letters of Allen Ginsberg*, 109–10; "Angkor Wat," 104–05; "Beginning of a Poem of These States," 106; "Chicago to Salt Lake by Air," 110; "Continuation of a Long Poem of These States," 106; "Crossing Nation," 112; "Howl," 32, 41, 96, 97, 98, 100–02, 125; "In the Baggage Room at Greyhound," 102; "Kaddish," 102; "Kansas City to St. Louis," 108, 119; "Lion for Real," 116; "Meditation and Poetics," 99; "Notes for *Howl*," 5, 41, 98, 115; "Outline of Un-American Activities," 109; "Poet's 'Voice'," 100; "Seabattle of Salamis," 102–03; "These States," 106–07; "Witchita Vortex Sutra," 107–08

Gioia, Ted, 210n4, 211n11, 211n16, 214n2

Gizzi, Peter, 85

Golding, Alan, 57

Grenier, Robert, 191–93

Guest, Barbara, 19

Guevara, Che, 108

Hall, Stuart, 15–16, 193

Harris, William J., 147, 151

Hawkins, Coleman, 121

Hawkins, "Screaming" Jay, 103

Henderson, David, 114, 125

Henderson, Stephen, 155–58, 160, 178

Hendrix, Jimi, 164

Hernton, Calvin, 159

Hickman, Ben, 26, 130

Hoffman, Tyler, 3–5

Holiday, Billie, 6, 50, 59, 70–74, 76, 77, 81, 83

homosexuality, 16, 20, 34, 61, 63, 66, 73, 77, 85, 101, 143, 151, 192

Hopkins, Gerard Manley, 43

Howe, Susan, 194

Hughes, Langston, xi–xiv, 20, 114, 140, 156, 157, 174, 180, 202

Jacobson, Matthew Frye, 16

Jim Crow. *See* segregation

Joans, Ted, 96, 125, 163

Johnson, Mark, 9

Jonas, Stephen, 61–68, 94, 172, 205; early life, 61–62; *Exercises for Ear*, 67–68; friendship with Jack Spicer, 20, 58–61, 63, 65–67, 78–83, 85, 88, 90–92; friendship with John Wieners, 20, 58–61, 62–63, 69–71, 73, 77, 91–92; "Cante Jondo for Soul Brother Jack Spicer," 65–67; ". . . . . An Ear Injured," 63–64; "Gloucester," 62–63; "Morphogenesis," 64–65; "Word on Measure," 63

Jones, LeRoi. *See* Baraka, Amiri

Jones, Meta DuEwa, 15–16, 174

Kane, Daniel, 3–5, 9, 160

Katz, Daniel, 58, 78, 80, 87–90, 212n5

Kaufman, Bob, 1, 21, 75, 76, 92, 93, 94, 96–97, 100–02, 112–28, 129, 156, 163, 205, 213n3; early life and career, 112–15; friendship with Allen Ginsberg, 112–28; marriage to

Eileen Kaufman, 113–14, 116, 122; relationship with Lynn Wildey, 114; self-imposed silence, 113, 128; "Abomunist Manifesto," 93, 123–26; "ABOMUNIST RATIONAL AN-THEM," 126–27; "Crootey Songo," 127; "Excerpts from LEXICON ABOMUNON," 125; "Ginsberg (for Allen)," 112, 116–20; "Jail Poems," 118–20; "October 5th, 1963," 115; "O-JAZZ-O War Memoir," 122–23; "Walking Parker Home," 120–22; "War Memoir," 122; "War Memoir: Don't Listen," 122; "West Coast Sounds," 115–16; "Would You Wear My Eyes?," 124

Kaufman, Eileen, 113–14, 116, 122
Keller, Lynn, 35, 50
Kennedy, John F., 108, 126, 137
Kennedy, Robert, 108, 176
Kerouac, Jack, 95–96, 104, 112–16, 120, 128, 156, 163, 212n1
King, Basil, 154
King, Martin Luther Jr., 108, 139, 176
Kohli, Amor, 96, 120, 213n3

Lakoff, George, 9
language poetry, 190–92, 194–97, 201, 203
Lawrence, D. H., 151–52
Lee, A. Robert, 95
Lee, Benjamin, 101
Levertov, Denise, 19
Lhamon, W. T. Jr., 32
Lindsay, Vachel, 79
Lorca, Federico García, 20, 58–59, 65, 72, 78, 80–82, 85–91, 114, 135, 212n9
Lott, Eric, 31, 34, 210n8
Lowney, John, 30
Lumumba, Patrice, 108, 176

Machado, Gerardo, 185
Mackey, Nathaniel, 5, 9, 20, 22, 201, 205; and performance, 196–97; *From a Broken Bottle Traces of Perfume Still Emanate,* 199; Interview with Charles Bernstein, 196–97; and "post-bop," 198; *Eroding Witness,* 199; *Paracritical Hinge,* 198; on race in contemporary poetry, 195, 201; *Splay Anthem,* 198; "Breath and Precarity," 5, 98; "Cante Moro," 64; "The Changing Same," 130, 135; "Expanding the Repertoire," 195, 201, 213n3; "Song of the Adoumboulou," 200
Madhubuti, Haki, 177
Magee, Michael, 18, 131, 209n5
Mailer, Norman, 32–34, 75, 76, 92, 102, 126, 210n9, 210n10
major, devorah, 114
Marcoux, Jean-Philippe, 168, 173
Margolis, Bill, 118
Marshall, Ed, 70–71
Mayer, Bernadette, 202
McCaffery, Steve, 192, 194, 202
McClure, Michael, 135
McGann, Jerome, 86
McKay, Claude, 114
Measure, 63–64, 83
Monk, Thelonious, 24, 99
Monroe, Marylin, 81, 83
Morris, Adalaide, 197
Moten, Fred, 11–14, 130–31, 213n4
Mullen, Harryette, 201, 204, 205; on Bob Kaufman, 113; *Muse & Drudge,* 201, 203–04; on race in contemporary poetry, 201–02; "Kinky Quatrains," 202, 204; "Poetry and Identity," 201, 202
Munch, Edvard, 74

National Association for the Advancement of Colored People (NAACP), 109, 140

Neal, Larry, 157–59, 186

New American Poetry, 18, 21, 22, 23, 59, 97, 134, 155, 156, 158, 168, 190, 205; and jazz, 7, 17, 157, 159, 164, 174, 178, 198; and poetics of breath and voice, 3, 5, 6, 12, 17, 22, 23, 25, 37, 56, 57–58, 61, 91, 93, 96, 100, 115, 128, 130, 131, 139, 154, 160, 162, 165, 166, 184, 187, 188, 191–94

New Black Poetry, 155–56

new thing. *See* free jazz

Nielsen, Aldon Lynn, xv, xvi, 4, 5, 20, 59, 60, 61, 63, 75, 76, 92, 96, 133, 212n1

Norman, Jessye, 14–15

Nowak, Mark, 214n1

O'Hara, Frank, 17, 72, 160, 211n3

Oliver, Joe "King," 49

Olson, Charles, 1–4, 6, 11–12, 17, 20, 21, 22, 23–56, 57, 59, 60, 62, 63, 64, 68–71, 73, 75, 77, 79, 80, 81, 84, 86, 91, 92, 93, 99, 101, 103, 114, 115, 128, 129, 157, 163, 165, 168–69, 174, 178, 180, 182, 193, 210n1, 210n2, 211n12, 211n14, 211n21, 212n6, 213n6; and Berkeley poetry conference, 193; as civil servant, 26; friendship with Amiri Baraka (LeRoi Jones), 25, 46, 96, 132–35, 137, 140–42, 145–54, 205–07; friendship with Robert Creeley, 23–56; *Letters for Origin*, 150; *The Maximus Poems*, 26, 34, 47, 62, 101, 205–07; in Mexico, 44–50; relationship with Jack Spicer, 91; *The Special View of History*, 12, 60; as teacher, 26–29; "Duende, Muse, and Angel," 212n6; "GrandPa Goodbye," 133; "Human Universe," 48–49; "The Hustings," 137, 148–50; "Memorial Letter," 58; "Muthologos," 24, 33, 165, 212n6; "The Present Is Prologue," 207; "Projective Verse," 3, 5, 20, 23–24, 33, 36–39, 60, 63, 69, 73, 79, 99, 128, 130, 131, 133–35, 148–50, 157–58, 160, 165, 167–69, 174, 192, 207, 210n2, 211n21; "The Is Yeats Speaking," 147

O'Meally, Robert G., 210n4

open field poetics, 41, 56, 60, 67, 130, 132, 149, 158, 207

Oppenheimer, Joel, 131, 132, 154

Origin, 2, 36, 57, 58, 150

Oulipo, 202

Panish, Jon, 95–96

Parker, Charlie "Bird," 5, 6, 20–21, 24–25, 28–29, 31, 33, 37–38, 40–45, 50–52, 54–56, 57–59, 65, 78, 81–85, 91, 95–97, 99, 120–22, 128, 132, 144, 162–65, 174, 198, 205, 211n11

Perelman, Bob, 6–7, 194

Perloff, Marjorie, 53

Pound, Ezra, xv, 6, 20, 26, 30, 31, 36–37, 39, 40, 46, 47, 48, 56, 59, 70–71, 88, 114, 121, 133–35, 147, 149, 180, 209n1

Powell, Bud, 29, 37

Pozo, Chano, 45, 49, 184–86, 214n2, 214n3, 214n4

Pritchard, Norman H., 159

projectivist poetics, 3, 21, 23–25, 33, 36–41, 44, 47, 55, 56, 60, 61, 68, 69, 71–74, 76, 79, 99, 128, 131, 133, 138, 148, 150, 153, 157, 158, 165, 180, 184, 185, 210n2, 211n21; as breath or voice, 3, 5, 37, 43, 53, 87, 130, 131, 134–35, 149–50, 167, 169, 192, 207; as score for voice, 160, 186

Ra, Sun, 1–2, 165, 206–07
race, xiii, xv, 7, 15, 17–21, 26, 27, 30, 33,
    36, 46, 48, 60–62, 75, 101, 109, 116,
    125, 142, 145, 147, 149, 156, 159, 189,
    204, 206
Rainey, Ma, 181, 204
Ramey, Lauri, 15
Redling, Erik, 8–9
Redmond, Eugene, 159
Rembar, Charles, 151, 213n8
Rice, Dan, 25, 50, 131–32
Roach, Max, 24, 37
Rodgers, Carolyn Marie, 159
Rodgers and Hammerstein, 175
Roediger, David R., 16, 209n4
Rollins, Sonny, 5, 9, 143–44
Roosevelt, Franklin D., 28, 137, 140
Rosset, Barney, 151
Rothenberg, Jerome, 194
Rumaker, Michael, xiii, xiv, 26, 28–29,
    132

Sanchez, Sonia, 3, 17, 21, 158–59,
    160, 167–78, 179, 181, 182, 187, 190,
    201, 205; on Allen Ginsberg, 168;
    Conversations, 168, 169, 172, 173, 176,
    177; friendship with Amiri Bara-
    ka, 168; on performance, 168–69,
    177–78; "a/coltrane/poem," 173–78,
    181; "homecoming," 169–72, 173; "I
    Have Walked a Long Time," 172–73;
    "Queens of the Universe," 160;
    "Sequences," 173
Santería, 184–85
Saussure, Ferdinand de, 202
Schoenberg, Arthur, 14
segregation (Jim Crow) xi, xiii, xv, 5, 26,
    27, 28, 30, 85 104, 108, 123, 164, 192,
    195, 202, 206
Serres, Michel, 7

Shaw, Lytle, 213n2
Shaw University, 27
Silliman, Ron, 191, 194
Sinatra, Frank, 106
Sinclair, John, 109
Siraganian, Lisa, 26
slavery, 141–42, 157, 185
Smethurst, James, 115, 156–57, 160, 176,
    189, 213n3
Smitherman, Geneva, 31
Snyder, Gary, 104, 111
Southern Christian Leadership Confer-
    ence (SCLC), 140
Spellman, A. B., 159
Spicer, Jack, 20, 78–93, 94, 155, 163, 172,
    196, 205; affection for Joe Dunn,
    82; *After Lorca*, 20, 58, 78, 80, 82,
    85–90, 114; on Billie Holiday, 81;
    friendship with John Wieners, 20,
    58–61, 70, 91–92; friendship with
    Robert Duncan, 91; friendship with
    Stephen Jonas, 20, 58–61, 63, 65–67,
    78–83, 85, 88, 90–92; life in Boston,
    58, 78; on the poetry of "outside,"
    79–80, 84–85; relationship with
    Charles Olson, 79–81, 84, 86, 91–93;
    and translation, 87–88; "Dictation,"
    79–80, 87; "Forest," 87; "Letters to
    Robin Blaser," 58, 78, 88; "Ode to
    Walt Whitman," 88–90; "A Poem
    Without a Single Bird in It," 85, 204;
    "The Poems of Emily Dickinson,"
    85–86; "The Poet and Poetry," 78;
    "Some Notes on Walt Whitman,"
    90; "Song for Bird and Myself," 58,
    81–85, 92
Stein, Gertrude, 37
Stevens Lee High School (Asheville,
    NC), 27
Stevens, Wallace, 38–39, 126

Stewart, Michael Seth, 68, 70, 212n4
strategic essentialism, 15, 193
swing, 24, 30, 49, 142

Taylor, Cecil, 143–44, 198
This Is Poetry (WMEX Boston radio show), 57
Thomas, Lorenzo, 3–5, 20–22, 158, 159–67, 169, 170, 174, 178, 187, 190, 205; early life, 159–61; on the Black Arts Movement, 3, 21, 158–59; *Extraordinary Measures*, 3, 160, 167, 169; friendship with Ted Berrigan, 160–61; friendship with Tom Dent, 159, 166–67; on Umbra, 21, 158; "Alea's Children," 159; "Ascension," 166; "Discovering America Again," 166–67; "Evolution of the Bop Aesthetic," 163; "Historiography," 162–65; "Liner Notes," 162–63; "Low Speech," 166; "My Calling," 166; "New and Old Gospel," 167; "The Offering," 166; "Political Science," 160–62
Touré, Askia, 3, 159
Turrentine, Tommy, 8

Uher (tape recorder manufacturer), 106
Umbra, 3, 17, 21, 124, 158, 159, 162, 166–67, 179, 205

Van Vechten, Carl, xi, xv

Walker, Margaret, 202
Waller, Fats, 24

Warhol, Andy, 108
White Panther Party, 109
whiteness, 16, 103, 109, 168
Whitman, Walt, 62, 66, 88–91
Wieners, John, 58–61, 68–77, 79, 81, 83, 85, 90, 91, 92, 135, 163, 172, 205; on Billie Holiday, 71–73, 77; friendship with Charles Olson, 68–71, 73, 77; friendship with Jack Spicer, 20, 58–61, 79, 81, 83, 91–92; friendship with Stephen Jonas, 20, 58–61, 62–63, 69–71, 73, 77; *Stars Seen in Person*, 58, 70–73, 75, 77, 91, 212n4; *Yours Presently*, 68, 69, 71 "Act #2," 76; "Cocaine," 73–74; "Hanging on for Dear Life," 68–69; "Memories of You," 76; "A poem for cock suckers," 75–76; "A poem for museum goers," 74; "A poem for record players," 73–74; "A poem for the dead I know," 69; "Stationary," 75; "We have a flame," 69
Williams, Alma Stone, xiv
Williams, Robert, 108–09
Williams, William Carlos, 29, 30, 35, 37, 39, 70, 71, 135, 156, 193, 211n19

X, Malcolm, 108, 205–06

Yeats, William Butler, 33, 147
Yépez, Heriberto, 46–47
Young, Lester, 121
Yugen, 133

Zukofsky, Louis, 6–7

CONTEMPORARY NORTH AMERICAN POETRY SERIES

*Bodies on the Line: Performance
and the Sixties Poetry Reading*
by Raphael Allison

*Industrial Poetics: Demo Tracks
for a Mobile Culture*
by Joe Amato

*What Are Poets For?: An Anthropology
of Contemporary Poetry and Poetics*
by Gerald L. Bruns

*Reading Duncan Reading: Robert
Duncan and the Poetics of Derivation*
edited by Stephen Collis
and Graham Lyons

*Postliterary America: From Bagel
Shop Jazz to Micropoetries*
by Maria Damon

*Among Friends: Engendering
the Social Site of Poetry*
edited by Anne Dewey
and Libbie Rifkin

*Translingual Poetics: Writing
Personhood Under Settler Colonialism*
by Sarah Dowling

*Purple Passages: Pound, Eliot,
Zukofsky, Olson, Creeley, and the
Ends of Patriarchal Poetry*
by Rachel Blau DuPlessis

*On Mount Vision: Forms of the Sacred
in Contemporary American Poetry*
by Norman Finkelstein

*Writing Not Writing: Poetry,
Crisis, and Responsibility*
by Tom Fisher

*Form, Power, and Person in Robert
Creeley's Life and Work*
edited by Stephen Fredman
and Steve McCaffery

Redstart: An Ecological Poetics
by Forrest Gander and John Kinsella

Jorie Graham: Essays on the Poetry
edited by Thomas Gardner
University of Wisconsin Press, 2005

*The Collaborative Artist's Book: Evolving
Ideas in Contemporary Poetry and Art*
by Alexandra J. Gold

*Gary Snyder and the Pacific Rim:
Creating Countercultural Community*
by Timothy Gray

*Urban Pastoral: Natural Currents
in the New York School*
by Timothy Gray

*Nathaniel Mackey, Destination
Out: Essays on His Work*
edited by Jeanne Heuving

*Poetry FM: American Poetry
and Radio Counterculture*
by Lisa Hollenbach

Poetics and Praxis "After" Objectivism
edited by W. Scott Howard
and Broc Rossell

Ecopoetics: Essays in the Field
edited by Angela Hume
and Gillian Osborne

*Racial Things, Racial Forms: Objecthood
in Avant-Garde Asian American Poetry*
by Joseph Jonghyun Jeon

*We Saw the Light: Conversations between
the New American Cinema and Poetry*
by Daniel Kane

*Ghostly Figures: Memory and Belatedness
in Postwar American Poetry*
by Ann Keniston

*Poetics of Emergence: Affect and History
in Postwar Experimental Poetry*
by Benjamin Lee

*Contested Records: The Turn to Documents
in Contemporary North American Poetry*
by Michael Leong

*History, Memory, and the Literary Left:
Modern American Poetry, 1935–1968*
by John Lowney

*Poetics of Cognition: Thinking
through Experimental Poems*
by Jessica Lewis Luck

*Paracritical Hinge: Essays,
Talks, Notes, Interviews*
by Nathaniel Mackey

*Behind the Lines: War Resistance Poetry
on the American Homefront since 1941*
by Philip Metres

*Poetry Matters: Neoliberalism, Affect, and
the Posthuman in Twenty-First Century
North American Feminist Poetics*
by Heather Milne

*Hold-Outs: The Los Angeles
Poetry Renaissance, 1948–1992*
by Bill Mohr

*In Visible Movement: Nuyorican
Poetry from the Sixties to Slam*
by Urayoán Noel

*Dissonant Voices: Race, Jazz, and
Innovative Poetics in Midcentury America*
by Joseph Pizza

Reading Project: *A Collaborative Analysis
of William Poundstone's* Project for
Tachistoscope {Bottomless Pit}
by Jessica Pressman, Mark C.
Marino, and Jeremy Douglass

Frank O'Hara: The Poetics of Coterie
by Lytle Shaw

*Renegade Poetics: Black Aesthetics
and Formal Innovation in
African American Poetry*
by Evie Shockley

*Questions of Poetics: Language
Writing and Consequences*
by Barrett Watten

*Radical Vernacular: Lorine Niedecker
and the Poetics of Place*
edited by Elizabeth Willis